ENTREPRENEURSHIP & MENOPAUSE: THE HARD ROAD A NURSEPRENEUR JOURNEY

by

Dr. Sylette DeBois

Copyright Notice © 2020

All rights reserved, including any right to reproduce this book or portion thereof in any form whatsoever.

This book is designed to provide accurate and authoritative information with regard to the subject matter covered. It is sold with the understanding that there is not a professional consulting engagement. If legal or other expert advice or assistance is required please consult with a licensed professional in your area.

Table of Contents

Foreword 1

Laughter Saved my Life
By Nikita B. Williams 7

From Dust to Gold
By Shawny Jackson 17

5 Star Nurse: A Journey Into Entrepreneurship
By Monique Moore, RN 27

Transformed: A Journey to Self-Preservation
By Sade Nichole Griggs MSN-Ed, APRN, RN 35

Blind Faith: The Journey to Entrepreneurship
By Kamilah J. Lyon, APRN 47

Behind the Mask: My Journey
By Dr. Jerwanda Johnson 59

Restoration: A Nurse Practitioners Journey toward Entrepreneurship
By Dequindra Quinn Blakey 71

A Silent Epidemic: Nursing and Depression
By Charlene Owuamana, LPN 85

The Golden Rose: My Journey towards Conquering Stress
By Keeonna Williams, MSN, RN 101

Challenging Path to Sublime Destination: A Journey towards travel and adventure
By Michele Graham, RN 115

Boss Nurse: One Class at a Time
By Dr. Bridgette Turner Jenkins 125

Nurse Entrepreneurship: The Journey to Securing 6 Figures and Beyond
By Sherri Lynch, MSN, RN 135

Entrepreneurship & Menopause: The Hard Road A Nursepreneur Journey
By Dr. Sylette DeBois 147

Journey through the Dark
By Beatrix Curry, LPN 157

From Seed to Bloom
By Denise Cadet, RN 167

Dreams Realized: A Nurse's Journey to Entrepreneurship!
By Katina Dorsey, RN 179

How Student Loan Debt Lead to the Journey of Purpose and Becoming a Nurse Boss
By Dr. Janel Willingham, DNP APRN, NP-C 191

The First Step is the Hardest
By Oreal Perkins, APRN 207

The Nurse Boss Collective From RN to Vsteam Queen
By Raven Diana Montgomery, RN-BC 217

Living Large- A Nurses Journey Toward Resilience
By Rasheda Hatchett, MN, RN 231

A Nurse's Journey to Entrepreneurship & Purpose
By Jessica Sinclair, BSN-RN 243

Lifting the Veil of Fear
By Casaleen Humber MS, RN, PCCN, CCM 257

Ordained Steps: My Journey to Nurse Entrepreneurship
By Flobrenne Joseph-Spaulding, RN 269

PURPOSE MANIFESTO : Unleashing the Covert Entrepreneur
By Sandra D. Cleveland, PhD, MSN, RN and CEO 279

Unshakeable: Bitten by the Entrepreneur Bug
By Dr. Valerie E. Green 293

A Nightingale's Journey 2 Business
By Diane Ehrig, MSN MBA RN-BC 305

Tending to the Spark: The Power of Dreaming Big
By Kecia Hayslett, RN 315

At the Right Time
By Sharon Addison, RN 327

Making A Definite Difference
By LaTonya Mims, CRNA 339

A Journey on an Untrodden Path - A Nurse's Story
By Victoria Y. Buggs MPH, RN 351

This is my Year to Grow: Journeys and Strategies for Nurse Entrepreneurs
By Michelle Greene Rhodes, MHS, RN 363

Resource List
By Marylyn R. Harris, RN, MSN, MBA 373

Foreword

This book, this profession, this life is all about a journey. One that has been defined as an act of traveling from one place to another. It becomes something that we call can relate to in one form or another. From baby to toddler. Toddler to School Age. School Age to Teen and so on. When you look back on your journey in life what do you see?

Happiness? Trauma? Neglect? Joy? Triumph? Is it something that you would do again the same way or differently if we could? I tell you, as I look back, I suddenly feel as though I was being prepared to become a "Nursepreneur" all along the way.

Every degree, certification, place of employment and relationship all play a part of whom you see today. I know it might sound cliché, but treasure those memories… and I challenge you to treasure each moment in which you now live and breathe.

As the collaborator of this treasure that you hold in your hand, let me briefly share my "journey" with you. Yes, my parents were married but quickly divorce a year after my arrival. So to say it was "just Mom and I" would sum it up pretty generally. Yes I had plenty of cousins, aunts, uncles and grandparents that nurtured me along the way. But you know, the love and presence of a Father is something that I don't feel you can ever replace with a substitute. You just learn to "make a way" and to find love along your journey that makes you feel whole again. Funny thing is, my Father was a natural entrepreneur and here I am… 46 years later working in my own business like he always did. God has a great sense of humor.

I would call my journey equivalent to taking that trip that we spoke of in the summary on the back of this book. One filled with scarcity, fear and plenty of stops at the rest areas to take a breather. Did I know where I was going initially? Nope, I just got on the road and began to drive. Hey, they told me to do it afraid! So, I did and the journey began.

As I built up speed along the highway, did I noticed that I was driving alone. Wait a minute, who takes a cross country trip all alone? Hardly anyone. So I made it a point to stop and pull over and picked up a few of my nursepreneur friends along the way.

I didn't want to go it alone, heck they even asked for a ride. So year one of this authorship journey, yes it was just myself and my new book and brand! We began to catch the eye of the Nation, social media, and communities as we arrived at landmarks. Year two, we launched 15 Nurse Entrepreneurs into Authorship and took pride of serving as a starting line for them. I see them now writing more books on their own, teaching others how to self publish, creating their own events and even capturing the eye of their tribe. Its such a great feeling. Fast forward, and now we are "on a roll". Yes!

Year three rolled around and my thoughts were, hey, lets launch on a cruise the next time. That way we could have fun, learn from one another yet launch our books along the way! So our travels took us to Jamaica and other ports where we were happy to showcase these authors and now international speakers as they launched their speaking careers upon that ship. Great fun was had by all and we were blessed to add the exotic Caribbean to our journey story.

Now, look at this beauty. We have arrived at Year four! Wow is an understatement.

In the heat of this race, I took on a challenge to go faster than we ever have before.

Go, Go, Go Michelle, they said! Let's see you bring on 30 Nurse Authors the next time!

Whoa! Pump the brakes! Look out, danger ahead! Danger of what? The unknown?

We had made it 3 years with the help of a small measure of faith and my heart said

GO FOR IT! Challenge accepted and had I not, these 30 Nurses would not have been able to stand together as co-authors today! We are here, we made it and the journey has been a beautiful thing!

So, sit back and enjoy this reading, I am almost certain that these journeys, may mirror your very own in life, profession or in business. Please, drop us a line to let us know how your nurse entrepreneurship journey is coming along, and how we can help you?

Are you taking the trip towards your best self? Are you taking a few folks with you who need help getting "there" as well?

I will be awaiting at your destination, so email at me
Michelle@MichelleRhodesOnline.com
Michelle Greene Rhodes, MHS, RN
CEO Michelle Rhodes Media LLC
www.MichelleRhodesMedia.com

Acknowledgement

To my husband Tarrance

Thank you for always being my soft place to land. You have been so selfless throughout my journey and I'm forever grateful.

To my family and friends I love you all.

Dad, what can I say besides you are simply amazing.

To God be the Glory!

Laughter Saved my Life

By Nikita B. Williams

I finally got my thoughts together and decided which road I wanted to take. My journey became enjoyable as well as profitable. I was a nurse consultant, I had a home health business as well as several small assisted living homes. Life was great. One day, I was visiting my mom and noticed a small knot under her left armpit. The k-not didn't give her any issues; she noticed it but thought it might have been from her soap or deodorant or something simple. A week passed, and I noticed that the area had gotten a tad bit bigger, and I encouraged her to schedule an appointment and seek the advice of her physician. We went to the appointment, she had a biopsy, and we patiently waited for the results. After we received the results, we found out she had "the big C." Oh my goodness; when I heard the word, I stopped breathing. I couldn't hear anything beyond that point. All I saw was the doctor's lips moving, but nothing made audible sense. Because I am a believer, and I had faith that we could beat whatever came our way, I got myself together so that we could focus on the battle ahead of us - until we went to Mom's follow up appointment after her surgery. I will never forget how I felt as I traveled to the hospital. I can't put into words what I felt, but once I got to my mother's room, and the doctor made his rounds, the feeling I experienced made sense at that moment.

"You have six months," the doctor said. "For what?" my mother asked. "To live," he responded, and he walked away. That one sentence changed our lives forever. It all started from a small knot in the armpit of my mother's left arm. A painless, not so big knot that came from nowhere, or so we thought. That's until we discovered that it came from somewhere that was a place of no return. Stage 4 triple negative breast cancer was the official diagnosis. And that six months that the doctor predicted was so precise that she took her last breath exactly six months after he came and spoke with us. The things I thought I had figured out no longer made sense. I didn't have the same desires; neither did I want to deal with sick, vulnerable or needy people. I fell into a dark depression and found myself questioning my existence and the value of even being here.

I quickly learned the truth of the matter was that I allowed the facts of my life to distract me from the truth; trust me - there is a huge difference. Like most of us, I allowed the facts to keep me from following my dreams. I was surrounded by those who had limited beliefs and didn't want anymore than they had, and if they did want more, they didn't believe that it was available to them. I was afraid to start, because I was afraid to fail. When I finally got started, I was afraid to go higher, because I didn't want to lose my current status or hear the "I told you so" comments from my naysayers. Then it got to be even worse. I was afraid that I wouldn't have the support that I needed because it seemed as if the ones that I loved couldn't relate to me, so they were unable to meet my support needs. I was so afraid of the "what ifs" that I wouldn't allow myself to think on any extravagant level, because sadly, I just didn't believe that it was possible. All these things were factual for me, but the good news is that none of them were true. The truth is (and remains to be) that fear is an emotion that we attach to the choices we need to make. Whether that choice is to stop, continue or start something, we have to conquer the strength to muster through our emotions and decide. Once I realized that fear was something I created to protect myself from what I thought could happen, I replaced my thoughts with those that added value and had positive results and would help me reach my goals.

Acceptance was also a huge barrier when it came to being successful and it can affect you, as well. Regardless of how much you may have accomplished in your life, there's always this small nudge of doubt that creeps in when you're thinking of doing something new. The desire to be accepted is the perfect environment for the imposter syndrome to set in. We begin to wonder what others will say and how you will be perceived. Sometimes, we even go so far as to create scenarios of why we won't be successful in the things we know we're capable of doing. I remember a time when I really wanted an opportunity to advance in my nursing career, doing what I was training others to do. I mean, I did the tasks on a regular basis. I was the go-to person when anyone had questions. I was their problem solver, or as we like to say, "I was the aspirin to their pain." The only difference was I didn't have the title; therefore, I wasn't "responsible" for the outcomes because I was merely assisting - it wasn't technically my job. I know, a silly way to think, right? But it took away the emotions that bombarded me when I thought of the idea of me being responsible for the outcomes of others. The problem was that I knew I was capable and was equipped to be successful in the new role, but I didn't believe that I could do it. When your belief system is limited, you not only doubt yourself - you also doubt that others will see the value that you have to offer. This is where the "little me" comes into play and infuses your thoughts with doubt and disbelief, reminders of past failures and negativity. You will soon start feeling like you're in the same place and situation that you were once in and immediately start to minimize who you truly are. When I did this, I began to see myself as the once timid person - with low self-esteem - that I once was. Because of this mindset, anytime I thought to do something, I would immediately replace the thought of moving forward with self-doubt. I would ask myself, why even try? Who would support me? Or I would ask for advice from someone who could not add any value to the conversation. I needed a listening ear and didn't care whose it was.

I didn't realize at the time that this was only contributing to self-doubt. Nobody wants to feel inadequate, neither do we want to seem as if we are not suitable for something. What I learned about being accepted was that no matter what you are trying to get accepted into, or who you desire to accept you, if you accept yourself first, the way that things and people respond to you won't affect you as much as they once did. I learned to accept me - flaws and all. I focus on my strengths and the things that add value to both myself and others. If I couldn't do something, I didn't look at it as an inadequacy, I understood it was an opportunity to learn or either partner with someone who was more proficient in the area in which I was weak. My biggest takeaway regarding acceptance was to not internalize all things that were said or done to me. We never know what other people have been through and because of that, we don't know their true intentions when they do things. I no longer processed other people's inability to function and need of comparison to put me in a position of not appreciating who I was and how I could contribute to the world around me. Instead, I accepted the fact that some people were unable to be a true friend or to support me due to their own personal reasons that had nothing at all to do with me. The bad news was I spent over half of my life accepting things and people in my life that should not have been accepted. Thus, I had to spend the better part of my adult life unlearning this habit. But the good news is what I thought about acceptance was never true; now, I no longer allow unqualified people to disqualify me.

I have been an overthinker for most of my life. I've never been able to just say a thing and do a thing. I was the one that would have a thought, rethink it and then decide…and then rethink that decision, then decide…then rethink that one…and the cycle continued. If that wasn't bad enough, not only did I talk myself out of making decisions, but I also made excuses for myself to make it okay. I would analyze things to the point where I would be paralyzed with indecision. As a creative, I'm always thinking of new ideas. This could be a beautiful thing for those who implement things from start to finish.

Unfortunately, I wasn't that person. I was the one who had what they call the "shining object" syndrome. This is when you have what seems to be a great idea but then, when another idea comes along, you pause on what you're currently doing and start on the new one. In the words of my grandmother, "I was doing a whole lot of nothing." When you hear others brag about being "a jack of all trades but a master of none," it's not always a positive thing. Having a lack of clarity was one of my biggest delays of being financially profitable. A confused mind does absolutely nothing. If I was entertaining different ideas and not giving my full attention to one thing until it was completed, I accomplished hardly anything.

For months I questioned God, asking him "WHY?" Out of all people, He took my mother - someone who loved her family and whom we all loved so dearly. She was my father's first and only love. I often wondered what would he do? How would he go on? All these questions went through my head as depression began taking me on a journey that I no longer desired to adventure on. I began isolating myself from everything and everyone because I just wanted to be alone without distractions or anyone else's responsibilities. Of course, these weren't realistic thoughts and wouldn't sustain me for long, but at that point, I didn't care.

On the weekend of my father's birthday, we planned him a big birthday celebration and hired a comedian. I decided to dress up in character and entertain my father as "Sis. M&M" but you pronounced it "Umm-Humm." It was hysterical. He loved it. The audience went wild, and after it was all over, someone approached me wanting my booking information. I was in shock. I didn't realize I was "bookable." The joy that I saw on my father's face (that I hadn't seen since my mom passed) and those who were in the audience rejuvenated my hope. I performed a couple more times as "Sis. M&M" until I could no longer tolerate her ridiculous costume. Then, I presented "Nikita B" - the fiery, no nonsense, empowering comedienne that the world sees today. I didn't understand how beneficial laughter was for your life until I no longer desired to live.

My comedic career took a world of its own and I decided to leave corporate America and do what made me and so many others in my audience happy. But that wasn't without the opinion and unsolicited advice of others.

The more I separated myself from the busy bodies and negative Nancys of my world, the more I was able to think about what I really and truly wanted out of life. If I was around others who thought their idea for me should supersede what I envisioned for myself, I always achieved less than I would have had I just continued to move forward. Like many other "first timers" of the family, I was the first child to obtain a college degree, the first to earn a six-figure salary, the first to own her own business as well as the first one to move away. I had a few other wins, but it seemed as if "my first" should have been the last in the eyes of others because I was the baby of the family. Although I was the youngest, and everyone seemed to have an idea of what I should do and who

I should become, I had to make up my mind that I was going to take control of my own life and do what made me happy.

It was time that I open myself up to become teachable again. I was on a new journey, doing something I had never done before. I knew how to be funny, but I didn't know that there was a strategy to telling jokes. I learned there were different types of jokes; you had punch line jokes, storytelling jokes and, of course, adult jokes. Like any other preacher's kid, my method was storytelling. I learned how to command a stage, engage my audience, live in the moment and accept the applause. This career change afforded me the experience of being able to tell my story, conquer my fears, accept who I was called to be, become clear with my purpose and learn how to present the "new me" in a strategic way.

But, that wasn't enough. I continued to question God and petition Him to give me answers and ease my mind concerning my mother. It wasn't until almost three years later that I was awakened out of my sleep to the words, "I heard your prayer, but I answered hers." Instantly, I felt a weight lifted off my shoulders, and my heart and mind were at ease.

All this time, I was thinking that I was forgotten. It was my belief that none of my prayers were being heard, my family was abandoned and all the things that I was once taught were lies. My faith had finally been restored, and I felt as if my mother was at peace, and I could finally move forward. Being a nurse has allowed me to connect with people who have encountered similar scenarios as mine. Being both a stroke and cancer survivor, I encourage others to laugh for the health of it. When asked how I got through things, I smile and reply, "Hope, dope." I can truly say laughter saved my life.

Biography

As an award-winning comedic speaker and best-selling author Nikita is affectionately known as the Hope Dealer and Purpose Pusher to her growing 625 thousand social media fan-base. Combining her healthcare experience as a former director of nursing, certified clinical nurse consultant and witty personality; Nikita, has been able to build a successful home health agency, several small assisted living homes as well as a nurse consultant firm. Hilarious", "Original", "Honest" & "Stylish" Are just a few words to describe the comedic styles of Comedian Nikita B. She has been seen on TV One, BET networks, BOUNCE TV and All Nations Network to name a few. Due to her notable success Nikita has also extended her services to other creative entrepreneurs as a brand and social media consultant to assist them with growing their audience as well as building and scaling their brand. You can find Nikita daily on her social media platforms @iamnikitab (Instagram) and Nikita B (Facebook) You can also stay connected by plugging in on her website: www.laughwithnikitab.com or www.nikitabwilliams.com email: nikita@nikitabwilliams.com

Dedication

If it had not been for the Lord on my side, where would I be?!

I am grateful for an overflow of blessings and support on this project. Mi amor, Mr. Jackson, I am grateful for your love, friendship, patience, and endurance.

Chantira, Devante, Chavez, Shamyla, Joshua, Jordon and Jamari you will always be "my reasons" and "dulzura de mi vida".

Very special thanks to Michelle Greene-Rhodes for your mentoring and guidance!

~Shawny

From Dust to Gold

By Shawny Jackson

As a leader in healthcare, I see a need for gentlemen and young ladies to have guidance in the area of interviewing skills and resume writing. I also note that while we may teach skill, many lack compassion. I have a passion for teaching and instilling these important details. Thus, this year, I decided to own my life and start RLegacy, which will launch an Allied Health Career Center and subsidiary Nurse Consultant division. RLegacy's career center mission is to encourage and empower students to be steadfast in their pursuit of long term, personal and professional success. RLegacy is committed to our students' success. We strive to help our students achieve the skills they need to be gainfully employed in healthcare.

RLegacy hired a legal firm to complete and manage all paperwork, and I consulted an accountant to manage our financial affairs. We secured a location and began purchasing supplies. We attended small business owner workshops. We connected with community leaders. Currently, we will be working on all licensure, building approvals, etc. over the next few months.

Most importantly, RLegacy will utilize our resources. My husband and I have plenty of friends and family who are successful business owners. We made calls. We asked questions. I decided to be the boss of my own business, as I have only previously been the boss of someone else's business (you will share in my excitement when you read about my road to this point)!

My journey to entrepreneurship is one of many bumps and bruises along the way...

When I was a child, my dad would say, "Nothing beats a fail but a try." To my mind, I would fail 100% of the time if I never tried. So, what took me so long? Well, I'll tell you. I was afraid to fail. My mind was bombarded with questions - what if I started a business and it didn't work out? What if no students enrolled? What if I didn't get funding? What if it was not financially profitable? What if...? I procrastinated. I continued to support my friends and cheer them on as they left the bedside and became their own bosses. Yet, I was still in the dust.

Gold can be heated to temperatures greater than 1000 degrees Fahrenheit and withstand

All I have endured, I should have no fear of failure or loss. I lost my parents at a young age. I was blessed as a child to have an aunt and a couple of childhood friends who loaned me their moms. Many of my childhood memories include abuse and me entertaining a lot of foolishness in the streets of Chicago.

Gold has countless uses

In 1994, I became an LPN. In 2012, I completed an LPN-BSN program. In 2015, I achieved my MSN, clinical nurse executive leadership. Lastly, I enrolled in a doctoral program to attain a doctor of health administration degree. As you see, I invested a lot of time and money into everything other than my business ventures.

While on this journey, I have held positions in utilization management, dialysis facility administrator, long-term care director of nursing, MDS coordinator, regional reimbursement consultant, ICU nurse, clinical manager of IMCU and house telemetry. As you see from above, I have held several reimbursement and financial responsibilities for other companies; again, investing time and energy into "other folk's business," as Granny would say.

I came to the realization that I represent one of the most respected professions on the planet. If I can challenge myself enough to be a nurse leader, then I can succeed at anything. During my tenure as a nurse leader, I earned a couple of affectionate nicknames: boss lady and boss baby (due to my vertical challenge). I also came to realize that, as nurses, we are bosses; we own every experience, good or bad. We are accountable for everything that happens on our unit and to our patients. The one thing we do NOT own is our time, control over our pay rate, our vacation time off bank or our tenure with that company. The only way to have ownership of these things is to become your own BOSS!

Sometimes, you must encourage yourself. I learned there were times when there was no one there to pat me on the back, or to push me forward, or to tell me I could do it. But I knew I had what it takes!

In June 2012, my family visited Disney in Florida and stopped in Georgia to visit my god-sister on the way home. That visit lead to us breaking ground to have a house built in Hampton, Georgia. I did some research and decided it would be a good place to open a certified nursing assistant (CNA) school. My biggest fears and doubts were how to become successful without support from my friends and family. My husband has been my biggest cheerleader and supporter throughout all the degrees, business ideas and ventures. He said, "Go for it, I got your back"!

Gold can be pressed and won't lose its value

A few months later, in August 2012, several suspicious cells and 2 masses were discovered in my right breast. In October 2012, I had my first lumpectomy.

We were supposed to close on the house in November. I was delayed, not denied. In February 2013, we closed on the house. All plans for opening a school were on hold so I could restore my health and finances. I spent the early part of 2013 back and forth to the oncologist. We moved into our newly built home in September 2013. In 2014, all was well with my health and finances. I was introduced to a very successful and well-known mentor. We discussed my plans for the CNA school. She introduced the idea of multiple streams of income. She pointed out that I have much knowledge to share and shouldn't limit myself to one service line.

I was a CPR instructor, so we planned to open with CPR, lifesaver, health and wellness instruction and CNA. Later, we would add CEU's, phlebotomy, home health aide and expand from there. The plan was to begin with mobile CPR while gaining approvals for the school. I was so excited to begin; I could hardly contain myself!

I filed the paperwork with the state for the LLC. I discovered my county doesn't allow my home address to be my place of business for the type of business I was attempting to open. At this point, I had an LLC with no location. I was so discouraged and over it all. I had invested months in lesson and business plans to be told NO. I was devasted and felt I had been denied. My mentor gave me several ideas to continue. I felt defeated and did nothing. I gave up and continued to punch a clock, while thinking about how I wished I could work for myself. I continued to assist someone else's organization achieve financial success, while dreaming about my own.

How do you continue to trust God for success when your world keeps falling apart

In 2015, I was told I had early stage heart failure and to avoid stress and make some diet changes. No big deal. God has sustained me through the worst weather. In 2016, I was driving to work and got a phone call - my daughter had been hospitalized (in Chicago) and the doctors didn't know if she would be okay. She was being life flighted to a different hospital under an alias. She had a traumatic brain injury. She was attacked and left for dead. I was 800 miles away! Every bit of nursing knowledge I had went out the window, and mama bear came out. I rushed home, packed and looked up flights from Atlanta to Chicago. There were NONE until that night. My only thought was, "This is unbelievable!" I packed very light, called my job, called my husband (who attempted to discourage me from driving). He asked me to wait for him, and he would come home right away and take me to Chicago. I got in my car and drove to Chicago. I had to get there. About a month later, my daughter was discharged from the hospital. If I didn't know before, I knew at this point that success and the school were not options. First, I had to help rehab my child. I spent the next year devoted to her recovery. I am now ready; I started a new job (need money to make money). I scouted out locations for a school. I completed a market analysis. I spoke to an owner of the location I wanted, and all was well. I go for my breast follow up. It's been 5 years and I haven't had any bad news pertaining to that; what could go wrong? I received a call - a new mass had formed in the same breast and I needed surgery…AGAIN.

How will it change? How can I come out on top? How will it get better? When will things change? When will it get better? But…does God ever swing and miss? God had to get me back to a place of longing, yearning, wanting and needing Him. And I thought I had it all together. I thought that my faith was solid and my walk with Christ was on point. This journey taught me otherwise. It showed me my room for growth. There are times when God must remove you from your comfort zone so you will rely totally on Him. Self-care is as important as your service to others. My journey was a lesson and a true test. It is one of molding and strengthening. My journey was always one of GAIN. I lost nothing along the way!

Gold doesn't tarnish

We possess no natural substance that can destroy gold! When you are faced with challenges that seem unbearable, keep in mind you are more precious than gold. Gold can withstand extreme temperatures, being pressed and it never tarnishes, cannot be destroyed and lasts forever. Get up and dust yourself off!

Pure gold lasts forever

You can and will leave a LEGACY that lasts forever.

For inquiries, Contact Shawny Jackson
At 404-938-4318
success@rlegacy-e.com

Biography

Shawny is a native of the south side of Chicago, Illinois. She currently resides in Hampton, Ga with her husband and children. She is the CEO of RLegacy, LLC.

Shawny is Quality and Process Improvement black belt. Her educational background includes executive leadership and she is completing her doctoral studies in health administration. Shawny dedicates much of her time to research. She was invited to present her research to Congress in 2020. She is member of Sigma Theta Tau, International Society of Nursing.

Shawny is a wellness champion. When not working out, she enjoys reading, traveling, good movies, attending church, spending time with her family and her sorority sisters.

Dedication

To my father who taught me strong faith no matter the circumstance, to my mother who showed me strength and independence and to my children for being my push and motivation to keep going when the going got rough.

~Monique

"For your shame ye shall have double; and for confusion they shall rejoice in their portion: therefore in their land they shall possess the double: everlasting joy shall be unto them."

Isaiah 61:7 KJV

5 Star Nurse: A Journey Into Entrepreneurship

By Monique Moore, RN

This journey started for me as a young girl. There I was, a 16-year-old preacher's kid, pregnant and embarrassed. But because I was so curious and nosy, I wanted to try everything that my father told me not to. He would say, "Keep your pants up and your dress down." That statement just intrigued me more. So needless to say, by the time I was 17-years-old, I had given birth to two children, and they were not twins. My mom and dad divorced when I was 2-years-old, so I lived with my mom - a single mother who was already struggling as a certified medication technician in a long-term care facility. She also had my two younger brothers to care for, so she could not afford two extra mouths to feed. Since I had made this choice, I felt I needed to make some hard decisions - and quickly. Thus, my journey began.

I met my soon-to-be husband after my family moved to the inner city to stay with my aunt. He was my dream guy - I was so intrigued by this bad boy, and I fell in love. We quickly became a couple as I started my career path. I enrolled in a job corps program and completed the certified nurse's aide class, but I believed that that was not the stopping place for me. I had heard that there was a program in my area that would pay for young women to go to the next level of nursing, as well as pay for their insurance and transportation to and from class. I immediately felt that this was for me and signed up. I enrolled in the licensed practical nurse program at a local community college in my area. I graduated from that class as a 22-year-old woman, found a job and started working full-time. Even though I felt accomplished and was happy with my success, I felt that this was not enough - I needed more. They say that a trait of a Virgo is to be a leader and in control, as well as mentoring and leading others to greatness. I'm not sure if horoscopes are true or false, but I was still not satisfied. Those Virgo traits were burning inside of me, and my father always told me to never be average; that Parhams were not average and to always go as far as you can and be the best you can be.

So, I decided after three years of working as an LPN it was time to move forward from where I was. I enrolled in registered nurse school full-time. This was a hard task, as I was still working full-time and dealing with personal issues. This was the start of the hardest time of my life. Nursing school was difficult, but moving forward, in my personal life, I was dealing with infidelity, betrayal, financial struggles and daily arguments. But I kept my eye on the prize the future of my children and myself.

I finished RN school and got promoted to assistant director of the nursing facility I had been working at as an LPN. I was so excited to be in a position where I could effect change and assist others to become better in their positions. This was the beginning of my career as an RN. I went on to become a director of nursing, regional nurse and so much more. My dream had come true - I was right where I strove to be and felt successful.

However, my personal life was still in shambles. My husband was still having multiple affairs, my children were now graduating from school and entering college, one right after the other, and then I was diagnosed with cervical cancer. I was, like, *what more can I take Lord; I need to get things together in my life and then comes this diagnosis.* I had to take 3 months out of work and complete radiation and chemo. Our home finances suffered tremendously with one income, our family was facing eviction, utilities were being shut off and we struggled to keep food on the table for our seven children and ourselves. My faith in God kept me going; I prayed for healing and I got it; I prayed for favor and I got it. If it was not for Jesus, I believe we would not have made it. Thank GOD I have been cancer free for 10 years.

Then, as I was coming out of that, my daddy - my rock and my protector – fell through the ceiling of a house and died. I felt as if my world was destroyed, and I could not go any further. I wondered, *Why my daddy? He was good man and didn't deserve this…not my daddy.* I had started the journey to get my BSN, but with cancer and the death of my dad, I put that on the back burner. I started telling myself, *Just stay where you are; you really don't have the strength or the time to deal with school with all that is happening in your personal life. Just forget about it.* In 2016, a light bulb came on for me; a shift happened. It said, *Monique, get up and make changes. I have bigger plans for you. You have been putting everyone and everything before yourself and your dreams. Now it's your time.*

I decided to finally leave my husband and release myself from those years of pain and betrayal. The kids were all grown and moved away with the exception of the 15-year-old, who at that time was 12 but mature enough to understand what was happening. I enrolled in class to get my bachelor's in nursing, and then the struggle of being a single mother with one income set in and I dropped out. I couldn't concentrate on studying when my world was being turned upside down. Even though I was working as a director of nursing, the struggles of adjusting to a different way of living after 28 years of marriage was difficult. Fear was conquering me again, and I let it.

Fast forward to 2019 - I finished school and I am now Monique Moore, BSN, RN. I am super excited, but I'm still not satisfied, which is the reason for the birth of this book. I went on Facebook and called out for help, and I met an awesome woman who has become my mentor in authorship, and more importantly, entrepreneurship, and I could not be happier. Fear will not get me again; no, not this time.

I just wanted you all to know that no matter what you go through or what you're dealing with, keep your eye on the prize. Fear held me back for so long, and I let it stop me numerous times. I finally officially freed myself from a toxic relationship and am starting a new chapter in my life, just in time for 2020: "The Year of the Nurse" as my mentor has said, and I am ready. I want to do things and make the moves I am destined to make. I'm still a work in progress, and I'm still working toward my goal, but I want you to know that if you believe in yourself and you keep yourself surrounded by those who celebrate you and not just tolerate you, it can be done. Whatever your "it" is. Everyone has different goals and aspirations, and we will all deal with a few roadblocks and detours along the way but stay on course - if you get knocked off, get right back on and keep moving. You are only defeated when you stop moving forward. This year of 2020, I will be walking into my next chapter of my life as an entrepreneur. All these years of experience, knowledge and education will now be used to push me to my next level. If I can do it, so can you. Push through it all.

So, I give you a little of my story to let you know that fear has no place in your life, and if you believe in your dreams, keep your eye on the prize and keep God and prayer constant in your life, you can conquer anything. I can't wait to share with you guys the next chapter in my life. Stay on the lookout for Monique - she is coming with both barrels loaded and ready to destroy fear, and you can too. Let's get it done; no better time to start than the present. This is our time, 2020, the year of perfected vision according to my Apostle, and I believe and receive that prophetic word.

Thanks for reading. Have a blessed year.

Biography

Monique R. Moore-Parham RN, BSN has been a high-performing nurse professional and currently works as a Director of Nursing in a Long-Term Care Rehabilitation Center in Independence, Mo where she has been for the last 4 years. She is the owner and operator of Parham Nurse Consultants & Education, LLC. She has over 25 years in the nursing field working as a Director of Nursing and Regional Nurse for a large corporation in the Missouri metropolitan area.

Monique earned her Associates degree from Sanford-Brown University in St Louis Missouri and her Bachelors of Science degree from Grand Canyon University in Phoenix Arizona. She is currently pursuing her Master of Science in Nurse Leadership from Grand Canyon as well with the expected completion date in 2021.

Monique has worked closely with Missouri state surveyors in understanding and perfecting the skills needed to be successful in the CMS star rating qualifications. Monique has led her team in several facilities on making the necessary changes in improving their star ratings from 1 star to a 5 star in a short time span and has maintained that rating for years after. Improving reimbursement rates, decreasing hospitalizations and partnering with Magnet Programs and Partnerships at the acute care hospitals in the Missouri area. The geriatric population has always been her passion and she strives to assist nurse leaders on making the best decision on providing quality care for the senior population they serve.

Acknowledgments

To my mother.

You are the epitome of perseverance which has inspired and led me on the same path

To my grandfather.

Thank you for believing and supporting me on my nursing journey when no one else would.

To my siblings.

My only hope is that I am and continue to be a positive influence.

To my Lord & Savior.

Thank you for the life you have purposed me to lead and for loving me despite my shortcomings.

Sade Nichole

Transformed: A Journey to Self-Preservation

By Sade Nichole Griggs MSN-Ed, APRN, RN

A train moves through an array of landscapes. It climbs mountains, descends into valleys and dives into tunnels. It moves through rain, snow, fog and sunshine at its own consistent pace. There is something so reassuring about a train – the path is set, the track is laid and the train moves along the route undisturbed by the activity around it. Even despite occasional delays, the train is reliable. It will arrive eventually, if you remain patient.

I have always felt that the tracks of my life's journey were set long before I even knew to contemplate my future. My life's circumstances determined where my track would be laid, and my ride wasn't built to be smooth. The tracks I had to follow were laid through the most treacherous of terrains, and there was no map or manual for me to follow.

My nature and my circumstances combined in a way so that my childhood evaporated before I even had a chance to notice it. I was the oldest of seven and was born a natural helper and a quick study, so when my mother was absent or preoccupied with the man of the moment, I instinctively filled that open role. I handled the daily responsibilities around the house and took care of my siblings since I was physically able to do so. My mother never thanked me or even smiled at me appreciatively for helping in this way. She seemed to think this was my purpose, and in a way it was. My longing to help would never go away.

I did want to help, but it shouldn't have felt so cold and lonely. The extent to what I could do and provide for the family was limited, being so young. I was only a child after all. We never got new clothes. Whatever we had came from either family or the Salvation Army, so I took to pinching a shirt or sweatshirt from the men that my mom dated and brought home. She never registered that my true motivation was purely having a nice comfortable hoodie to bury my head in. Instead, she assumed I was stealing and sleeping with her men. This always ended in severe "whoopings" and verbal abuse. I had a new piece of clothing, but I would also have bruises as I continued my endless chores.

Having a laundry list of responsibilities was not the only way in which I grew up quickly. I also physically grew up more quickly than any of the other girls in my grade, leaving me looking much older than my nine-year-old spirit. Unfortunately, this gave the men around me ideas - ideas that they eventually acted on. This only fueled the discord between my mom and me. She refused to believe the truth about what one of my brother's fathers did to me. For me, it was becoming very clear that my train tracks were headed into some dangerous territory. I couldn't change direction, but I could make myself stronger. I could erect walls around my heart. I could lock away my vulnerability.

I tried hiding under baggy, tomboy clothes throughout high school. I easily fell in with the guys at school and was happy to have them befriend and respect me rather than desire me. That was just the way I wanted it. And when they did start to notice me in a way that was less about friendship and more about sexuality or romance, I soaked up the attention. School came really easily to me, and I knew that it was important to make this a priority, but sometimes the attention they gave me trumped school. I was so excited to be accepted and appreciated that I started missing classes and misbehaving. I had no idea that I was looking in all the wrong places for validation and self worth in those after-school romances.

After high school, I took a year off before college to work and save money. I moved out of my childhood home and was able to rent a place of my own. Many of the people around me thought that this was a bad idea and that if I didn't go to college right away, I'd likely never go. It was discouraging to hear, but I was used to this sort of talk. Listening to their pessimistic outlook on my future felt disheartening. It was like even they could see the railroad path my life was set on, and they saw no room for improvement. I was simply on a path to nowhere.

Their feedback caused me to work harder. I did return to school as I said I would, and I enrolled in a four-year nursing program even though I wasn't sure how I would pay for this expense. It turned out that maintaining a "B" average was difficult to do while maintaining a full-time job, and I had to cut back my hours to ensure I could keep my grades up. A lot was going on in my personal life at this time, and I had to constantly make sacrifices in order to keep my grades up and keep going along this career path. I refused to give up - even when my bills inundated me, and I lost my apartment. My health was starting to slide as well. Things were looking dire. I wasn't sleeping, exercising or eating well, and I often wondered if I had the strength to do this.

My family and friends couldn't understand why I was working so hard. I remember one day my brother called and told me I was stupid. He said I could easily quit school and get a good-paying job or even two jobs, and I'd easily be able to support myself. He couldn't see why I was paying for an education that was just making my life more difficult. If I was just looking for the easiest thing to do in the present, I could understand his point; but I wanted more for my future, and I knew that nursing was a steady and reliable career. Putting the work in now would be uncomfortable, but it would pay off in time. I didn't let myself get deterred by his words. Instead, I focused on the light at the end of the tunnel and kept on.

I ended up graduating cum laude with my Bachelor of Science in Nursing. My family came out to support me with tears of happiness in their eyes, but I felt a dark regret in the pit of my stomach. I felt like I could've done so much better if only I had been more focused. The entire time I was in school, I was also dealing with the ups and downs of yet another unhealthy relationship. The thorns of my past continued to disrupt my life, and I was feeling that unease on my graduation day. My emotional health was so wounded by my childhood and everything I hadn't gotten as a little girl. These longings continued to show up and wreak havoc on my life even though my rational mind understood the importance of school and career. I was always being distracted in my personal life. I was proud of myself, but felt like I was balancing on a very precarious bit of track, and that my train might fall over the edge at any moment.

I decided I needed to dream bigger. Nursing was such a vast profession and it was brimming with opportunities. When I envisioned my ideal career, I saw myself as a Navy nurse, helping soldiers in the middle of the battlefield. I knew that's not how it would look in reality, but I was compelled with the idea of working as a nurse in the military. I worked for a year in a hospital and assisted living facility to gain experience as I explored the requirements I needed to enroll in the military.

But my demons were still chasing me. No sooner had I gotten admitted into a military program did the same old habits find me yet again. I quickly got involved with my recruiter. He was older than me, and though I didn't completely trust him in the beginning, he was manipulative, and I was in need of supportive attention and care. This relationship had to be kept secret because of his position, and so he only saw me in private. Things progressed quickly until I found out he was keeping a big secret from me. He had a terminally ill wife that he never mentioned. He finally brought it up when it was determined that she was not going to make it, and he had to fly to the hospital to be with her in her final hours.

I held back my anger since this was not the time to unleash it. Instead, I made my plans for relocation to another base for boot camp. I was hurt and devastated, but I needed to move forward. Little did I realize that another threat – dressed in the uniform of a high-ranking official - was already waiting for me at boot camp.

Against my better judgment, I fell for him right away. Everything happened faster than I could process. Within six months, we were married. He took me to the courthouse in the morning, and by that night, everything had devolved. He drank heavily, and when he drank he got aggressive. Things had turned quite ugly in just a few hours. The entire episode would take months to resolve in court, and because he was the high-ranking official, justice was not on my side. My dreams of becoming a military nurse faded quickly, all because I got involved with this man. His rank protected him, and I was put out into the cold.

I was disappointed in myself and crushed. I had truly thought I was moving in the right direction with this man. I thought all of my dreams were coming true. Instead, my dream of being a military nurse was stripped from me, and I was left with the scars - physical, emotional and mental - of his abuse. In time, I was able to look back at this experience with gratitude for the things I gained, but that took time and work. Eventually, I was able to see that I had a reservoir of great strength in me, and I could access it even in high-pressure situations. Having come out of that experience in one piece, I knew that I could achieve anything I put my mind to. I simply had to start getting out of my own way. It was so easy for me to fall back into old patterns and to end up prioritizing love from someone else over my own self worth.

At this point, I knew I still needed a career. The military was out the question, but there were plenty of other careers available to a nurse. The idea of becoming a travel nurse appealed to me for all the same reasons as being a military nurse. I would get to travel the world and work autonomously. Being a travel nurse would give me flexibility with both my schedule and my finances, and I would finally be able to live my best life. So, I packed my bags and moved to California to start this new life. And at first, everything seemed to be falling into place. I was making plenty of money, I had more control in my career than ever before and I was seeing the world from a new vantage point. I finally felt as if my train tracks had turned a corner, and I was in a totally new landscape where my little engine didn't have to work so hard for once.

Just as I was settling into this new life, depression, self-doubt and self-sabotage came knocking at the door. I was burnt out and fatigued. The hours were long, and my body was tired. Nursing no longer lit me up. It felt like my passion for the job was fading and that made me very worried. The only reason I kept going to work was for the money, and I didn't want my life to be reduced to simply working for a paycheck, even if it was a good one. I wanted to enjoy what I was doing.

I needed to do something different, so I reflected on what had inspired me earlier in my life. When I thought back to my time in the military, I realized that I really enjoyed educating the sailors. I enjoyed the act of teaching, and people seemed receptive to the way I taught them. That dynamic felt gratifying. That's when I decided to pursue a Masters in Nursing Education.

During my schooling, I kept working as a travel nurse. The money was good, and I needed to pay my way through school. But even after graduating, I still wasn't quite ready to leave that profession. I knew I wanted to teach and that I wouldn't truly be fulfilled until I was doing that, but I wasn't yet sure what that career looked like. I needed to come up with a plan.

Recently, I enrolled in a Doctor of Nursing program and have started to obtain the certifications I need to become a healthcare provider instructor. I am in the process of working to open my own CNA/allied health school. This is my new trajectory, a path that can both support and fulfill me.

When I reflect on my life, the missing piece has always been support. No matter what stage of my life, I never had anyone in my corner. I fought and persisted despite this void, but not having a community or even one person around me who believed in me was always my downfall. It led me down dark alleys that were not in line with my true mission and purpose. I wanted someone to fight for me and to believe in me, and so I ended up seeing mirages many times along the way. And it sent me down tracks that are better left untraveled. I don't regret them, because all of my travels have allowed my strength to manifest, but I have not taken the easy path.

No matter what type of nursing you do, at one time or another, you will experience trauma, setbacks and roadblocks. As nurses, we constantly battle with the stressors of life outside and inside the healthcare facility. It's a challenge to show up at work everyday and continue to care for our patients when our own lives are in constant turmoil. I have learned throughout my nursing journey how important it is to do what you love. Life is about finding your purpose and sharing that gift with others. Pay attention to what sets your soul on fire, embrace it and move toward it. Your purpose in life will present itself over and over until you do.

I am a better nurse today because of the trauma I have endured. I am a diverse, flexible and experienced nurse who can now master any situation I am presented with. I am more innovative and creative because of where I've been, and these qualities are the foundation of my entrepreneurial mindset. My hardship has literally paved the way for my success, because I chose to not get stuck in my circumstances. I am learning more each day about managing a work-life balance in order to give my very best to my patients while still maintaining my own well-being. My advice to any new nurse or aspiring entrepreneur is to uncover the thing that lights you up. That is the only thing that will be worth fighting for. In the meantime, process your experiences in a healthy manner and work on healing traumatic experiences. Dwelling on where you are will not and cannot move you forward. You have to set your eyes on something different in the distance and go toward it.

I feel now, more than ever, that I am finally like the train that moves through various climates with ease. I move through hardship, up hills and through dark tunnels with a strength that I learned on the tracks. And I've learned that the only way forward is by working on your self and making yourself strong. It's not the simple, thick walls I built in my youth to keep out the hurt. Those walls keep out everything. The type of strength that truly moves a person forward is the ability to be vulnerable, to be scared and to be honest about reality and move through it anyway. And that's why my purpose is to educate. In education, I can teach others not just the basics of nursing, but also the basics of living and thriving. I can be the support to others that I never had myself. I can be the light at the end of the tunnel. That's the path that's mine to navigate.

Connect with Sade

Website: www.sadenichole.com FB: sadegnichole
Website: www.onelifeinspired.net IG: @sadenichole

Biography

Sade Griggs was born and raised in Martinsville, Virginia as the oldest of seven children in a single-parent household. Sade attended North Carolina Central University, graduating with a Bachelor of Science in Nursing. She then obtained a Master of Science in Nursing Education from Norwich University and continues to pursue a Doctorate in Nursing Practice at Walden University.

Sade has also served as a nurse in the U.S. Navy and participates in medical mission trips abroad. She is the Founder and CEO of OneLife Inspired Enterprises LLC, a life coaching group that supports and empowers teens and adults who have experienced childhood trauma/abuse. Her firm commitment is to provide compassionate nursing care, educating those from similar backgrounds on what is possible, and inspiring others to heal in order to live a full life.

Ms. Griggs has paved her way as a nurse, author, speaker, life coach, and entrepreneur. All of which have afforded her the opportunity to generate multiple streams of income, gain personal freedom, and leave a legacy for her family. Sade looks forward to her future and all that is to come.

Dedication

This book is dedicated to all the people who positively impacted my life and empowered me through prayer, encouraging words, and acts of kindness. Thank you

To Christopher: I deeply respect and love the way you stepped up to be my support system. Thank you for your love and for being my protector as I went through this process.

To My Nephew: Delexius: I know I would not be a nurse if it had not been for you. Life gave you a hard hand, but you are doing your best with that hand. Auntie is so proud of you. Keep fighting.

~Kamilah

To My Four Children:

Cameron: Thanks for holding the fort down when mom had to study. Thank you.

Christian: For stepping up and becoming the man God has called you to be. Thank you.

Serenity: For keeping everyone in line when mommy was not able to. Thank you.

Khaleel (KJ): My preacher and 7-year-old prayer warrior; thank you for all the hugs, kisses, and random prays. They all come right on time.

Thank you for being such excellent children and never giving up on mom in a hard time during the process. Greater is coming.

To My Cousin: John Plattenburg: Thank you for your support during this process. I would have given up without your example of pushing when the odds are against you. Thank you.

To Pastor Keion Henderson: Thank you for all the blood, sweat, and tears. We don't see behind the scenes, but I know it cost you everything. Then in spite of what you are going through, you give us a word that will change our lives. Thank you for allowing God to use you. You have truly changed my life.

Blind Faith: The Journey to Entrepreneurship

By Kamilah J. Lyon, APRN

"What do you mean it is not working out? I have been working since I was 15 years old, and I have never been fired! Plus, I have given this company everything. Can I at least get a reason other than the doctors said, "It's not working out?" Tom replied, "In the state of Texas, we can fire you for no reason." Confusedly I replied, "What about my contract for the whole year?" "That applies to that also?" Tom responded. At this time, in my head, I start knocking everything off the desk and screaming, "OH YOU GONE FIRE ME!" in my David Ruffin voice. But in reality, I politely said, "Okay, I'd like some paperwork stating this, and can I finish my last chart, please." Tom replied, "Yes, you can do that. It has been a pleasure working with you, and we hate to see you go. The doctors had a meeting without me and said that it's just not working out. They did not give me any reason, and they are making me be the bad guy. I am so sorry you are going through this. I see how hard you have worked for this company. At least, you will be paid to the end of the month."

Earlier that month, I began working as a nurse practitioner at a doctor's clinic. I was working with several MAs who had been working for this particular doctor for several years, one of which had been with the doctor for five years. For this book purposes, we will call her Becky-with the-good-hair. For some reason, she did not like nurse practitioners. She made this clear daily. She felt like she was untouchable because no one was trained to do her job.

She was allowed to yell at the doctor and curse in front of the patients and staff. I could not understand why this culture was allowed, but it was not my practice, and I was just working there.

I saw several signs that I need to move on, but I was too comfortable with my lovely paycheck every month. God showed me that he wanted greater for me, but I was stuck on having a monthly income that was secure, at least I thought.

On this particular day, I asked Becky-with-the-good-hair to give the patient in room five some assistance. Becky-with-the-good-hair stepped in the hallway and started yelling, "You have to do your own patients too!" I replied, "Please stop yelling at me. I still have three rooms to see, and two people have been waiting for an hour, and no, that was for yesterday when there was only 1 MA for both providers. Today there a three of you." The patient in the hall's eyes got very large when he heard her yelling at me. I then had to begin to get my bearings because I was in shock. Becky then came to me, yelling again, "I was not refusing. I was just telling you!"

I stated, "Please lower your voice! Please don't yell at me! Please leave me alone." I continued to face my desk and say this repeatedly in a very low voice. This apparently made her angrier because she came closer, yelling and pointing her finger in my face. "I am not raising my voice! You haven't seen nothing yet. You don't even know our f**** names." Then she stepped closer, stating, "You need to learn our F***** names. I am Becky, and that is Shirley!" I then closed my eyes, continued to face the desk, and repeated, "Please leave me alone."

At this point, I saw my whole nursing career going down the drain. See, I am a veteran of the US Navy; I have been trained to protect myself. I felt threatened in the movement with the aggressive hand gestures towards me. If she had touched me, I would have gone to jail because I was going to drag her in that office. But to God be the glory, when I did not face her or look at her, she turned and walked away. At this point, I realized that I could not work with her anymore because I had worked too hard for my license, and nobody, including Becky-with-the-good-hair, would make me lose them. This was a point where I had to turn on emotional intelligence. I wrote a formal letter, and she was removed from that office.

From that day on, they began to try to get rid of me. I would see 10-18 patients with no medical assistant, and three medical assistance (MA) were in the office. The MAs would be sitting at the desk while I roomed, treated, and checked out my own patients. At first, I was upset, but then I realized it was training for the future. I knew my vision was more significant than this position. But I refused to let it go because I enjoyed my check every month. I knew my season was up in that position, but I refused to let it go. Multiple times people asked me, "When are you going to start your own business." I would always reply. "I like my check." When God has called you to do something greater, you must move when he says to move. If not, he will push you. After this experience, I declared that this would never happen to me again.

I have never been a stranger to struggle. I have struggled my whole life, and I have accepted that I am a WINNER. See, God brought back some of the victories He has won for me. Against all odds, God allowed me to become a nurse practitioner while being a sing mom with four children and receiving my niece in my last semester. The last semester is one of the most critical semesters because you see the like, but you still in the tunnel.

Earlier in February, I was sitting in church and my Pastor, Keion Henderson, stated, "There is someone here who is about to take a test to be a nurse." I was looking around and thought in my head, Well, he can't be talking to me because I'm already a registered nurse, but I do have to take a test to become a nurse practitioner. He questioned, "There is no one here?" I looked around again and slowly raised my hand, and he said, "Come here, the only thing you lack for this test is confidence. What's stopping you from taking the test?" With tears in my eyes, I stuttered, "I just got my niece. She has not slept in 3 weeks. She has horrible night terrors.

My car was repossessed last week, and then I got her with the clothing on her back and nothing else." Pastor Henderson began to pray for me. I began to sob uncontrollably.

I was tired and ready to give up. It would have been so easy just to give up and go back to work as an RN, but I was walking in blind faith. I had no idea how I was going to be a mother, work full time, and do clinical and class full time. Talk about not enough time in the day, month, or year. My pastor did not know earlier that morning; I sat at my clinical site with tears in my eyes because I had to make a decision. See, I had been blessed with the task of caring for my niece due to unfortunate events. She was two years old at the time and had been through a lot, which resulted in her having horrible night terrors. That day had marked the third week of me literally being up with her from 12 AM to 3 AM praying and feeling helpless because she was fighting people and things that I could not see. Many times, I could not fall back asleep, and when I did, I had to get up at 5 AM and get all five children to daycare and school, then go to class or clinical myself. The process had worn me down.

I could not figure out for the life of me why I was still going to Nurse Practitioner (NP) school and putting myself through this torture. I heard rumors about NPs never finding a job and NP being paid less than my current pay at my intermittent job. This just added fuel to the fire. I was tired and wanted to quit. One of the hardest things is to go through the process for the greater good when you know you can end it and not go through the pain. While I was going through all of this, God chose me to be the chaplain for Prairie View A and M University, class of 2019. I really did not want to do anything extra because, at that time, I was struggling working, paying rent, keeping the lights on, and being a mother. My grade was surviving only through prayer. The class itself became torture due to fatigue. My brother and sister-in-law would assist sometimes, but they refused to take my niece full time, and her own father would disappear on me. I did not receive any government assistance, either. My classmates paid daycare and bought diapers for her. My church gave clothing and a car seat. And the daycare that God opened the month before allowed her to be there for free many of days. See, God will provide. I was already struggling before I got her and could not for the life of me figure out why God put more on my plate.

See, my car had been repossessed just one week earlier. But the God I served brought the car right back the same day and had it dropped off at my clinical site. Now, where in the world, does that happen? I can't make this stuff up, and no, they did not make a mistake; they were supposed to come and get it. I was confused about why they had not come earlier because I was definitely late for a few months. Any other time, I would have been ashamed to go outside and get my car, but that time I proudly went in the rain to meet the repo man. Only God can touch hearts and provide the way He does. God has shown me who he is so many times, but I still suffer from unbelief sometimes. I'm human. See, that was indeed a miracle that day because I did not have the money and had no way to get it.

When I say God provides, He truly provides. Many times, God calls us to do something so crazy that it makes no sense to us or anyone around us. I have always known that I have been destined for greatness. My Father in heaven says I am the lender and not the borrower. I am the head, not the tail, above only and not beneath. I just did not want to go through anymore struggle. I was in a great place where I was making money and paying my bills without any issues, but God would not let me get comfortable. Uhhhhh. Why can't I get comfortable? Your purpose is greater than you. You are destined for greatness, and your lesson has been learned in this position. Your time is up, and since you won't get the hint, I'll help you. I did not want to hear that.

Abraham had faith, and he obeyed God. God called him to go to a place he would later receive as his own. So, he went. He did it even though he didn't know where he was going. Hebrews 11:8

This was truly Blind Faith. My people have been called to do extraordinary things, but they can't see where they are going or how to get there. It may even look too hard. Has God called you to do something to change the world or change one person's life? Do you feel like you want to leave a legacy for your children and your children's children? If you don't build your own dream, someone will hire you to build theirs. This is the time when you must have blind faith. If God told you to do it, do it. God will provide.

Dear Past Employer,

I am writing this to thank you for firing me. It was really the best thing you could have ever done for me. I did not realize that you noticed that the vision God had for my life was bigger than your current practice. I was asked several times why I had not stepped out on faith and started my own business. Well, because that paycheck was a security blanket that held me back from stepping out on Blind Faith. See, I fell for the most addictive thing in the world, a paycheck. It makes you so dependent on a job that you never fulfill your dreams. I did not want to break this addiction, but God used you to break my habit of a paycheck. See, I have never been fired in my life. I gave you everything for the 10 hours that I was there. I know I was only required to provide you with 8 hours, but I went above and beyond for you, investing time and money into your dream and not my own. Now it's time for me to invest in my own vision. Dreams are something that everyone has, but only a few are motivated and determined enough to reach them.

The journey isn't comfortable, but it's definitely worth it. As I sit here thinking back over my life, all I can say is thank you, My Lord and Savior. You have been so good to me. See, I did not start this journey with a silver spoon in my mouth - It began in the slums. But that's neither here nor there. God brought me from the bottom, and now I'm here, and I came to encourage you today and let you know that all you have to do is take action and determine that you are not going to stay where you're at. Your life is what you make it. The journey is not comfortable, but it's worth it. Let your faith be greater than your fear! Step out with blind faith, and God will provide.

Biography

Kamilah J. Lyon MSN, APRN, FNP-C, dared to defy all the odds. She was born and raised by a single mother in Livingston, Texas. She is the youngest of 4 children in which she was the first to graduate high school and go to college. She was determined not to become static and had a dream to become a nurse. She joined the US Navy. In 2004, Kamilah lost her sister and mother, which propelled her desire to educate people about health issues such as diabetes, HTN, renal failure, HIV, and AIDS. She stepped into nursing as a CNA in 2005. Then in 2006, she attended Medical Careers Institute in Norfolk, VA, and became a Licensed Practical Nurse. In 2011, Kamilah obtained her RN from Lone Star College System. In 2013, She earned her BSN in Nursing from the University of Houston-Victory. In 2019, Kamilah reached her goal to become a Family Nurse Practitioner obtaining MSN in Nursing from Prairie View A&M University.

Kamilah launched her entrepreneur early in her nursing career because of the acquired role of a single mother to her children, nephews, and nieces. She began by contracting herself out to different agencies, including surgery centers, hospitals, adult/pediatric home health, and hospice.

Kamilah is passionate about helping people reach their goals and dreams. She enjoys encouraging them to never give up on their dreams, no matter how hard it gets. Kamilah also enjoys community outreach and teaching vulnerable populations about health and wellness. Kamilah is a servant leader on the Emergency Response Team at the Lighthouse Church in Houston. Kamilah is the mother of four wonderful children, Cameron, Christian, Serenity, and Khaleel (KJ), which motivates her daily to keep pushing to her goals to leave a legacy for them.

Kamilah J. Lyon is a mother, entrepreneur, author, speaker, and mentor.

Kamilah resides in Houston, Texas where she is the owner of Lyon Health Services PLLC. She is currently expanding the services of this organization. Stay tuned to the new and exciting services. Kamilah also speaks at churches, schools, and community events on various health and wellness issues. She is a member of Sigma Theta Tau National Nursing Honor Society, American Nurse Association, Texas Nurse Association, Texas Black Nurse Practitioners, and Texas Nurse Practitioners. Kamilah is a part of Texas Nurse Practitioner's Legislative Ambassadors Program – a grassroots network which consist of 181 nurse practitioners who serve as the official TNP liaison to their state representative or senator.

Connect With Kamilah J. Lyon
Lyon Health Services, PLLC,
Phone: 832-616-0698
Email: kamilahlyon@gmail.com
LinkedIn: linkedin.com/in/kamilah-lyon-4b5b21191

Dedication

To My Family, Mentors, and Struggles,

As I continue my journey, there are memories of joy despite the stumbling blocks before me. My heart overflows with gratitude. The poem "BE TRUE TO YOU" reminded me of the darkness and pain; somehow, tears of joy are present. My parents would often tell me that 'life itself is a task.' Although it may seem as if life isn't going the way you have envisioned it, remember that life itself is a blessing. Keep following your path because faith and determination will lead the way. A final thought as my dad would say, situations don't control you because you control the circumstances.

With love,
Jerwanda Johnson
Dr. Jai

Behind the Mask: My Journey

By Dr. Jerwanda Johnson

It's so easy to fall into the trap of confusing the **person we are** with the **path we walk**. Often, we look around at our lives, our accomplishments, our setbacks, and we judge it all so harshly. Our inner monologue is filled with sentiments like, "How did I end up here?" and, "I can't believe I'm dealing with this." Somewhere deep inside, it's like there is this metronome ticking, telling us what we should've accomplished at different stages of our lives. We are continually looking at others' lives and comparing what we see to our progress. As humans failing to meet our harsh standards, we tend to look down on ourselves. We feel inferior, frustrated and defeated.

But the truth is, we measure the wrong thing. If life were a race, then the winner would be the first to pass through every rite of passage and wind up at the end. But in that story, death is the final stop. If you got there first, what did you achieve? A true satisfaction in life doesn't come from getting anywhere early, but living each moment to the fullest, through every struggle, doing the best we can, and squeezing out every last drop of meaning from even the worst of times. When we live life in that way, we can be proud of what has accomplished in spite of all the obstacles. And isn't that where the real beauty lies, in all the scars we've collected through the years? In that version of life, success might mean resilience.

I've fallen into this exact trap. Sometimes when I think about my life, I get discouraged that so many of my years have been swallowed by setbacks. I look at my path, and it is painfully circuitous - even when I had a clear sense of my destination.

In my lowest times, it's this frustrating sense of disappointment that bubbles inside of me, and I think I've failed. I'm not remotely where I thought I'd be at this point in my life. Sometimes, I feel like I'm in a car headed toward this idyllic destination, but I keep stopping at places that I shouldn't. I stop at a rest area, and I drive over broken glass and get a flat. I stop to visit a friend I know is distracting and get caught up in their toxic plans for way longer than is beneficial. I stop to help someone on the road, and my car gets sideswiped. No matter what I do, I can't reach my destination.

My life has been playing out this way since I was in high school. My dad was winding on his circuitous path when he struck a bridge. We were all in the car with him and absorbed the impact of the crash. I was hospitalized for several months as I recovered, missing the final months of my senior year. My brother nearly lost his arm as a result of his injuries, and I naturally came to his aid as best as I could, even while dealing with my injuries. The healing process was long and slow, and we all dealt with it in our ways. I remember having to miss my senior prom seemed like a new, cruel joke. It had been a bright spot and a source of excitement all year and losing it seemed like a punishment for something I didn't even cause.

Missing a dance doesn't sound like such a big deal. Lots of people lose their prom, but the action represents what would become a troubling habit of forgetting myself because of others' reactions and mistakes. All of these complications that were out of my control were dictating what I could and couldn't do. Missing that dance seemed like an acceptance of something that I wouldn't shake for years to come. For whatever reason, I was learning that I deserved to suffer for things out of my control. It was okay to disregard my wants and desires. That habit of ignoring myself is the root of why my path became so winding in the first place. Though I'd also say, it's a significant contributor to my passion for nursing.

I was always helping others. I loved working with the elderly at my church and taking care of my grandparents. Whenever anyone needed a helping hand, I'd be the first to volunteer. There was nothing more significant than witnessing the appreciation in a person's eyes when a kind word or action reached them in a time of distress. I knew this gift of compassion was my purpose. I knew I needed to become a nurse.

But though I knew this was my intended destination, the path wasn't so straightforward. My dad's car accident shook my family. Though it planted the seed of nursing within me, it did nothing to help me move toward that seed. I couldn't focus on studying after the experience. Instead, I was filled with frenetic energy. My concentration was scattered. I wanted to help others, but my energy was spraying out of me in a million different directions. Instead of walking straight toward my goal, I turned left.

Soon after college, I met the man who would become my husband. This was no fairy tale romance. He broke me down steadily and consistently with his words until I no longer believed in myself. Already having the tendency to put others first, I put a person first that treated me like garbage. In terms of my career, I had managed to make it into the medical field, but I wasn't a nurse at this point. The desire to help others was still buried deep inside of me, but the verbal abuse that I bore from my husband took its toll. He made me feel as if I was worthless. It was impossible for me to rustle up the motivation to better myself surrounded by this negative energy.

His harsh and demeaning words left me feeling on edge. Because this person, who was supposed to love me, said such hurtful things to me and seemed to be going back on the promise he made to me, I no longer could trust men at all. I was always waiting for the other shoe to drop. A compliment or a kind word would inevitably still be followed by betrayal. That's just what I had become accustomed to. I wasn't the sort of person who deserved honesty or kindness or love.

Despite the darkness of my marriage, I never stopped praying to God for guidance. God was the only one who knew my pain because, in my life, I presented a strong face. I didn't let anyone in to see what was eating away at me on the inside. I felt like my situation was unchangeable, or at least I couldn't see the way out. So I did the only thing I knew to do and prayed. I felt like I was drowning. My life was just an endless series of verbal attacks and successive fear. I couldn't even imagine it being any different than that.

The answer came, like a light bulb going on in a dark room. A voice in my head said, "What are you doing?" At that moment, I knew that I was being called to stand up. I couldn't let him destroy me. It was like I suddenly remembered that everything negative he said to me wasn't right. With that realization, I finally had the courage to tell him that I was leaving.

As I was going through the divorce process, a tornado tore through my neighborhood. At the time, I was home with my two children and my niece. Before I could I even process what was happening, the house was uprooted around us. The detritus swirled and then dropped out of the sky on top of us. We all survived, but the impact caused me to lose my memory for some time. This medical setback did nothing to improve my journey and made it more challenging to pick up the pieces as my marriage ended. My memory may have been compromised, but the muscle memory of feeling "less than" and "not good enough" still lived inside of me. At times, I even wondered if I deserved the wrath of that tornado. Maybe the world was trying to tell me something.

As I waited for the divorce to become official, I stayed with my sister and slowly came up with a new plan for my life. Now that this painful and energy-consuming marriage was over, I was finally able to focus on my career again. I worked for a while as a Surgery Technologist, and though I enjoyed working in the OR in this capacity, I wanted something more interactive with patients.

I went back to school to become a registered nurse and was then able to work as a bedside nurse. After that, I got a Business degree and later went on to get a Master's and a Doctorate in Nursing. During all of my schooling, I worked as a nurse, eventually moving up to Director of Nursing. Later becoming Dr. Johnson DNP, FNP and Legal Consultant.

In terms of distance, I made it so far from where I started. I was counseling other nurses on my floor, had worked bedside and was doing what I always intended. But then I hit a wall. I eventually found myself in a position where I could no longer move forward. I started to feel stuck and overwhelmed. I was working all the time, and though my position was reputable, I wasn't happy. I felt guilty thinking about all the school I had just gone through. I had invested so much time, money and energy, that I knew I couldn't just give up. But the actual job didn't look like what I wanted for my life.

And I knew all too well the lesson of sacrificing my own needs out of responsibility or guilt. I didn't want to fall back into the trap of believing that tough circumstances were signs of my worthlessness. But yet, I still wasn't sure what to do. How could I make use of my education and my degrees AND have a fulfilling career that lit me up each day? I prayed some more.

That's when I got the idea to start an after hours urgent and primary care clinic. Being in the medical field, I understood the need for such a practice, and I had the experience and desire to make it a reality. So many people I encountered daily didn't have the means or insurance to seek out medical care. I could create a place that was both affordable and accessible for this underserved population. It wouldn't be easy, but I could work this business in addition to my job until it got going.

I was suddenly filled with a newfound passion. Maybe my entire life had led me right here so that I could be there for others in this innovative way. This endeavor would take a lot of re-balancing to make it a reality, but I was determined. I found a mentor who gave me guidance and support. I had a business degree, but this was going to be a practical exercise, not just the theories and ideas I was used to.

Just as I was getting underway, and in the early stages of building my business, my mentor passed away suddenly. This loss threw me. I moved from feeling healthy and motivated into a place of doubt that was difficult to shake. A part of me thought that maybe I was attempting something that was just too big to do all on my own. And I thought about giving up.

But then I thought some more, and I realized that my mentor would never give me that advice. He would tell me that I could do it, that he was giving voice to things I already knew inside. So with that, I brushed aside my feelings of fear, and I moved forward. When I finally opened my doors, he may not have been there in body, but he was there in spirit and heart.

From that point on, I knew I could handle any obstacle that surfaced. Some setbacks arose around the opening date, but I pushed through and found the answers. When a new challenge surfaces, like trying to get the word out to new clients or deciding how best to market the services, I don't hesitate. I keep moving forward, looking for solutions, doing the research, and seeking out guidance. I may not be perfect, and I don't have all the answers when it comes to building a business, but I do know how to persevere through adversity. My life has provided me with all the tools I need to be successful because I know how to change course. I know how to adapt and to find new paths when the old ones are worn. I know how to move forward, even when it feels like the world is against me.

When I struggle with something new, I try not to let it derail me from my journey. I take a step back and look for a positive impact. After you move through enough obstacles in your life, you learn to look at these setbacks differently. Even though it might seem like it sometimes, the world is not out to get us. In my early days, I always felt like I was cursed; the world was set on forcing me to fail. And instead of moving through my struggles with confidence, I let myself feel like a victim. I didn't deserve anything good. But that's not true. When I felt like a victim, I became it. I attracted situations in my life where I got to play that role. And I was comfortable with it. The reason for attracting those victim relationships was not because I deserved them. It was so that I could learn that I deserved [a1] more. And until I learned that lesson, I was destined to repeat it. But I am not my path. I am who I am today because of what I overcame along my way, but I am not the path itself.

I like to think about my life's journey as a work of art. If it were easy to make a beautiful painting, we wouldn't look in awe and amazement at paintings by great artists. A painting that is easy to create wouldn't enthrall the viewer. It would look like the doodles someone might sketch as they sat through a tedious chemistry class. But a work of art has a history. Lots of thought and care go into a detailed painting. Sometimes the perspective or color doesn't work, and the artist has to step back and try again until the figures coalesce into the perfect scene. That might happen on the first go, but more often than not, it would take hours of diligence and hard work to come up with a finished piece that is the true vision. That's what our life's journey is like and why it's unimportant the path we take or the length of time spent journeying. The thing that is most important is what we create in the end and if we create that sense of awe in another person when all is through.

No one says in a eulogy, "I loved that she took such an efficient path in life. What a great person." But they will say something like, "Her life was hard. I don't know how she did it, but her strength inspired me." That's the difference between purpose and path. The path will be forgotten, but purpose will live on in the hearts of everyone it touches along the way.

We live our purpose when we move through the struggles - no matter what - when the goal seems impossible, and somehow we keep plodding along.

Let's Connect!

Facebook: Facebook.com/divinmed/ or IG @divinemedical

Biography

I am Dr. Jerwanda Johnson DNP FNP-C, a graduate from Chatham University and a Medical Provider at my very own clinic. My greatest strength as a provider is my ability to connect with people. I was introduced to my purpose at a young age. As a teenager, I realized my passion for the medical field was rooted in me. Having survived a tragic car accident with my family and having a house collapse on me and my children from a horrific category five tornado, the love for medical became profound. I knew that being able to give back to society using the therapeutic avenue as a vehicle was my calling. Striving for excellence has led me to provide quality care to everyone. No matter where my patients are from or what their circumstances are my goal is to bring personalized, high-quality medical care to each individual. My goal is to treat my patients with the same love and care, which I treat my own family. Helping others to maintain and improve well-being is a burning desire that keeps me focused while promoting excellence from all eight aspects of health and wellness. After all, family comes first. The relationships that I build with my patients last for years. It is an honor to be able to take care of multiple generations within a family and to offer my skills and experience to the community.

Acknowledgements

I would like to thank my Lord and Savior Jesus Christ, without whom nothing that I do that is worthwhile would be possible.

My husband Rodney, who has been patient and supportive despite the many late nights.

I have spent while working on this project.

My Coach Michelle Greene Rhodes for training, supporting, and challenging me beyond my comfort zone, believing I could rise to the occasion, and providing a platform to do so.

My mother Brenda Marshall, Lakeila Deloach Lucas and Laronda Gracia Allen for reading, editing, feedback and encouragement.

My father Willie Cottle for teaching me that I can do anything I put my mind to.

This is the knowledge that fuels my entrepreneurial perseverance.

Dequindra Quinn MSN, RN, FNP-C

Restoration: A Nurse Practitioners Journey toward Entrepreneurship

By Dequindra Quinn Blakey

A legacy nurse?

My dad's four sisters and my stepmother are nurses, so I decided I was going to be a nurse too. But graduating from high school with a 2.3 GPA, my destiny as a nurse was in question.

I was ecstatic when my area supervisor said he would make sure that I received 80% tuition reimbursement for my prerequisite courses for nursing if I remained employed until I started my nursing program full time. I took all my science prerequisites for my program at the local community college and maintained a 3.5 GPA, but it seemed as if I had an argument with my husband before almost every exam. I started leaving the house to study with a classmate.

Where my help comes from

My desire to enroll in an accelerated second-degree nursing program for students who already had a bachelor's degree in another area would mean fierce competition. There were over 400 applicants for 80 spots, and grade point average was a major determining factor. I have always had faith in my Lord and Saviour Jesus Christ and the power of prayer to move mountains. I called my grandma and asked her to pray. Thanks be to God, I was accepted - one of only five African-Americans in a class of 80 students.

I began the CD2 program at Wayne State University in August 1994. Henry Ford Hospital in Detroit paid my tuition in exchange for 20 months of employment after graduation. The program required me to be in clinical and class from sun up to sun down most days, which meant I could not work. My dad and stepmom supported my household and me financially for the next 18 months. My best friend Veronica took me grocery shopping monthly, and to help offset expenses, I took in a roommate. By the grace of God, I finished the program in December 1995.

Insult and the power of unity

The day of final exams, the hospital notified us that there were no jobs available for registered nurses; however, there were nursing assistant positions until RN jobs became available. This was a ludicrous suggestion, but being unemployed for 18 months with bills piling up, many of us actually considered accepting the offer. We met and decided to obtain legal counsel, who advised us that we would not be bound to the terms of the contract if the jobs we signed for were not provided. All 40 of us refused employment as nursing assistants and were placed in positions as RNs.

I worked with an infectious disease unit for six years. Because of my assessment skills and ventilator experience, I was often asked to fill in on ICU units due to staff shortages.

I trained the patient care assistants to do phlebotomy, respiratory treatments, EKG's and insert NG tubes. This unit provided me with a great clinical foundation for my nursing career.

One of the best pieces of advice I have ever received came from my stepmother, Diane Cottle: "Never burn your bridges in nursing; the healthcare market is small around here. The same people move around and you will keep running into them. You don't want to get a bad reputation because then you will have a hard time finding a job."

Curious, assertive and effective

In 2004, I began a position as supervisor at a medical care facility while I pursued a Master's in Nursing. During that time, I was taking a course on quality improvement. One day, the medical director came to the facility for a continuous quality improvement meeting. I escorted him to the conference room. Because I was curious, when we arrived at the meeting, I took a seat, expecting to be asked to leave since this was an invitation only meeting, but I was allowed to stay. After that day, I attended monthly and just listened. After about 3 visits, I began to speak about how I had been doing chart audits and querying staff because some of what I heard as departmental reports did not correlate with my observations on the units.

I spoke to the nursing and social work staff, as well as supervisors and facility administration when I discovered deficiencies and developed plans of action to address them. I often worked well past my shift without prior approval for these projects. The administrator approached me one evening. "Quinn, I cannot justify you working all these extra hours, so from now on, unless I ask you to stay over, I need you to go home at the end of your shift." "Okay," I responded, but the very next week the facility consultant who assisted with compliance and survey readiness came in to do a chart audit and asked who had been doing quality improvement because the charts looked better and things were more in order than she had ever seen them. The administrator now had her justification. "If you have something you need to work on, it's okay for you to stay over - just let me know when you are going into overtime." I learned that my value as a nurse exceeded the care I provided at the bedside. That experience taught me the importance of process. Quality of care within a facility is a reflection of established processes or the lack thereof. I had an epiphany!! Because I had been effective in utilizing process improvement to facilitate quality improvement within this facility, I could utilize the same principles in any healthcare environment.

Creative change agent

In 2007, I had a surgical procedure that required me to be off work for 8 weeks. Out of boredom, I began applying for jobs online. I applied for a job at a local skilled nursing and rehabilitation facility as staff educator. I was called for four interviews, the fourth after an offer of employment had been extended. I wanted to tell them where to stuff it but my husband advised me to take it in stride and keep my cool.

After accepting the position, I immediately began making PowerPoint presentations, videos and interactive games to use to train staff as an alternative to traditional lectures and paper tests.

About 3 months after I accepted the position, the infection control nurse retired, and I was asked to assume the responsibilities of that position also. About 6 months into the job, we had our annual survey and received a citation for outdated policy and procedure in the infectious disease department. This meant that I had 30 days to rewrite an entire infection control manual. This is where my knowledge of research from my Masters of Science in Nursing really came in handy. Staff, including physicians, was trained in the related procedures with great results; we passed our revisit for our survey with flying colors and significantly reduced the facility infection rate - especially in terms of urinary tract infections.

After holding these positions for approximately 3 years, the director of nursing resigned. Another was hired but only stayed in the position about 2 months. After the 2 of us attended a conference, she resigned and suggested the facility hire me in the position, which they did.

This facility had a long history of providing excellent care and having several citation-free surveys, but some of the business models needed to be revamped to increase and strengthen the bottom line. I was given the title Chief Administrative Nurse/ Director of Nursing Services and my administrator/ mentor allowed me to renegotiate contracts with supply, equipment and pharmacy vendors. I was ecstatic to be granted the opportunity to educate the board of directors about quality measures. Several of the board members thanked me for explaining how the activities of daily living documentation done by the certified nursing assistants affected minimum data set assessment reporting and drove Medicare reimbursement.

That experience taught me the importance of process. I assisted with retraining the staff to focus on caring for rehabilitation clients who were more skilled needs, faster turnover and higher reimbursement-generating than traditional long term care residents. I was successful in managing a $4 million per year budget with a good level of staff job satisfaction even though raises were frozen for a few years. I was the only African American in administration at the facility - I was confident, assertive, opinionated, educated and not Catholic like those at the facility where I was employed. I realized that being a change agent is not necessarily a recipe for upward mobility. However, the changes that were put in motion during my tenure at that facility remain visible walking those halls today.

This is when I believe the seed of entrepreneurship was planted within me. If I could successfully run a $4 million per year business for someone else, surely I could run a small business of my own.

One door shuts, another opens

All of the success that I had in that facility did not prevent me from being let go from my position despite never having a single negative performance review or disciplinary action. After I was walked out of my office and told that HR would pack my belongings and meet me with them, I made a call to my former assistant administrator. "How are you, Quinn, good to hear from you," she said. "I'm good...and UNEMPLOYED; I just got fired," I replied. "You're not serious," she stated.

"I swear to God - they just walked me out." "Great," she said, "I need an interim DON at the facility where I am. Do you want $50 per hour or $60 per hour?" "What kind of question is that? If I have an option, I want $60." Two days later, we met at a restaurant to complete new hire paperwork, and the following week, I started my position as Director of Nursing at the new facility. Remember how my stepmother told me not to burn bridges? I was allowed to train, interview and recruit my own nursing supervisory staff. I attempted to train several of the RN's to perform shift supervisor and infection control nurse duties, but to no avail. I was able to convince my regional consultant to approve me hiring my former assistant, an LPN from the previous facility, to perform these duties. After a little intense fellowship, we were able to form a strong team and get to work. Within 60 days, the CMS rating went from one star to three stars. The facility was part of a nationwide chain of over 100 nursing homes. Every policy, procedure and form came from corporate headquarters. When I realized several forms did not comply with the federal register guidance to surveyors, I created my own facility forms with the approval of my regional director. When our survey took place, there were five citations in the nursing department, none at the level of actual harm and no civil money penalties.

Each position that I held taught me valuable skills in the clinical setting, leadership, managerial, training, policy and procedure development, quality improvement, mentoring and budgeting and finance that I carry into my life as an entrepreneur.

CANCER!!!

Shortly after I began my family nurse practitioner program, my dad was diagnosed with prostate cancer. It was almost unbelievable. I knew he had lost a lot of weight in a short period of time, but it seemed like he went from being okay to bedridden almost immediately. There were times I felt work, school and watching him slip away was too much to bear, and though I never said it out loud, I believe he sensed it. 'Whatever you do, promise me that you will finish school," he said. "Okay, Dad…I promise," I replied.

The stress of it all caused me to checkout mentally on occasion. I remember completing and turning in an assignment, and the assignment I had turned in had nothing to do with the syllabus, although it was a great paper. I shared my situation with the teacher, and she graded my paper with a C and allowed me to resubmit it with no penalties.

My dad did not live to see me finish my program or practice as an NP, but every time I set a goal for myself and begin to doubt my ability, I can hear my dad saying, "You can do anything you put your mind to."

I completed my courses and passed the American Academy of Nurse Practitioners' certification exam to become a family nurse practitioner in April 2016.

I was happy about passing my exam and started to apply for jobs. I found it difficult to secure a full time position due to lack of experience. Dr. Terry Baul, who has been in private practice in Detroit for over 30 years, allowed me to do 3 clinical rotations at 2 practice locations while I was in my nurse practitioner program.

To strengthen my skills while I sought employment, I decided to assist him in his practice. I worked with him for two years and he agreed to be my collaborating physician so that I could pursue starting a practice of my own.

I began by contracting with the State of Michigan foster care system, performing initial medical examinations on children who had been removed from their homes. Dr. Baul allowed me to utilize his space during his off hours and on Saturdays.

One of the gaps in knowledge from most nurse practitioner education is that programs do not teach billing and coding, though we need to understand basics since this is part of our responsibility whether we are employees or entrepreneurs. I utilized a friend who owned an independent billing company for the first few months I was in business but decided that a practice management system that was integrated with my EHR and generated multiple reports would be more useful.

I lost $22,000 in uncollected revenue the first year in business due to multiple shortcomings within an electronic health record billing system. I spent countless hours logging complaints and explaining to the billing staff how to rework rejections and denials. I went to do a group home visit and saw 7 patients. One was not submitted, and when I asked why, I was told that they did not have electronic means to submit a claim.

I had to return to my friend and biller with my tail tucked between my legs. She received me with open arms and an "I told you." She immediately started submitting corrected claims for denials, but about 50% of the revenue was never recovered. Going into my third year, I am now operating a profitable practice. My advice to nurse practitioners who want to own a practice is to get a business coach who has experience in your area of interest and can help you avoid costly mistakes.

Entrepreneurial nursing provides a myriad of alternatives to traditional primary care. The experiences we have in every area of our nursing careers - as well as our understanding of the nursing process and patient education - translates well into virtually any area of business. The business aspects are the essential elements that may be unfamiliar to nurses. A practice must be carefully planned and will require at least contract or part-time assistance from financial management, tax and accounting personnel, marketing specialists and medical billing and coding professionals. An investment into a business coach or mentor is the best investment you can make for your future in business.

Restoration Health LLC provides individualized primary care and wellness for the body and soul in an urban community.

Dequindra Quinn MSN RN FNP-C can be reached at 734 489 9863

Restoration2health@gmail.com

Restoration Health LLC on Facebook Dequindra_quinn on Instagram

Biography

My name is Dequindra Quinn, and I am a family nurse practitioner. I am from the East Side of Detroit and a graduate of Finney High School, which was featured in Ebony magazine in 1990 due to the student violence that takes place there. I graduated with a 2.3 grade point average and went to Oakland University through a program for minority students who were underachievers.

I currently have a Bachelor's in Human Resource Development with a minor in Sociology, a Bachelor's in Nursing, Master's in Nursing and a post Master's Certification for Family Nurse Practitioner.

I am the sole provider of the primary care clinic at All Well Being Services in Detroit and the CEO and founder of Restoration Health LLC, a nurse practitioner run family practice in Detroit, just around the corner from where I graduated from high school. I am also the founder of Vision NP Consulting, a coaching and education service for nurse practitioners who want to own a primary care practice.

I believe that when I sat down and determined that I wanted to speak about the interconnectedness of health, acquiring wealth and living your best life, I began to live in my intention. Intention comes from the heart, and the entire Universe begins to assist in bringing these desires into view. Within six months, I have accomplished more as an entrepreneur than I ever imagined. NP Vision Consulting is an affiliate of Restoration Health LLC and offers practice start up coaching and business education for nurse practitioners.

I want nurses to know that despite challenges, we can meet and exceed the requirements to be successful, to own our own businesses and to make an impact in our local communities. If you are young, you will be ahead of the game if you get a mentor and develop a strategic plan. If you are mature, it's still never too late!

I can be reached at Restoration2health@gmail.com

Dedication

I dedicate this chapter to my parents – Elizabeth "Dorothy" Fullard and Oliver W. Harrod, Sr. My Heartbeat and Rock!!! To my siblings - Deborah Gaters, Oliver W. Harrod, Jr., Kenneth W. Harrod Sr., Dawnika Houston and Melvin Coxs, Jr.. Legacy for my nieces and nephews – Gregory, Juanita, Kenneth, Jr., Justice, KenShaun, Jasmine, Jamera and Jayla; great nieces and great nephews – Jayla, Jameria, Juan, Javon, Morgan, Gregory, Jr and Amiyah.

Thanks to my family and friends for your support.

A Silent Epidemic: Nursing and Depression

By Charlene Owuamana, LPN

The only thing more exhausting than being depressed is pretending you aren't...

Depression in nursing is not often talked about, but it is something that definitely affects this profession. As healthcare professionals, we need to speak more about depression and how to support and heal the #1 most respected healthcare team. By being open about it, we can become more powerful in how we relate to self-care, when it comes to providing for ourselves and others. Everyone deals with depression differently. Being open with family and friends and expressing our feelings can be the starting point for healing. Supervisors/bosses need to educate themselves on how to recognize symptoms of depression, how to approach nurses and support their feelings and how to assist them with appropriate professional assistance.

I knew it was time to talk about this subject when I read online how a nurse took her life after working a 12-hour shift. In the letter she left, she talked about working long hours and being unable to have a social life. She also talked with her friends about pills and wine being her way out. Family and friends need to start LISTENING to what their loved one is saying. During one of my crises, I spoke with my family and friends. And they, too, did not take me seriously. Not that I wanted to harm myself. But I needed their support to get me through. Although we are trained healthcare providers, sometimes we feel as if we are letting others down. Believe it, when it comes to our mental health, sometimes we do not recognize the sign and symptoms. Or we do not feel like it's that serious. Healthcare professionals need to have a general conversation with ourselves and our peers because we spend most of our days and nights at work with our extended families.

According to the Robert Woods Johnson Foundation Interdisciplinary Nursing Quality Research Initiative (INQRI), nurses experience clinical depression at twice the rate of the general public. Depression affects 9% of everyday citizens, but 18% of nurses experience signs and symptoms of depression.

Seven Early Signs and Symptoms of Depression for Nurses

It's difficult to explain to someone about depression if they have never recognized they're experienced it...

Signs and symptoms of depression can include sadness, irritability, absenteeism, apathy, changes in sleeping habits, somatic complaints and weight fluctuations. While this list is not exhaustive, these signs and symptoms can help nurses recognize depression in themselves or their colleagues. Sadness in a state of depression is more than a temporary feeling; of course, everyone gets sad at times. Sadness is a normative emotional state and a normal reaction that is triggered by something. In depression, a person tends to be sad about everything in the absence of any trigger. Irritability can become accentuated as the threshold of a person's outlook is lowered. A nurse might become quicker to anger, frustrated or subject to emotional outbursts. They tend to break down faster and take longer to bounce back. Apathy is a loss or decrease of interest; a lack of any compelling emotion to direct behavior. This type of behavior is displayed as indifference, detached and unresponsive. These qualities are detrimental to the care of patients, where emotion drives nurses to respond to issues on their behalf, whether it's calling the physician to address a concern, pain management or coordinating care. A nurse who doesn't care can be dangerous. Changes in sleep vary from person to person in depression and can include anything from sleeping too much to insomnia. Sleep complaints are one of the key symptoms of depression and are one of the few proven risk factors for suicide. Restless sleep can significantly reduce quality of life and can exacerbate depressive symptoms. Night shift nurses are particularly at risk for disturbed sleep due to the unnatural sleep-wake cycles they must maintain in their jobs. However, day shift nurses who rotate to nights are more vulnerable to sleep disturbances, which can lead to depression. Fluctuations in weight and changes in appetite are common in depression. Weight fluctuation can be difficult to tease out from typical weight gain seen on the units resulting from families bringing in treats: donuts and other high fat foods. People who are depressed tend to gain weight faster, according to researchers. Foods that have a high fat content, or "comfort foods," provide a sense of contentedness that people with depression may experience.

Why Coping With It Isn't Enough

Depression isn't something you just "get over" or deal with. Nurses wouldn't expect their patients to just smile to make everything better. The consequences of depression in nursing are high not only for themselves, but for patient and professionals as well. Studies show depressed nurses make more errors, have a higher incidence of chronic illness and obesity and are at increased risk for having cancer and cardiovascular disease. Nurse managers need to be aware of signs and symptoms of depression and let their nurse know that confidential treatment is available. Advanced practice nurses are positioned to recognize depressive symptoms in nurses with whom they work. A study in 2012 points out that using standardized depression screening tools can accurately identify nurses at risk.

Stigma behind Depression in Nursing

There are wounds that never seem to show on one's body but are deeper felt in their hearts.

Healthcare workers have issues with admitting to being depressed, due to the misinformation, sense of shame and negative perceptions surrounding mental health. Nurses are concerned about the way their peers respond to their diagnosis. Healthcare workers believe that if you are diagnosed with depression, you might not be able to handle your assignment. But what they should be focusing on is making sure they notice the signs and symptoms of depression and supporting their fellow nurses - by urging them to contact their primary care provider, call the 24-hour helpline and/or seek mental health care. Early detection and treatment can make the difference in anyone's care, especially a fellow nurse. Nurses and other healthcare workers should assist one another to prevent the condition from becoming worse. If not treated properly, depression can result in social isolation, causing pessimism and lost hope for recovery.

My Personal Experience with Depression

You can be a nurse with clinical depression, and no one knows, not even you I experienced depression 10 years ago, when working in home care. We had the most compassionate clinical leaders (supervisors) who had an open door policy. They understood what it took to be an excellent leader and cared for their staff members. During our monthly department meetings, we would talk about our patient outcomes and how it personally affected our lives - whether the patient's health declined or he/she passed away. The social worker in the company would offer assistance to the staff, checking to see if they had a concern or just needed someone to listen. Depression was a topic that this agency focused on throughout my career. Nursing turnover was never an issue at this home care agency because the leadership team took pride in the staff's well being.

One day, I spoke with my supervisor about how the time between November and December was challenging for me due to my mom passing several years ago, plus the patient for whom I had been caring for over a year had passed away the previous week. I had been very depressed, and I informed her that I had contacted the Employee Assistance Program (EAP) and scheduled an appointment to see my primary care provider the next day. I asked if I could have a different assignment for a week or two until I received the help I needed. She granted me the time and changed my work schedule for the next 6 weeks. I went back to work and worked for a total of 8 years for this company. I was so grateful that my supervisor understood the way I felt. It took everything I had left in me to recognize my feelings and be able to share them with my supervisor. That's how I knew I was at the right job. I remained working for this agency until my supervisor retired.

My Signs and Symptoms with Depression

It is okay to admit that you still being held because the healing process takes time.

Suddenly, I felt tired, unable to sleep and an urgency to be alone. I did not want to be hear, listen or be bothered by others – I wanted to be still and quiet. Although tears flowed from my eyes, my body remained still. Even time seemed to remain still. My body felt weightless, and I couldn't even think of eating. It was as if nothing mattered. The sounds seem to have not existed, although birds chirping and water flowing down a stream comforted me. It was like a dream and/or a fairytale, where all the scenes and scripts were written with happiness. But when reality set in and one recovers from those emotions. You wonder how long they been stuck in these emotions. One starts to think differently and react differently to those who have experienced life with depression. What is the definition of depression? What are the stages and different types of depression?

Different types of depression

Major depression, persistent depressive disorder, bipolar disorder and seasonal affective disorder.

Stages of Depression

1. Denial and Isolation – Both are usually short lived.

2. Anger – As denial begins to wear off, you may start to feel angry that you're having to go through this, angry because you see no way of overcoming the feelings of depression, and even angry toward the world as you wonder why this had to happen to you.

3. Bargaining – As the illness progresses, the depression takes on a life of its own. It tells you horrible things about yourself. You begin to engage in negotiations, trying to stave off the thoughts brought on by the depression in favor of something more positive.

4. Depression – When you're in the depths of depression, you may feel you're lost in the wilderness with no way out. You may feel you'll never be happy again. During this stage of your depression, you'll have obsessive, debilitating thoughts, further perpetuating the depression, making you feel increasingly desperate and alone.

5. Acceptance – When you've reached this final stage, it means you've come to accept the reality of your illness. At this point, you'll likely realize you need help, so you see a therapist, take your medications and follow your treatment plan. Eventually, you start to feel better! The fear of a relapse is there, but eventually you come to recognize you need to keep focusing on the positives.

Increase Staff Engagement with Depression

Despite all their medical training, professional nurses are sometimes unable to recognize symptoms of illness when it happens to them, even something as life changing as depression. With vague symptoms like moodiness, exhaustion, distraction, weight fluctuation and even sleep problems, nurses can easily shrug off disruptions to everyday stress. But depression isn't something to shrug off because it affects everything from a nurse's daily life to the patient care he/she provides. There's no denying nurses endure enormous work stress, but depression isn't the same thing. "There's a big difference between depression and stress. Stress can be a strong contributor and can be a precursor. It's important to recognize the symptoms of depression. Depression can be insidious in nature and can develop over time - the symptoms can creep up on you."

Clinical nurse specialists can provide essential education to nurses on the high prevalence of depression and confidential treatment options. It is imperative that more attention be given to screening and early intervention of depression to ensure a satisfied, productive and high-quality workforce. Nurses who are suffering from depression need to be diagnosed as soon as possible, so they can obtain appropriate treatment and minimize the impact on their ability to deliver safe care. Never has this been so imperative, as the current nursing shortage is likely to worsen with the imminent retirement of aging nurses. Health-care organizations should strive to provide less stressful, more respectful workplaces in order to support the physical, emotional and mental health of their employees in a proactive and responsive manner. It is my hope that, in the future, interventions to prevent stress in nurses and health care workers will be offered as a standard part of a benefits package within all health care organizations. Stress prevention can be a win-win situation where everyone will benefit. Most nurses are aware of the Employee Assistance Program (EAP), but what nurses really need is some support when a crisis arises on the nursing unit – especially when a patient's health declines and/or death occurs. Before that nurse provides care to her remaining patients, make sure there is communication on the unit; maybe even give the nurse an extra break to pull herself together. During monthly meetings, have a conversation to recognize the passing of a patient. This will be the perfect opportunity for the staff to have closure. Nurses will have decreased stress and increased coping mechanisms, which will increase job satisfaction and lead to a better quality of life. Also, nurses will be superior employees and better able to provide care for themselves and their patients.

In addition, these findings substantiate the need for regular stress reduction programs to be offered through hospitals and other medical employment organizations. The use of these and similar programs provide far-reaching benefits for the nursing profession. Anticipatory measures for the reduction of stress can increase job satisfaction and potentially increase nurse retention. Goals for these programs could include guidance in stress management techniques, increased social support, open communication, role strengthening and empowerment and individual growth to fully utilize positive interventions.

Future studies in programs for stress intervention should include additional similar studies offered to a larger sample with long term and ongoing evaluations of the effectiveness. Consideration of other alternative adjunct intervention therapies, such as yoga and meditation, which assist in stress reduction, could be examined. The use of these physically and emotionally stress-reducing techniques may also be effective in stress lessening and coping measures increasing. I hope this chapter has opened your mind when it comes to depression and you understand the importance of early detection, early prevention and provide safe care for the nursing staff and the patients nurses are caring for daily. It paves the way for treatment interventions and better outcomes.

Thank a nurse – it's important for her/him to know how her/his care is going. Nurses are human, too. But their profession and career are important in that they provide excellent care and commitment to the institution and facilities where they spend most of their seconds, minutes, hours, days, months and years.

I thank God for giving me the strength to endure all the challenges I have been through and able to share with all those who are able to read this chapter. Take some time and complete a depression-screening tool so you can identify signs and symptoms of depression early so, you can obtain treatment. Calling the 24-hour help lines can assist with education, support the individual or family/friends calling for advice, treatment – questions about treatment & facilities in the area, links – connect to facilities, information about therapies and crisis support and guidance through suicidal thoughts, psychotic breaks or manic episodes.

Here is the 24-hour mental healthcare number:

1. In Maryland, dial 211, press 1/text your zip code to 898-211
2. Baltimore Crisis Response, Inc.: 410 433-5175 (MD relay dial 711)
3. Substance Abuse and Mental Health Services Administration SAMHSA: 1 (800) 662-4357
4. National Suicide Prevention Lifeline: 1(800) 273-8255
5. Veterans Crisis Line: 1(800) 273-8255; text a message to 838255. Operated by the Department of Veterans Affairs

Please - do not forget to help someone if you believe that they are experiencing some type of mental health disorder. A mental mind can survive if the brain receives assistance in a timely manner. Here are some extra solutions to destigmatize mental health issues:

- Develop self-awareness biases about mental health treatment
- Talk about seeking assistance with depression and other mental health issues
- Become a member of the National Alliance on Mental Health (NAMI)
- May is Nurses Week

Start a campaign centered on mental health in nursing *depression, 24-hour mental health helpline and bereavement, etc.

*****While there are many emergency mental health hotlines, if you or someone you care about is having thoughts of suicide, call 911 for immediate help.

Biography

Charlene Harrod-Owuamana is a Best-selling Author, Professional Speaker and Educator to youth; in Baltimore City. Where she started her business as a "Kid's Coach" for her personal Brand "Nursz's HIVE & CEO/Founder of Owuamana Enterprise, LLC.

Nursz's HIVE, Inspire youth from ages 8 to 24 years old - to focus on a Career in Healthcare. There are many occupations and career choices in healthcare. She teaches and educate the youth to prepare them for their future. She has been in the Healthcare System for over 36+ years. With 18+ years as a Licensed Practical Nurse (LPN); Graduated from Baltimore County Community Colleges (Essex Campus) with an Associate of Science Degree.

Despite all the challenges that her city has been faced with over the years. She returned to the neighborhood where she was raised after 40 years. To strengthen the Healthcare System and show the community her commitment and dedication. She managed to collaborate with top city leaders and educators; such as, Baltimore City Mayors Office, Baltimore City Fire Department and others. Remaining busy in vulnerable communities doing what God intended her to be nurturing, caring and inspiring Nurse.

I AM A NURSE!!

One of the lessons that I grew up with was to always stay true to yourself and never let what somebody else say distract you from your goals. And so, when I hear about negative and false attacks, I really don't invest any energy in them. Because I know who I am.

Michelle Obama

Email/Social Media

Nurse4travel@gmail.com

Owuamanaenterprise@gmail.com

Facebook:

Charlene Harrod-Owuamana

Heartbeat of Medicine

Nurseologist

Revision after Bariatric Surgery

Acknowledgements

I humbly thank my Heavenly Father for the opportunity to transform my mess into a message, without him, I am nothing. I am forever grateful to my mom for the unconditional love, support and wisdom she shared. Thanks to my seven children for inspiring me to go beyond myself, we are one. I appreciate my dad who still finds time to say that he is proud of me. And to my longtime friend Robbie for being there in the darkest hours to remind me Im-still-a-rose!

**~Keeonna

The Golden Rose: My Journey towards Conquering Stress

Overcoming Overwhelming Obstacles

By Keeonna Williams, MSN, RN

I dropped out of high school in the 11th grade because I was expecting my second child, Christian. Approximately a year later, I met a very outgoing and fun-loving individual, who later became my husband. We were young, in-love, happy but naïve about the essential ingredients of building a healthy, productive relationship. Sometimes we grew together, but most times we grew apart; however, our family continued to increase in size. I was a mother of five kids by the age of twenty-one. Even after marriage, we continued to have an unstable relationship, and my husband and I often lived separately.

Nevertheless, I knew it was up to me to provide a better and quality life for my kids and myself. The first step in this plan involved earning a GED. I was determined to reach my goal, and nothing was going to stop me. I humbly rode the Head Start bus with my three young daughters since my classes were in the same building. I did not give it a second thought, and I was extremely grateful.

How It All Began

No one in my immediate family had pursued a career in a medical field, and I had successfully completed this stringent nursing program.

Initially, I had not considered nursing as a career choice, but after receiving my graduate equivalency degree (GED), the counselor suggested that I complete a career assessment test. The tool helped identify my strengths, weaknesses, interests and soft skills.

My original plan was to become a licensed practical nurse (LPN) and later bridge over to RN. However, my TABE test results were two measly points shy from acceptance into Louisiana Tech. After receiving the results, I cried so hard that overflowing tears obscured my vision as I drove across the Greater New Orleans Bridge. God revealed to me that all my struggles were my plan and route and not His. Subsequently, I completed the required pre-requites and applied to Charity School of Nursing. I successfully passed the entrance exam and was accepted into the RN program; that is how I embarked on my exhilarating journey of becoming a registered nurse.

I began the program as a single mother of six children and although the odds were against me (as one of the professors harshly shared), I graduated with seven kids. Motivation is often disguised as discouragement. With God and the support of my mother, I knew it would come to pass. I remember it all like it was yesterday. May 12, 2005, I graduated with an associate degree from Charity School of Nursing in New Orleans. All the long hours of studying, preparing for clinicals and sacrificing had finally paid off. My family and friends were proud and excited about my achievement, and so was I!

Living the Dream or Not

Nursing is such a diverse field; there are so many different areas to practice. Originally, I wanted to work in labor and delivery. However, those plans came to a halt after the closure of the University Hospital due to damages from Hurricane Katrina. I worked in several areas: med-surgery, postpartum and long-term care, but I knew it was temporary because I wanted more. I was in search of my professional niche as a nurse. I was grateful for the opportunity to serve as a nurse, but I was not satisfied. It felt like something was missing. There was a void that needed to be filled.

The Adventures of the Operating Room

The operating room was unlike any previous training or professional positions I have held as a nurse. Therefore, it required extensive and rigorous specialized training. Although the transition into perioperative nursing was challenging, it seemed like I had found my 'happy place' professionally. I took pleasure and pride in my role as a perioperative nurse at a level I trauma center. [a6] It was a teaching facility loaded with ambitious and anxious surgery residents who kept ORs full of medical emergencies and traumatic injuries.

I was extremely thrilled to share my experiences with my mother, children and friends. There was an excitement in being part of a team that removed aggressive tumors from internal organs, fixed fractured bones and repaired holes that tunneled through human flesh from ammunition. However, I later discovered that the adrenalin rush and continual response to traumatic incidents came with a substantial price.

Losing My Focus, Peace and Motivation

For a significant part of my adult life, I was a confidant, nurturer and caregiver to many others. Therefore, as a nurse, I would occasionally over-extend myself in these areas. The result would be me feeling as though I had been submerged in an active sea of chaos, imbalance and turbulence. My mother was the life preserver that helped salvage my breath and balance. She was my confidant, nurturer, best friend, biggest supporter and so much more.

My mom was influential, wise and multitalented. The dreadful Saturday morning that my three sisters and I made the agonizing decision to withdraw our mother's life support was the worst day of my life. After suffering a subarachnoid hemorrhage as a result of a ruptured aneurysm, our beautiful and vibrant mother's life abruptly ended.

I was consumed with agony, misery and guilt of not recognizing the signs and incapable of saving my mother. Honestly, if I did not have my children, my mourning and heartache would have easily transitioned into a severe depression that would have eaten me up. However, I was the single mother of seven children, ages ranging from 4 to 18 years old. For that reason, I had to pull myself up by the bootstraps and somehow maintain my sanity - at least for their sake.

The Cost of Self-Neglect

It was challenging, but eventually, I resumed my personal, social and professional duties. I was more actively engaged with friends, family, colleagues, patients and whoever needed me. In resemblance to the root of a carrot, it was the optimum soil in which to bury my emotions, fears and pain. It was an ineffective way of coping, but it worked momentarily.

One evening while working the trauma shift (2:30 pm – 11:00 pm), I began to feel awful. I did not immediately acknowledge what it could possibly be - not the dizziness, blurry vision or the sudden confused state of my mind. My disoriented thoughts only led me to accept sitting down as a reasonable solution.

However, my colleague did not agree and decided to intervene. The frightening and rapid sequence of events was the effects brought on by a (TIA) transient ischemic attack. It is extremely horrifying and intimidating to hear "Room 4, stroke activation!" when you are the patient being triaged. My thirty-four-year-old body had just issued a major warning, and I neglected to resume self-care.

Getting Back To Me

Although I took pleasure in working in the operating room, the uninterrupted evenings of responding to fatal motor vehicle accidents, traumatic amputations and performing postmortem care to lifeless bodies of young adults who lost their lives to gun violence, had taken its toll on me. Furthermore, I did not feel I was progressing professionally. My career was stagnant, my employer focused on maintaining employees, while overlooking the significance and value of further developing professionals.

I accepted the position of a procedure nurse in the urology department at another hospital just a few blocks away. My role as the procedure nurse provided more opportunities for growth, autonomy and flexibility. It also allowed me the freedom and convenience to pursue a higher level of education as a nurse.

The Pursuit of Personal and Professional Fulfillment

I had many professional reasons for enrolling into Concordia University's RN-MSN online program: expand my knowledge base, have more influence as a professional, increase career marketability and earning potential. However, it was predominantly a personal goal and challenge because I am a woman of perseverance, and my heavenly Father created me this way. Nevertheless, I had not anticipated the emotional turbulence I would soon experience.

To gain additional control over my work schedule and allow availability for courses, I began to explore nursing contract opportunities, both local and travel. Considering most of my nursing experience was in the surgery, I returned to perioperative nursing. Initially, I signed a 13-week local contract that extended into a year assignment. It was convenient, as I would have three 12-hour shifts a week, and I was very familiar with the residents, surgeons and staff. It was "Mr. Right Now."

Incidentally, the contract was not my only encounter with "Mr. Right Now." I remarried after eleven years of being divorced and single. Unfortunately, my second marriage did not last as I hoped. We married in March, separated in September and divorced in November. Many newlyweds experience hardships within the first year of marriage, but my financial struggles, health issues and the unexpected death of my stepdaughter were among the extreme difficulties I faced at the time.

Once again, while taking care of everyone else, I heard those frightening words being repeated, "Room 4, stroke activation!"

Unfortunately, I had experienced a second TIA. So many images and thoughts filled my head, while tears silently streamed down my face. As I defenselessly lay on the hospital bed assigned to the intensive care unit, it became painfully clear that things had to change. It was also evident to my professor, who assertively advised me to withdraw from my courses and other activities in which I was involved. She reassured me I could resume classes once things improved, especially my health.

A Moment of Silence: Where In The World Is Kwajalein?

Once I was medically cleared, I returned to work. It was near the end of the contract, and I was offered an extension opportunity. I had become well acquainted with most of the staff members and established a good rapport. I was also familiar with departmental policies and procedures.

Those two aspects are essential for every agency nurse and are half the battle of new assignments. However, in opposition to the Cheers theme song, for a moment, I longed to exist where no one knew my name. The familiarity that was once reassuring had suddenly evolved into an over-stimulating and mind-boggling scene. It felt like my world was falling apart, and I had no balance or peace.

As a contract nurse, I receive many inquiries about my availability for new assignments. In response to one random email I had received, I accepted an invite to apply and interview for a 13-week contract at Kwajalein Atoll hospital, located in the Marshall Islands. Two days after interviewing with the DON via phone, I was offered the position.

There was no drawn-out, lengthy and deep deliberation, and I immediately accepted the offer. Afterward, I excitedly began the onboard hiring process and paid additional fees to expedite my passport application. Somewhere in between Hawaii and Guam would be my new home for the next three months.

The Divine Bench of Balance and Healing

Although it was a professional assignment due to limited external distractions, Kwajalein presented a rare opportunity to take personal inventory and identify internal triggers of unmanageable stress. This reflective practice often took place outdoors on a wooden bench. This single bench was strategically placed in an open space facing the breathtaking and peaceful Pacific Ocean.

Sometimes I would read, other times I would write in a journal but mostly, I would practice deep breathing and mentally filter my thoughts and suppressed emotions. Periodically, I would have the pleasure of sharing the bench with an intriguing individual. He was a world traveler and was well grounded. He challenged my perception with two simple questions: (1) How has my past experiences affected me; how was I dealing with them? (2) What do I want for my life? Until that moment, I had convinced myself that I was too busy and mentally unavailable to ponder the answers to these questions.

My living quarters were equipped with everything I needed: a bed for rest, a kitchen for nutrition, a bathroom for personal hygiene and a television for entertainment. Most importantly, there were no interruptions to inhibit the flow of accumulated, buried tears. There was nothing or no one to interfere with my intimate conversations with God.

Growing Forward

The island life was full of sunshine, blue skies, beach huts, salty air, flip flops and starry skies—the perfect environment to focus on what is, instead of what is not. The attitude of gratitude is the breeding ground for hope and healing.

During the healing process, my perception of life experiences began to shift. In my world, things no longer happened to me; instead, they happened for me, and the best component of that is how I choose to respond.

It was time to get back into the active arena of life and get the best out of it.

I reached out to my professor via email and we created a schedule for the resumption of academic courses upon my return to the States. It was never my intention to follow the traditional career path of working many years for any organization and then retire. However, it was toward the end of completing the RN-MSN program that a light bulb went off, and I realized I needed to expand my career horizons beyond the bedside.

Discovering Balance & Pursuing Entrepreneurial Opportunities

In the course of laboring as a travel nurse, I have worked in different facilities in many locations. However, the demeanor and mindset of hopelessness seem to be spreading like wildfire among healthcare workers from one scene to the next. I recall being infected with the malicious contamination of mental exhaustion and discouragement. It affected every area of my existence, mentally, physically, emotionally, and spiritually.

Unrealistic expectations and self-neglect became toxic to my productivity, happiness and health, which impacted on me negatively.

I finally recognized the significance of self-care—mental, physical and spiritual. Once I gained clarity of my thoughts, it became less challenging to effectively prioritize and organize each area of my life.

I am a part of an amazing organization that encourages nurses to utilize their skills and expertise to become successful entrepreneurs. Writing this chapter is an exciting introduction to my coaching, speaking and writing journey.

My vision is to support and empower other nurses with strategies that promote stress resilience and self-care. Balance is not a classified or mysterious location, nor can we put coordinates in Google map to find it. Balance is not found; rather, it is strategically and individually created.

I can do all things through Christ who strengthens me. Philippians 4:13.

Believe, breathe and be balanced.

ImStillARose

Biography

Often referring to her kids as her inspiration, Keeonna is a caring mother of seven children: Ronald, Christian, Chloe', Chantrell, Constance, Allen and Alonzo - ranging from ages 15-28. Keeonna is a native of New Orleans, Louisiana, and an alumna of Charity School of Nursing. She obtained her Master of Science in nursing from Concordia University of Texas, with a concentration in healthcare project management and emphasis in leadership. She describes her blood type as RR, which denotes rich in resiliency. Her professional experience cuts across school nurse, postpartum, long-term acute care, operating room, in addition to gaining international experience as a travel nurse.

In response to the steady increase in nurse suicide, compassion fatigue, and nurse burnout, she has been inspired to identify opportunities to counteract negative effects associated with the challenge's nurses are facing.

She is creating her path as a speaker, writer and coach, with the focal point of educating and empowering others with support and self-care strategies to prevent burn-out, manage stress and restore a healthy work-life balance. Keeonna is the Founder and CEO of Holistic Balance LLC.

She is an example that non-traditional pathways and unique journeys can lead to fulfilling destinations.

"Just because my path is different, doesn't mean I'm lost."

~ Gerard Abrams

Acknowledgments

To God be the Glory.

To my Children and my family for all the support.

~Michele

Challenging Path to Sublime Destination: A Journey towards travel and adventure

By Michele Graham, RN

No challenge is too great to overcome. I am proof that suboptimal circumstances cannot prevent you from achieving your dreams. If you are willing to work for your dreams, you can have anything you desire. If you choose to use your circumstances as an excuse as to why you can't have the life you want, that is also an option, but recognize that it is a decision, not a fact.

I was born in the Ivory Coast in the late 60s. I often refer to myself as a "poor girl from nowhere," because we were poor according to American standards, but we actually lived a decent life in our country. My father was a politician and my mother worked as an RN. We lived in a nice house in a community of good people who looked out for one another. I attended University and worked for the government for a little while. We didn't think about careers or big houses or extravagant lives. Our dreams were much more modest, but we were happy. Unfortunately, civil war changed this dynamic drastically, and I knew that I needed to make a change if I wanted to live a comfortable life. I'd heard about the American Dream, and the thought of creating a whole new life intrigued me.

So when I was thirty years old, I decided to move to America to not only escape the war, but to start over and take my shot at the American Dream. I only spoke my native French and moved in with some friends and family upon my arrival. But staying with friends and family has a different connotation than it does where I'm from. When people offer to let you stay with them in America, they generally mean something very short-term, like one or two weeks. So within a short amount of time, I had worn out my welcome.

I ended up meeting a man from my country around this time. He was familiar. He spoke my language and was a reminder of home, so it was natural for me to form a connection with him. He told me that I could stay with him, and I jumped at the opportunity. But his kindness shortly wore off, especially when he took to the bottle. Many nights, he'd come home reeking of alcohol. On those nights, he got aggressive fast, as if for no reason. My body shouldered his punches and kicks. His attacks would leave me sore, broken and full of fear.

I wasn't sure what to do. There weren't many people I could reach out to, and I had nowhere else to go. It was difficult even to research my options because I didn't speak the language. Ultimately, I did find a shelter for battered woman that took me in. There were women from all over the world at the shelter, Mexico, India and Africa. Many of them were in similar situations to my own, far from home with no common language or alternatives. That sense of community became a soothing relief to me.

Once I was at the shelter, doors started to open for me. A friend told me I should learn English and said she would look around for a place that would teach me. She ended up finding a church that was teaching ESL nearby. I started attending regularly. The shelter helped me get my Green Card and asked if I wanted to attend school. I jumped at the chance to go to school; and they paid for me to learn how to become a CNA. This was where my nursing journey began. Not long after that, I was able to get my CNA license. The shelter even helped me find a job nearby in a nursing home.

After three months of working, I had saved up enough money to be able to find an apartment of my own and moved to Dallas. Things were really starting to look up. Soon after I started working at the nursing home, a friend introduced me to someone she knew at the hospital; they hired us as CNAs and cross-trained us in other disciplines like phlebotomy, medication and secretarial work. I learned and mastered all of those areas, and worked hard to do my best wherever they needed me. One day, a co-worker expressed to me how good of a caregiver I was and told me that I had the potential to become a nurse if I wanted to.

I knew that it was not as simple as it sounded, but I was willing to put in whatever was required in order to take on this new challenge. So I applied to a handful of nursing programs and was accepted by most of them. I had my choice of programs, but I knew that I needed additional income in order to pay for this schooling. Back in my country, it was common to braid each other's hair in the lower classes. I hadn't done it myself, but a friend taught me how to do it and soon I was braiding the hair of many local women. Eventually, I was able to turn braiding hair into a business since no one in the states was offering this type of service. I would work as a nurse all night and, then I would braid hair all day. The hours were long and I was often tired, but I had to balance both of these jobs in order to get through school.

I didn't realize it at the time, but the hair-braiding business taught me a lot about entrepreneurship that would end up resurfacing down the road. For the time being, it was a great way to generate extra income, to connect with other women and to work on my English. I kept it up all throughout school until I no longer had the need or time for it. At that point, my sister had joined me in America, and she was able to take it over. It gave me great pride to be able to hand her a business and a livelihood.

As the years went by, I worked my way up through the ranks. I've worked as a charge nurse, house supervisor and even as a traveling nurse. During this time, I also managed to raise two daughters. I met my daughter's father just a few years after I arrived, and shortly after that we found ourselves pregnant. But the doctor told me I couldn't have a baby. At six and half months, I had to be put on bed rest at the hospital. I ended up delivering my daughter at just 27 weeks. She weighed only 1 pound and 4 ounces. She spent eight weeks in the NICU, and I was wrecked with worry and fear. I remember the first day I picked her up, she only weighed five pounds, but it felt like a miracle. The joy I felt in my heart was inexplicable. I felt myself get stronger at that moment, knowing that I would do anything for that tiny little life.

I eventually got pregnant again, and though it wasn't as bad as the first time, my body was still not cut out for pregnancy and I went back to bed rest by three months. Luckily she was not born premature, but I lived with the fear of another premature pregnancy daily and prayed to God for strength. I later became pregnant with my son - so much for the doctor's pessimism. All of my children are smart and healthy now, and I make sure they know that nothing is impossible. My son has even served in the US Army, something I couldn't' have even imagined when I was back in the Ivory Coast. The doctors told me having them would be impossible, yet here they are.

A few years ago, I learned that I had cervical cancer. Hearing this news was horrifying, especially since it called for a total hysterectomy. Losing a part of your body is never easy, but I had no choice. I knew that I still had a lot in this world that I needed and wanted to do. I looked to God, and knowing that he had already blessed me with three beautiful children, I felt at peace. My uterus had served its purpose, and I could be okay sacrificing a part of myself in order to keep persisting and living my purpose.

Working as a bedside nurse is rewarding, but it's not easy. The hours are long and the quality of life is compromised. I knew that the lifestyle of a bedside nurse was not something that I wanted long-term. Luckily, I had already learned that nothing was impossible. If I wanted to make a change, it was well within my power to do so. That's when I knew that I wanted to start my own business. In 2016, I opened a shelter similar to a halfway house intended as a haven for felons after they had been released from jail. I called it Point of Grace Group Homes, and it was created as a place that offered a second chance and the resources to start a new life. Not long after I also started Point of Grace Health Care Agency, which focused on Home Health Care. Unfortunately, I had to close both of these businesses after my husband and I divorced. At the time I didn't have the resources to keep them open, but I do plan on reopening both in the coming years.

After the dust had settled from my divorce and I was back on my feet financially again, the entrepreneurial bug bit again. My history braiding hair as a business gave me an idea. I could combine nursing with beauty, and open a medical spa. That's when I started Sublime Body Spa, my current business. But I didn't want to just stop here. I noticed something during all of my interactions with people every day. There were so many women out there struggling with challenges of one kind or another. Often when I saw or met them, they were beaten down and feeling stuck and helpless. But they didn't have to be. There is always a path to the life you want no matter odds are stacked against you. My story was proof. And whenever I shared my story, I could see something lighting up inside of them, an understanding that they too could live a positive story.

In addition to my medical spa, I also help empower women to open up their own businesses. Anyone can live their dream life. It doesn't matter what you have or don't have when you start. The only thing that matters is that you have a goal and stick to your vision. Once you have that dream, it's only a matter of taking steps to get there. If the circumstances aren't favorable, change them. If you don't have the tools or guidance you need, get it. I came to this country alone, unable even to communicate, and here I am today with three beautiful children and a handful of businesses that I built from scratch. I got my start in a home for battered women in a forgotten neighborhood of Texas. But the circumstances that surrounded me at that point in my life didn't stop me. I wanted to live the American Dream, and so I got busy figuring out how to get there. The trick is to never give up. I was a hustler, an overachiever and I believed in God when things seemed dark. The Bible assured me that I could do anything, that I could move up, that it wouldn't be easy, but that God would never forsake me. I took those words to heart, and kept going.

I have plans down the line to open up a Free Clinic for women where I can offer health care assistance, mammography, pap smears, STD education and other resources. There is a huge need for these services. So many women put their health on the back burner because they don't have insurance or can't afford care. They put their children's care ahead of their own because they can't afford both. That is how cervical cancers go undetected, and how treatable conditions turn into bigger problems. It is my mission to put an end to these kinds of problems. I also plan to open a clinic and house call business that is geared toward helping the elderly and veterans.

For all the girls and women out there who are on the verge of giving up, I urge you to keep going. It might seem futile when you're looking around at your situation, and find yourself with no edge, no resources and no options. But God made us strong and resilient. It's not about what you have around you, it's about what you have inside of you. And we can all muster up some strength. We can make a better life for ourselves, and we can do it with nothing other than our own two hands. I know this because I did it. If you're reading this, then you have language, which is more than I had when I stepped onto American soil. That alone gives you options and opens doors. You are the only one responsible for putting up walls that constrain. You are just as capable of building ladders or tunnels to get out of your situation than you are for building walls that keep stuck and trapped in your circumstances. There is always a way to your dream. The bigger and better the dream, the more work you might have to put in, but it can come true. One thing is certain, and that is anything is possible.

Biography

Michele Graham, RN, BSN is a business mogul, heading several businesses simultaneously, while furthering her education. Michele endeavors to impact the world, especially women with the knowledge and education that will further them in life. She desires to serve our country and does so by giving back to our veteran population.

To learn more,
Email bryan4michele@gmail.com.
Website sublimebodymedspa.com

Dedication

This book is dedicated to my three beautiful children: Amber, Jairus and Amira. Thank you for packing cars, making copies and stuffing envelops to fulfill orders. Thank you for supporting me in all of my endeavors.

This book is also dedicated to my wonderful and supportive family and friends. Thank you for helping me set up tables and conduct sales at various events all over the country. A big shout out to Deirdre Moore & Dr. Yalanda White for helping me facilitate CPR courses.

I couldn't have done business without your support!

THANK YOU!!!!!

Boss Nurse: One Class at a Time

By Dr. Bridgette Turner Jenkins

I've always known that I was destined for greatness, and that I would do something good on this earth. I've also always wanted to be a nurse, and honestly never thought about being a business owner. I was happy and content being a nurse. I have worked in so many areas of nursing: labor and delivery, the operating room, plastic surgery, public health, pediatrics and academia. As you can see, I was quite experienced.

You see, I had my life planned. I was going to go to school, graduate, get a good job, and live happily ever after. Ha! Needless to say, things didn't go as planned. I learned the hard way that life is not a big puzzle where all the pieces fit perfectly into their special place. I don't care how much you write it out and put things into place: life is bound to happen, and life is unpredictable.

A lot of things have changed for me since I became a nurse. I never thought that my life would go in the direction that it did: divorced, diagnosed with multiple autoimmune diseases, my health failing and I could do nothing about it. I couldn't have prepared for this. No one could. As my health declined, I had to think of innovative ways to earn money. I decided to use all of my passion and skills to pursue the very best life possible, for both me and my children. I was extremely frustrated, but I was not giving up.

Although I felt like I couldn't physically do my job anymore, I still wanted to work in nursing. Instead of complaining about my situation or waiting for someone else to help me, I decided to help myself and start a business. Since I loved to teach, I thought it would be good for me to become an instructor for the American Heart Association (AHA).

I chose this route because heart disease is a major problem in America, especially in the African-American community. I had taught so many heart awareness courses that I felt like AHA would be a great fit for me. The statistics were staggering back in 2009. They are even more staggering today. Heart disease is the leading cause of death for both men and women, as well as most racial and ethnic groups in the United States.

Heart disease has hit very close to home in recent years. My maternal grandmother died in 2010 from heart disease. My father died in 2012 from a massive heart attack. And my best friend Dee has suffered multiple heart attacks, one of which I was there for. I performed CPR on her, and saved her life.

So it couldn't have been coincidence that my CPR training center was accepting applications for new instructors. When I decided to register for an instructor course, I wasn't really sure how everything worked. But I knew that I needed to supplement my income. What I didn't realize is that this would become my primary source of income for the next two years. I took the courses to become a basic life support, heartsaver, AED, and first aid instructor.

Becoming an American Heart Association instructor was relatively easy. I had to pay about $3,000 to learn all the courses that I wanted to teach. Then, I had to pay for all of the CPR equipment. I bought the economy pack of mannequins and two automated external defibrillators, which cost me another $2,000. Once I had completed the courses and purchased all the equipment, I went to register my business with the state of Texas. I called it Health Education Consultants. I chose this name because I wanted to offer more than CPR courses, and I wanted the name to be generic but healthcare-focused.

Starting this business was not difficult at all. The hardest part for me was finding a location to hold classes. I didn't have the money to go and get an office space. At this point in my business I had essentially no overhead and no debt. So I decided to put a little spin on my business-marketing tools. I decided to advertise "Mobile CPR in your location or mine." What essentially happened (and I was glad that it went this way), was that facilities like daycares and long-term care facilities started contacting me. Soon I was teaching 3-4 CPR courses every week. This business was becoming very profitable for me.

I've expanded my business since 2009. As a certified master nursing instructor, I can teach a variety of courses. I have been asked to teach awareness courses on breast cancer awareness, HIV, women's health topics, diabetes, domestic violence, lupus and other autoimmune diseases. I not only teach courses for the American Heart Association, but I also teach awareness courses for other national organizations. I teach courses for community organizations, social groups, and faith-based organizations. Or to whoever needs one of the courses that I offer.

I also offer continuing education units (CEU's) and professional development courses for nurses and other healthcare professionals. These courses include: conflict resolution, infection control education, medication administration in non-medical settings, medication errors: prevention is the key, culturally competent nursing, cultural diversity, fall prevention, nurse burnout, workplace violence, dealing with difficult people, OSHA and blood-borne pathogens.

Business was going very well for me until I suffered a stroke. Unfortunately, I had to stop teaching my classes. I was paralyzed on my left side. I have to admit, I was scared. I wasn't sure if I was going to make a full recovery, or if I was going to be paralyzed or weak on the affected side. Because I received plasminogen activator (TPA), I had a very good chance of making a full recovery, which was exciting news. TPA works by dissolving blood clots, which helps restore blood flow to the brain after a stroke, potentially preventing additional brain cells from dying.

I did well following the treatment. I went to therapy every day and worked hard to regain my strength. It wasn't always easy. I fell several times. My foot would get caught and I would tumble down the stairs. Sometimes it was discouraging, but I kept pushing and working to get stronger. I was not going to let a stroke win. I was determined to return to a normal life.

And God is so good to me. I persevered in pure determination and made a full recovery through the power of prayer from friends and loved ones. I didn't immediately return to my business. I wanted a smooth, easy transition. I also wanted to acquire more training and add more courses to my offerings.

I'm often asked what I would tell others who were interested in entrepreneurship. I always share with them what I personally do. I have six steps that I consistently execute when accepting an opportunity, considering a business, or writing a book.

1. **Write it down.** *Write the vision and make it plain* (Habakkuk 2:2). Seeing your written vision can give you the inspiration and motivation you need to push through challenging times. Dr. Gail Matthews, a Psychology professor, studied 267 people from all over the world and all walks of life, dividing them into two groups based on people who wrote down their goals[1] and those who didn't (Morrissey, 2016.) She found that the people who wrote down their goals on a regular basis were 42% more likely to achieve them. WRITE IT DOWN.

2. **Know your why.** *Why* is your goal valuable and important to you? What I've realized is that your *why* is not just your life purpose. It can be your vision for your big idea, or your reason for doing something extraordinary. When you know your *why*, your *what* (your business, your book, etc.) will have a greater impact.

3. **Do your research.** Research to find out what it will take to accomplish your goal. Before you start any business or major project, there are a number of questions and considerations you need to address. How much will it cost? How much time will you need to dedicate? Is it feasible? What are the chances of success? What laws or regulations are involved? I've seen a lot of people start a business and fail. Some of them had great ideas, but they failed because the necessary research and planning was not done. They didn't count the cost.

4. **Get motivated.** Start visualizing your goal already completed. Be intentional (do it on purpose; be deliberate) about working on your goals or achieving your dreams. My Apostle gives really good advice. He says, "Hang around like-minded people." He also puts it this way sometimes: "Find someone who has what you want, and find out what they did to get it."

5. **Watch your mouth.** *Death & life are in the power of the tongue* (Proverbs 18:21). I read the Message translation for a better understanding of this scripture. It says, "Words kill, words give life; they're either poison or fruit—you choose." We have to watch what we say about others. But we also have to watch what we say about ourselves. Your tongue is powerful. It has the ability to build or destroy. I hear people say things like; "Nobody is going to buy my book," or "nobody is going to pay this much for one of my programs," or "I'll never meet the man of my dreams." If you say these types of things enough, what do you think is going to happen? The Word says, *We call those things which be not as though they were* (Romans 4:17). Watch your mouth! Open your mouth and encourage yourself. Instead of saying, "Nobody is going to buy your book," say, "My book is an Amazon best seller." Start making bold declarations about your business every day.

6. **Don't quit.** You will encounter obstacles, frustrations, tragedies, and challenges along the way, but don't quit! Make the necessary adjustments. Take some time off if you need to, but do not quit. Remember your vision. Revisit your *why*.

I am truly grateful that when I was going through rough periods in my life, I made the decision to use the skills and knowledge I've acquired to do more and not less. That single decision, which I would say was part of God's plan for me, led me to many more opportunities, each of which have helped me with my purpose of making an impact on the lives of others. I've been in business for 10 amazing years now. I am enjoying every minute of this experience. I've also started several other business ventures that complement one another. I am a published author of four books, own an inspirational T-shirt line, and host a talk radio show. I have also added tutoring, coaching, and mentoring to my education business.

Through my career and business, I have taught so many people and come in contact with thousands more. Many of whom I have impacted and inspired through service, coaching, or teaching. Whether it was speaking engagements, sharing my story corporately or personally, career knowledge, published books, inspirational T-shirts, or my world-wide radio show, Bounce Back Mondays with Dr. B, I have empowered many.

Nurse entrepreneurship has been very rewarding in more ways than I could have ever imagined. It has allowed me to travel the world both personally and professionally, connect with people I may not have otherwise have met, helped others grow in their personal and professional lives, build new relationships, and build a legacy for my family. I am definitely enjoying the journey, and I'm excited to see what the future holds.

Biography

Dr. Bridgette Jenkins! Affectionately known as Dr. B or Professor is the daughter of the late John Turner & Rosie Turner.

Dr. Bridgette has over 20 years of nursing and healthcare experience. Dr. Bridgette has worked in many different areas of nursing throughout her career. She is currently a Professor at Houston Baptist University. She is author of 3 books and will be releasing her 4th book the Fall.

Dr. Bridgette has a heart for people! She mentors students and nursing professionals as they matriculate through the nursing profession. She also has a passion for people who are struggling in life and spends countless hours ministering to those in need.

She is the CEO & President of the Houston Chapter of Black Nurses Rock. She is committed to changing the lives of the citizens in the Houston area and surrounding communities through service and education.

Dr. B has been a Ambassador and Instructor with the American Heart Association since 2006. She is a trained speaker and certified instructor with the capabilities of teaching life saving courses to health care professionals and to the community.

She is single and mother of 3 adult children. In her spare time, Dr. Bridgette can be found enjoying life with her beautiful family & friends. She can also be found participating in activities that bring awareness to various diseases & serving the homeless population. She is a member of New Light Church.

Dedication

This book is dedicated to my parents for all their love and support throughout the years. I also dedicate this book to my life partner, G, for his love, encouragement, motivation, support, believing in me, and commitment to our family.

A special dedication also goes to my children.

~Sherri

Nurse Entrepreneurship: The Journey to Securing 6 Figures and Beyond

By Sherri Lynch, MSN, RN

When you set out to be a nurse, more than anything you want to make a difference in the lives of your patients. That is the driving force behind any nurse's intentions. We are on the floor and in the field working with real people every day. We see all sides of the struggles that they are going through from the uncertainty about their health to the fear of healthcare costs and everything in between. Aside from just our knowledge and skills, we are the main source of support that they experience during their healthcare journey. And that's the truly rewarding part of the job, when you know that your presence, your kind words, your quiet support are the small things that are making the difference in that person's experience.

The word, "revive" can mean many things, everything from "to restore life or consciousness," "to give new strength or energy to," and to become active or flourishing again." As a nurse, that it was I feel like I do with my patients. I help them find new strength and to flourish again.

But there comes a point when this satisfaction alone can't compensate for your own depleting energy, when I can no longer "revive" my patients because I, personally need to be revived. When the job starts to hollow you out and drain you of all of your life force, you begin to reassess what you are really doing out there. It's not unlike what they tell you on airplanes about the oxygen masks that would drop should the plane lose cabin pressure. They tell you to apply your mask first before helping others because without your life force, you will quickly become depleted. This truth is important in any profession that requires giving of yourself in order to help others, but in the nursing setting consequences start bubbling up as the nurse to patient ratio ascends, a problem that is all too common.

Like many nurses, I love to go the extra mile for my patients and provide them with everything they need. It's why I went into this field and it's the source of a lot of joy and job satisfaction, but in the hospital setting that I was in, as my list of patients increased, I realized that I was running on fumes. Not only was I getting more and more tired after a regular shift because there were so many patients and related paperwork piling up, but it was becoming increasingly difficult to get quality time off to recharge.

I was a single mom with two small children at home and an elderly father requiring my time and attention in addition, and I couldn't get approved for regular time off to simply do my own life. Holidays were out the question, and I was spending more time making arrangements for childcare at these times than with my children. None of this was okay with me. This was not a satisfactory quality of life. And with the increased number of patients, it seemed like no one was getting "A-game Sherri." I constantly felt like I was sub-par in all arenas of my life because I was so depleted from the relentless nature of the work.

And what's more is that I had no power to change anything. I was at the mercy of my superiors and what was best for the hospital. I had no autonomy over my schedule and consequently, over my life. If I didn't make some sort of move, I'd miss my children's entire youth. My own life was flashing past me in a whirlwind with little reward for all my effort. I was breaking my back, as they say, but I couldn't quite see what I was doing it for.

At the time of my breaking point, I was spending a lot of time caring for my father. My experience both taking care of him and witnessing the care he was receiving from his home attendants as he moved between hospice care and home care, was enlightening. The care he was receiving was simply not enough. He deserved much more than what they were able or willing to provide. What I could see from my position was that the agencies didn't have either the resources or interest to gather sufficient information on his situation and condition. As a result the, attendants that they sent were under-informed and didn't have the resources to provide him with the right care. They were stretched thin, and he suffered. That also left me to pick up the slack and provide the care that was missing.

To me, this was wrong on so many levels. His care was slipping through the cracks because of how the agencies are inherently structured. That's when a light went off. Most families that experienced what I was experiencing didn't have a nurse family member in the wings to fill in the gaps of service. This was something that I could provide others in similar situations. I had just been shown a giant hole in the industry, and I had the skills and the desire to fill this hole.

At that point, I knew exactly what I could do to get autonomy into my nursing career while simultaneously filling an important need in the community. My parents raised me to value education and hard work, and from an early age, I knew that I could have anything that I wanted as long as I was willing to work for it. So I wasn't worried that I couldn't succeed at starting my own business. However, I did know that that I still was the sole support to my two children. I couldn't simply quit my job and pursue this new idea full-time. Although I was confident that my exact skills and expertise were the perfect answer to this real problem, I had no idea where to begin creating a business. As excited as I was about discovering this niche, I still had a lot of questions and fears. I had enough ambition to get to my goals, but I also needed to be smart and not put my family at risk.

That's when I started to shift my mindset. I realized that if I was going to succeed, I needed to infuse my life with positivity in order to achieve my goals. Success wasn't only – if you want it, work for it. That could easily translate into what I was already doing, working long hours in order to get the things I wanted. But that was all at a cost. There was another component missing from the equation. Success was also about believing that I didn't have to drive myself into the ground and neglect my self-care in order to accomplish my goals. My business idea was a valuable one, and I deserved to be able to support myself through this passion and talent. I could work hard, but I could also have a high quality of life.

I needed a way to declare this truth and really spell it out for myself and see it on a daily basis, so I took out paper and a pen. I named my business Revive Homecare Services, LLC because of that inherent belief that not only could I help bring new strength and energy to my patients, but I too needed to become active and flourishing again. I affirmed in my notebook that Revive Homecare Services would attract and retain the ideal clients. I affirmed that this endeavor would eventually replace my current income. I affirmed that I'd connect with the most experienced individuals in order to scale this business. And I affirmed that I would acquire the knowledge I needed to help make this business a success. I revisited my notebook often, and never let these thoughts slip far from my consciousness.

It turned out to be much harder than I had anticipated to promote Revive Homecare Services and to simply get my name out there. It seemed like everything cost money, from creating a website to marketing on different outlets. And I didn't know which avenues made sense financially and which were akin to throwing money into the trash. When you start your own business, there are plenty of tasks that you think you should do yourself in order to save money, but sometimes those tasks end up taking up so much time that they would've been useful to outsource while you did other tasks. It was all extremely overwhelming in the beginning, and of course there was very little return on all of my efforts early on. In the beginning, it seemed like I was pumping lots of time and money into something that wasn't paying off in any real way that I could see.

During this time I also took a marketing class and used social media as best I could to try to bring in leads. Often what I found was people were calling me with questions about what I did and what I offered, but early on very few of those calls turned into paying clients. Everything that I was doing was in my downtime between jobs. I was still working nine to five, and I carved out time to work on my business during my two hour commute and after my children went to bed, but the leads were sparse. I tried to stay positive, but it was difficult not to feel defeated. Here I was ready and willing to provide this amazing and helpful service, and I just couldn't connect with the people who actually needed and would pay for my services.

From lots of trial and error, I ended up realizing that one mistake I was making was misidentifying my target market. On the surface, it certainly seemed like my market was the elderly who needed better care. But as time went on, I started to see that this demographic was actually NOT who I should be targeting. After all, my father wouldn't have been the one to call someone like me. It was ME who was looking for alternatives when his care was lacking. That meant my original demographic was all wrong. My target market wasn't the elderly, but the elderly's adult children who were fed up with the quality of care.

That one realization helped me reorganize my entire marketing approach. I could reach those people on social media. I could find them at networking events. I could refine my cold-call lists to reach the people I needed to find. I had already invested a lot of money and time, but this shift helped me regain some of my waning confidence and I started getting calls that lead to real clients.

About a year and a half after first deciding on my new direction, I saw the business start growing in ways that were no longer directly related to my individual efforts. People were referring me out to other individuals in their network. I was no longer deeply invested in every social media post and ad I ran waiting for the phone to ring because now word was getting out. My name was now in the conversation when people brought up home care. I could wake up one morning and receive a phone call seemingly out of nowhere, and that feeling was so liberating. In the beginning, I was the only one working in my business. I personally worked every home care job and did every bit of marketing and business admin on the back end, but eventually I was able to start hiring home attendants to send out. Being able to not only provide a healthy income for myself, but to provide others with good jobs was extremely rewarding and felt like its own version of success.

I also found my circle around this time, a group of like-minded individuals to help and support me on this up-and-down journey of entrepreneurship. Having this circle and hiring a business coach have been instrumental in my success. Having a business coach is so pivotal because that person knows and understands the path that you have for yourself and can give you advice that will help you stick to that path.

When you don't have a person like this, it's like trying to sail a ship without a compass or GPS. It's so easy to end up off course when you don't have a plan and a guide that can keep you accountable. It sounds simple and even like something you could just handle yourself, but I'd advise anyone NOT to be there own coach. Think about any diet you've been on in the past, and you'll understand immediately. When you have that outside accountability, it's so much more likely that you'll stay on the path. As humans, we naturally default to the path of least resistance, even when we desperately want a thing. Think about it: if you were out for a walk on your own and came to a fork in the road with a choice of a steep hill or flat road, which way would you go? I get it, I'd take the flat road too. But if you were with a coach that was encouraging you to push yourself, you'd be more likely to take the hill, do it well and feel great about yourself afterwards.

My journey from working bedside to having my own homecare business has not been an easy one, and it's not a journey that is near over. I still have many additional goals, one of which is to create an adult day care center in the future. My story and my struggle to make a name for myself and to establish a career in which I have autonomy and financial and time freedom is an example to any nurse that even when your current view seems dim, there is always an alternative path. It's just a matter of opening your eyes to see those less obvious paths.

Often when we are in the thick of a given circumstance, we look around and we can't even imagine a way out. Every path out looks like a dead end or way too steep to conquer or simply doesn't' seem like an option, but we create our own paths with every decision we make. When we face difficult times like the era when I was weighed down at work and had my children and sick father to shoulder in addition led to my revelation of a giant gap in the system. I would never look back on the period of my life and want to relive it, but I appreciate that time so much for the gifts that it revealed to me. If I hadn't been stressed and looking for alternatives, I might never have noticed that unique hole that my skills could fill.

If I didn't go through that difficult period, I might still be working as a bedside nurse. I might have succumbed to the idea that I simply don't get to have holidays off, and I have to work the schedule that is given to me. I might have found myself trying to get used to the idea that I don't deserve to live my dreams. But our lives' paths are revealed to us in mysterious ways. The trick is to stay aware, to be present to the circumstances around us, and to then think outside of the box when it comes to creating our lives.

I knew when I set out to create my own business that it wouldn't be easy. But I also knew that there was no way I could maintain the life that I was currently living. I wasn't happy. I wasn't fulfilled. And I was a dimmer version of myself to all who came in contact with me. I had the grace to realize that I was worth so much more to the industry and the world; and now I get to make a difference to people, which has always been my passion AND I get to show up for all the important people in my life. In reinventing my life and my career, I have revived my soul. I have renewed energy and new perspective on life.

If you're reading this, I want you to know that you have this option as well. You are not locked into a specific career path because you are nurse and that's what millions of nurses before you have done. You can create your own path. It might require some sweat and some sacrifice, but generally sacrificing some things in the short-term in order to invest in yourself in the long-term is always worth it. And when you are functioning as your best self, you naturally have a positive effect on others. And as I said at the start, making a difference to others is the core of who we are as nurses. Now we can be entrepreneurs as well.

Biography

Sherri Lynch is native New Yorker and grew up in Brooklyn, New York. She graduated from St. John's University in Queens, NY with a Bachelor of Science in Healthcare Administration. One year later, she entered the field of Nursing as an LPN. She attended and graduated from Helene Fuld College of Nursing after completing a one year accelerating Nursing program. She earned a Bachelor of Science in Nursing from Long Island University and also holds a Master of Science in Nursing.

Sherri is an intellectual and compassionate caregiver. She has extensive experience in many areas of Nursing from several notable institutions in NYC. Her work experience ranges from long-term care, medical, surgical, psychiatry, case management, care management, utilization review, nursing education and home care.

Sherri is passionate about following dreams, setting goals and attaining goals. She is the founder and owner of Revive Homecare Services LLC. But, her work doesn't stop there. Sherri is also an active member in her community and serves as a mentor to help fellow nurses through the journey of entrepreneurship.

Connect with Sherri: Instagram- revive_homecare_services
Facebook- revivehomecare
Email- info@revivehomecareservices.com

Acknowledgement

This book is dedicated to all the women in business who also suffer in silence. Let me be the one who inspires you to speak and to heal. And to my family, thank you for supporting me through my 10-year journey as an entrepreneur.

Dr. Sylette

Entrepreneurship & Menopause: The Hard Road A Nursepreneur Journey

By Dr. Sylette DeBois

I come from a family of strong women, the kind of women who keep moving forward in the face of great adversity. There is no doubt that this kind of strength is important. But somewhere along the way, whether taught to us by our culture or learned in response to a world that requires strong defenses, this type of strength also develops a more insidious side. What the women in my family did and the women in the community at large did, was to weather their suffering in silence. I, of course, understand the reason for divorcing yourself from sensitivity and vulnerability in order to portray the face of strength, but what I've only just learned is the great cost this comes with.

The reason to maintain a face of strength is obvious. It's not wise to let others see our weaknesses since that can lead to them taking advantage of us. It might make others think less of us or not respect us. Or sometimes it is simply to protect our children from seeing our pain. So instead of exposing our pain and talking about it, we decide to suppress it. If something takes us down emotionally, physically, or mentally, the best course of action is not to let it shake us. Instead, we gather up our inner reserves and persevere. But is this really strength or are we shutting something down within us in order to maintain the illusion. Might there be an even greater strength in vulnerability?

Hormones took me down. It seems crazy, I know. After years of handling challenges and obstacles with ease and a can-do spirit, in the end it was a natural ebbing of hormones that knocked me off my game. It was this simple drop in estrogen that nearly broke my business and destroyed everything that I had worked for. I had no control, no explanation and no clear course of action. And what's worse is that I felt unusually weak because I had never seen anyone experience what I was going through. If a similar lethargy and indifference affected my mother, aunts, grandmothers or any of the other female relatives in my family, no one had ever let on. They never let on when anything affected them. Suffering, pain, and weakness were not to be talked about. And because these things were swept under the rug, I didn't have any resources to deal with what was going on. Instead, I felt alone and hopeless. I was being attacked by something I couldn't even see, and it felt shameful to succumb to this invisible nemesis.

I started working as a nurse in 1999. I grew up with the spirit of entrepreneurship in my blood because my family owned a restaurant. I knew what it was like to toil in the trenches because I participated in that business since I was sixteen, but I really had no thoughts about becoming an entrepreneur myself. I was a helper, and I had an intense desire to care for others. I didn't see how entrepreneurship and nursing went together, so I started my career in the nursing field.

One of my early jobs was working for the state in the "Train the Trainer" program. It was my job to teach CNA instructors all the rules and guidelines of the program so that they could pass that information onto their students. That's where my job ended. It wasn't my responsibility to help them with anything other than the official rules. But the thing that was so fascinating to me was how many other questions these women had. What I understood immediately based on the questions they were asking was that no one was really helping them. They were being given this task of overseeing CNAs, but they didn't even know where to begin, where to get equipment, or how to make a name for themselves. They were taught vague notions of what their goals should be and the rules were made clear, but no one was giving them any real help in establishing their businesses.

Finding answers was also something that I was good at. At this time, I had never had my own business, but I consulted a great deal. So I was very resourceful when it came to figuring out how to get things done. I taught myself everything I needed to know about EINs, LLCs, state taxes, websites and anything else that came up. And when these women started asking questions, I started giving them real answers that they could use to move forward. I started teaching them things I wasn't supposed to be teaching them. I simply couldn't do what everyone before me had done and give them just enough information to bring up more questions. I'd teach them everything I knew. And when I didn't know the answers, I found them.

My time working this program ultimately sparked the idea for my business. There was a huge need for information and assistance in starting health care businesses, and I had the experience and ability to help. So I opened my consulting business, SD Nurse Consulting.

For awhile, everything was moving along beautifully. I was doing what I loved, leveraging my entrepreneurial roots, and helping others follow their dreams. I couldn't ask for more. That's when the rude awakening came. It seemed to materialize out of thin air. One minute I was fine, and the next it was as if a dark cloud had descended upon me, leaving me with no energy, no motivation and no interest in anything. I couldn't even talk, as opening my mouth seemed like too much work.

I was teaching at a University at the time in addition to running my own business, but the classes were the only task I could muster up energy for. And they took every last drop of energy in my body. When it came to my business, I couldn't answer the phone, I couldn't listen to my messages, I couldn't even hire an assistant to do these things for me. I completely checked out. My business still existed, but I was nowhere to be found.

My two adult sons and fiancée left me to my own devices most of the time. They saw that I was in a near-constant irritated mood and knew not to bother me. My fiancée would descend into his man-cave and leave me to myself. One of my sisters seemed to understand what I was going through. She wouldn't harass me or complain that I wasn't available like my other sister, who felt abandoned by me. Instead this sister and I would Facetime, but we would literally not say a word to each other. We'd just sit there, making random comments every now and then. That was all I could do.

This feeling of apathy lasted for months. I couldn't get out from under this heavy blanket of fatigue and disinterest. And I didn't understand it. I knew that my business was dissolving before my eyes. I hadn't been able to answer a phone call or take on any work in months. Though I understood what this meant logically and what I should do about it, I simply couldn't do the things. I couldn't lift the phone. I couldn't talk. I couldn't work my business. I had never experienced such a persistent helplessness that was so out of my control.

It wasn't until I had the good fortune of running into an amiable woman in her sixties. For some reason we got to talking about what I was going through, and she totally understood the feeling. She told me that what I was feeling was absolutely normal, and that she herself had gone through it. It turns out that estrogen is what keeps us vibrant, and the sudden decrease in estrogen takes time to adapt to. She said it could take as long as two years to start to feel like myself again, but that it was all a simple result of changing hormones. Her advice was to stop being so hard on myself, and to instead be gentle with my body and simply do things that made me happy. Beating myself up, feeling guilty or forcing myself to do things I didn't feel up to wouldn't help the situation. All I could do was be patient. Eventually, the foreign sensation would fade.

It was only after talking with her that I felt any sense of relief. I finally had permission to simply be where I was. I didn't have to pretend that nothing was happening. The things I was feeling were real, and they were out of my control. I wasn't imagining them. I wasn't suddenly an apathetic failure. I was going through a very real life process, and it was all okay.

Once I understood the cause, I also felt like I had more control over how I spent my time. Some things would still be out of the question for now, but the guilt surrounding them was gone. When I was ready, I could rebuild my business, but for now it was okay to just focus on what was important to me and to do just the things I could do.

This experience taught me the strength in vulnerability. We are all human and so we are all vulnerable by default. But it's not weak to ask for help. It is a sign of self-awareness and the willingness to open oneself up to possibility. We don't have to weather the storm alone. We can ask others for guidance, for help and for assistance. Going through difficult things is a part of life. It's not shameful to go through something that you don't understand and don't have any answers for. Those who are farther along on the path can share their wisdom with us, but we have to be open to asking, and they have to be strong enough to expose their own struggles.

That's what is lost when we maintain a face of strength during times of struggle. We have come to believe that we shouldn't show the cracks in our mask, but that doesn't help any of us. We can gain so much when we come toward each other when we are vulnerable and broken. For when we expose that side of ourselves, we teach those around us to navigate those darker times as well. When we don't learn how to do this, a simple biological struggle like my own suddenly has the power to completely derail my life.

It's not unlike the "Train the Trainer" program. Looking back now, I think of those women in that program with all their questions. They were in the dark. They were feeling lost and alone. And everyone around them was giving them vague answers pretending it was all so easy. But what they needed was for someone to get vulnerable with them. They needed someone like me to illuminate the unknown elements of what they were experiencing. They needed someone to shine some light into the darkness.

That was the same thing that I ended up needing when my estrogen levels began to plummet. Fleets of women acting strong, like nothing was happening to their bodies wouldn't bring me any peace or understanding. I needed that older woman to open herself up and tell me she had been there, that it felt foreign and terrible, and that it would eventually end. She didn't have to tell me any of that. She could've pretended like I was sick and sad or crazy. She could have been intimidated because it was like looking into a mirror and seeing a time in her life that she preferred to forget; and pushed me away never to be thought of again. But she didn't. She took a moment to relate to me and to make me feel understood and in good company.

And that's what my intention is in sharing this story. Our bodies are complicated miracles, but they can ultimately let us down. We can get sick or grow older. We can get hurt and injured in ways that mean learning to use our bodies differently. And all of it can happen so fast, that we don't even have time to process it in our heads. All of this is okay. And it's also okay to find others who understand what we're going through. There is no shame in that. We can have close families and loved ones who don't understand our journey. Not everyone will relate with every circumstance we experience, but that doesn't mean we can't seek out others like us. We are a community, and a community is meant to be relied upon. We are here for each other.

I've since rebuilt and rebranded my consulting business to Nursing First, LLC. Nothing is ever truly lost. Once I understood what I was going through, I was able to prioritize what needed to happen. I still had all the same skills I always had, but I now understood I could delegate out what was taxing for me to do. I could use my network and my community. I hired a virtual assistant to help with the daily tasks leaving me with more time and energy for the elements of the work that inspired me.

And now I make it my mission to be open with others. I share my story so others know it's okay to be vulnerable. It's okay to wander off the path. It's okay to crash and burn. The most important thing is not just to appear strong and unfazed, but to emulate how to cultivate strength in the midst of strong emotions, intense hurts and debilitating disappointment. We all have permission to be real. That is the greatest strength of all.

Biography

Dr Sylette DeBois has always lived by defying expectations. She became a mother at the age of seventeen and although that caused her to adapt and defer her dream of becoming a nurse until later, it did not stop her. Instead, it made her more resourceful. Once she became a nurse, she maintained that same spirit of boldness and tenacity. In her eyes, there was no reason why nurses couldn't also be entrepreneurs, even though that was not the common perception, and she set out to make that a reality for herself and to inspire others to do the same.

Dr Sylette understood that there were very few resources available to aspiring nurse entrepreneurs. She spent over twenty years working in an array of nursing positions, ranging from pediatrics to critical care to management and consulting. With that experience under her belt, she knew she had the experience and skills to become the resource that was lacking in her own journey. Therefore, she founded Nursing First, a company that focuses on educational community care and the professional development of nurses, and Nursing First Academy where she educates hundreds of new nurses each year. She works daily to provide these nurses with the resources they need to open and manage successful businesses in the healthcare arena as well as build their current knowledge and arm new nurses with tools to keep them learning and growing. Sylette's life mission is to educate and inspire as many individuals in the nursing profession as she can, and nothing will get in the way of this God-given purpose.

Dr Sylette currently lives in Atlanta, Georgia where she spends her quality time with her fiancé Cedric and her grandson Dallas. She now dedicates her company to combating Compassion Fatigue and Nurse Retention for Health Care facilities. You can reach her on her website www.drsylette.com

Dedication

This book is dedicated to my Mom and children, A'narius and A'ziah. I lost my Mom early in life and know what it's like when your greatest advocate is gone. My daily motivation is being there for my children as my mother was before her death and in all the ways she couldn't be after her passing.

~Beatrix

Journey through the Dark

By Beatrix Curry, LPN

Samuel 22:29 "For You are my lamp, O Lord; The Lord shall enlighten my darkness.

I lost my mother when I was a teenager, and that one loss sent my life spiraling downward. Since that loss, I've consistently felt like I was struggling to climb out of a black hole. It felt like the harder I climbed, and the tighter I clung to the jagged walls, the steeper and more perilous the walls became. I couldn't seem to free myself of that feeling that I was perpetually on the edge of sliding into utter darkness, a place of no support.

Through the years, I've spent a lot of time thinking about how this loss changed things for me, and how it set me back behind all of my peers. I know that my loss was directly related to most of my hardships. But it hasn't really been until recently that I've started to shift this thinking. Of course, losing my mom left me with a lot of unresolved pain and was most certainly the catalyst for many of the struggles in my life; but this deep loss also shaped me into someone who could persist in the face of hardship. I became stronger in the face of this sadness and hurt, and I learned early to always rely on what I could do with my own two hands because there was never anyone in my corner.

I learned how to cultivate an inner determination and drive even when the world around me had nothing to offer. I learned how to muster strength from nothing because I had to, but it took me years to realize that I had this skill within me. I didn't see my resilience as a gift. My belief has always been that when life pushes you, either you fall or you fight back. As far as I see it, if you fall and stay down, things are only going to get worse. I saw the odds stacked against me and did the only thing I knew to how to do. I fought back. For me, choosing to fight back came naturally and seemed like my only choice in the matter, so I never recognized that this ability to persevere in the face of adversity was actually a gift and one of my greatest strengths.

My journey of becoming a nurse started over twenty years ago. During the course of my journey, I faced many obstacles starting when I found out I was pregnant with my son while I was in nursing school. A difficult pregnancy meant I had to put my dreams on hold at that point. I attempted to finish my schooling years later but was met with another hurdle when I became severely ill, unable to see or walk. God was on my side through all of it, but it seemed like every time I took a step forward, I got pushed two steps back. I fought twice as hard for every degree and every position that I had. And so when I got to the point of finding a job where I could work and earn a living as a nurse, I initially thought that I had reached my destination and could relax. After all, I was lucky to have even made it this far, and I was constantly pushing aside the whispers in my head that told me I wasn't worthy of anything more than this.

As a nurse, the hours were long and the shifts spilled over into holidays, nights and weekends, times other people had off. I had no problem working these hours in the early years, but this was not what I wanted my life to look like in the long-term. I didn't work so hard just so I could keep working hard at the expense of spending time with my family and risking my own wellbeing. Something had to change.

The feeling was familiar and reminiscent of my earlier struggles. It was the feeling of watching others enjoy a life that you don't have access to. It was the story of my youth. I watched my bosses inundate me with excessive amounts of work and unreasonable shifts. I got tired and they got paid the big bucks. I knew that there was more to nursing than bedside care, exhausting hours and stress from working so hard. It was then that the spark of entrepreneurship really began to take root inside of me. I could have access to a better life. I wasn't knocked down yet, but I surely would be if I stayed in this role for the rest of my life. I had the skills, the compassion and the drive to do this job as my own boss. I simply needed to summon my fighting skills again. I would not be knocked down. I had come a long way in becoming a nurse, but this didn't have to be my final destination. I couldn't fathom putting in hours and hours of hard work only to miss out on all the important things in my life. I wanted the time and freedom to enjoy the life I'd worked so hard to build alongside my career.

So I decided to open my own Home Care Agency. This was where I had originally gotten my start, and I knew the industry. I encountered unexpected hurdles along the way. Getting the right balance of help was difficult, and not long after I started, a new Medicare policy essentially eliminated all of my profits. I learned that not all hurdles are for jumping over. Sometimes they are there to tell you to try a different direction. It was not feasible to hire enough help to support this business model, and once I got my hands dirty a bit, I saw that this wasn't the best path for me. I needed to rethink things. I wasn't ready to give up; I just needed to look at other options.

A few years later, I landed a decent job working as a mental health nurse consultant. I had moved up through the ranks and was earning a considerable living. Maybe I could have been happy here, but I still had a desire for something more. I struggled back and forth with the worker mentality that nurses are trained to maintain, because it felt secure to have this steady paycheck. I wanted the freedom and lifestyle of an entrepreneur, but it was difficult to keep my focus on entrepreneurship when things at my job seemed good and reliable.

I came down with the flu, and missed two weeks of work. A merger had taken place a few months before, and it was evident now that additional layoffs might be in the works. I had a bad feeling in my stomach that had nothing to do with the flu. When I came back to work, there were signs that things were shifting. Other workers had already been fired, or were leaving due to the changes; I worried that I could be next. I didn't want to believe that they'd fire me. I had lots of skills and qualifications at this point, and believed myself to be a valuable asset. But I was also grandfathered in at a pretty substantial salary and had a considerable benefits package that was no longer standard now that ownership had changed. Then just like that, I was fired.

This job loss struck deep. I had worked so hard to make myself valuable, and it was all taken away due to the behind-the-scenes politics of the merger. Maybe it had to do with the business's bottom line or new policies, but either way, it stripped me of everything. This was the final straw for me. I knew that I had to make a serious go at entrepreneurship. I didn't have a choice, but no matter what new job I got, I would always be at risk. My livelihood would always be in someone else's hands, and I couldn't stomach that.

Luckily I was able to collect unemployment for the short-term, but I would need a better long-term solution. I started researching how I could start my own CNA program. This seemed more in line with my strengths and what I could offer. Plus I knew how much a program like this would've helped me early on in my journey, and it would be gratifying to help others in this way. I could be a source of guidance to girls who struggled as I had struggled.

But the CNA program would take time to develop. I needed something even more immediate that could start earning me an income fast. That's when I opened up my Day Care. This had been percolating as a business idea in my mind for a long time. Affordable and reliable daycare was something I had desperately needed when I was first studying to be a nurse. I lost many jobs because I didn't have anyone to watch my kids, and I sometimes had to take my children with me to school because I had no other alternative. So starting a daycare was not just a business idea for me, it was something that meant a lot to me. If I could help women who were currently struggling with the same thing that was such a challenge in my own journey, I would feel like I was really making a difference. It only helped that I knew I could get the proper certifications quickly and start bringing in money before my unemployment ran out. I started the Day Care through word of mouth and grew it pretty quickly. In the meantime, I attended workshops and studied everything I could in order to come up with a plan for building my CNA program.

I also increased the attention I was putting on my spiritual practices and became a spiritual life coach to others during this time. This has not only helped me keep my focus, but has given a renewed sense of purpose. Since doing this, I've been offered other opportunities to use my spiritual coach skills including launching my own spiritual wellness online course. Once you start using your own skills to help others, and you see that this can actually bring money in, you become empowered in a way that you weren't empowered before.

I learned that its okay to change your mind. Just because you start something with a particular ending in mind doesn't mean that you have to stick to that. There are some things that you need to see through to the end, but there are many others when it's smarter to pivot into a new direction. There are also many lessons to be learned from all the mistakes and false starts. But these are all things that I learned myself simply by doing things and making mistakes. I never had anyone telling me that what I was doing or not doing was okay. It was all trial and error.

I initially started moving forward because I lost my mother. Later I kept moving forward because of my children. They needed me, and I knew that I had to figure out how to make things work. I needed to create a life that both paid and allowed me to spend time with them. When I started missing events and holidays, it was a sign that I needed to pay attention and think about what I was doing. If I wanted a different result, I would have to do something differently.

My journey has allowed me to appreciate life and everything it has to offer. That includes both the blessings and the hardships. If anything were changed or taken away, I would not be the person I am today. Right now, I am in the midst of building my own business. I have found another day job for the time being, but I understand its role in my life. I do not rely on that job for my livelihood. It is a simply a way to fund my real business, the one that I will be able to rely on. No one will be able to fire me, and I will work on my terms, create my own hours and decide what clients I work with. I am moving from a place of reliance on others into one of true empowerment.

The more I work on my business, the more it becomes evident how much of a gift my mother gave me by leaving me so early. Of course, I would do anything to extend the years I had her in my life, but the duration of her stay on Earth was not up to me. But there was a gift in her departure, and that gift was that it forced me to become resilient and strong. It created a determination in me that wouldn't be possible in me otherwise. Adversity has no power over me because I learned how to overcome it even in my saddest moments.

For years I didn't feel worthy of success or good news or even love. But through my journey, I've witnessed how I am valuable, and that I do deserve the life I want. And I have the perfect tool to help me get to any dream I can come up with for myself and for my family. I have strength. I have been through the worst and survived. I emerged from the dark hole I was thrown into in the beginning, and I didn't emerge weaker and worn from the climb. I emerged strong and with the wisdom that if I can do that, I can do anything. Darkness can't exist without light, but the only way out is through. There is light at the end of every tunnel. With enough steps in the right direction, you will emerge. Trust me, I made it through the darkness.

Job 29:3 When his lamp shined upon my head, and when by his light I walked through darkness.

Biography

Beatrix Marie Curry is a nurse, entrepreneur, consultant, author, spiritual coach and ordained minister, in addition to being a single mother of two wonderful teenagers. Her intense desire to help others stems from the loss of her mother at age sixteen. She has made it her life's mission and purpose to help others, sometimes serving as a nurse and other times inspiring women to start businesses or cultivate their spirituality. She is the founder Bee'z Kid'z and is in the process of developing her own CNA program. She derives her strength from her faith and inspires others to do so as well.

Twitter: www.twitter.com/currybeatrix
Facebook: www.facebook.com/beatrixcurry
Instagram: www.instagram.com/beatrixcurry
Website: beatrixcurrybooks.weebly.com
Email: Aziah10@hotmail.com

Dedication

This chapter is dedicated to some of the most influential people in my life. Thank you to my father, Pierre Sony Cadet for taking the chance to come to a foreign country. Thank you to my mother, Francoise Elise Cadet, for teaching me compassion and love by acting as both father and mother to four kids and fostering many others. Thank you to my grandma, Elda Celoy, who inspired my initial love of cooking and taught me the basics when I was just a girl. Every time I cook rice or beans I hear her voice dictating instructions. Thank you to my sisters Mimi Cadet-Patterson, who raised the bar and inspired me to pursue my ambitions and stay on course. And thank you to Lainda Cadet for never giving up on life no matter what hardships she faced. She is a true inspiration.

Thank you to my best friends Mayra Figueroa-Clark for taking me in as her little sister when I had absolutely no money as a new grad studying for my board. Thank you to Jackie, Cheryl, Mrs. White, and Mrs. Lanier for teaching me how to apply my knowledge as a new nurse. And thank you to all my friends who have listened and encouraged me countless times when I've been discouraged about life and business.

~Denise

From Seed to Bloom

By Denise Cadet, RN

Most journeys start with a seed. Sometimes that seed is literally a seed that will eventually bloom into a fruit, vegetable or flower. It's a physical gift from the Earth that will either nourish a body with its nutrients or nourish a soul with its beauty. Other times that seed is just an idea, a passing thought or the spark of a purpose making itself known. Both seeds require time, care and attention, but when that is given, something truly amazing eventually blooms. I'm about to take you on what that journey was for me. I moved through my life collecting seeds without completely knowing what they'd produce. Patiently, I cared for them, nurtured them and waited to see what might emerge. I never expected that it would all turn into such a gratifying journey and mission.

Being a nurse is one of the most helpful professions on the planet. On a daily basis, it's our job as nurses to care of those who need it most. It is truly amazing how a simple, intentional touch can ease a person's pain or relax a tense body. Ironically however, my role as a nurse uncovered how truly helpless I could feel even in the most helpful of professions.

In my early years, I was assigned to the oncology department. What soon became evident was that despite giving myself one hundred percent to the role, all of my effort seemed like too little, too late. I was helping my patients to the best of my ability, but it felt like just grasping at something that was just beyond reach. My patients were longing simply to survive, and I was giving them care and comfort and easing their pain, but there was a bigger problem lurking in the vicinity, and it was making me uneasy. I saw that the true help my patients needed was already in the past. Now we were just managing the symptoms, but if we could rewind time, there might have been diet and lifestyle changes that would have prevented their illnesses altogether. My heart sank on a daily basis as I watched patients dealing with these debilitating diseases knowing that the entire hospital team was much too late to the party.

Thinking about this devastating irony kept me up at night. The medical care we were providing was necessary and often helpful, but we were already so late. Plus there was also very little comfort offered in combination with the endless treatments. I longed to help these terminally ill patients find some comfort and nourishment for their soul on this long and lonely journey. There are plenty of facilities that specialize and focus on this type of thing, but I dreamed of opening a center of my own that had this focus. To me, there was something so much more important about nurturing the soul and reducing the anxiety of illness rather than strictly focusing on the prognosis and the treatments despite any side effects.

I was brimming with other ideas as well, and they all had to do with prevention in some capacity. I wanted to open up a healing center, I wanted to help people advocate for their health long before it became a life and death decision, and I wanted to intervene early so that people never even made it into the oncology ward. With every patient I saw, my mind raced beneath the surface. It eventually became so persistent that I couldn't contain the anxiety. I felt unsettled in my role as nurse because intuitively I knew I had to do more. My purpose was fluttering somewhere far beneath the surface. Finally, my friend Mayra recognized my anxiety and intervened. She sat me down and asked questions until she got to the root of what I was feeling. Once we established what was bothering me, we set out to coming up with a practical plan for how I could realistically help others outside of just being a nurse.

With her help, I decided to go to culinary school. The shift may seem drastic and contrary to what I was already doing, but cooking was a passion of mine. Also, I had witnessed firsthand how intertwined diet and health were. So many of my patients were diagnosed with diabetes, hypertension and other preventable diseases, and I knew that diet was critical. Every time a new patient was diagnosed, they were required to go through a two-hour dietitian consult. The results of this consult were never positive. Instead the patients left overwhelmed and discouraged with their new dietary plan. Those that followed the plan did so with resentment and despair, and many others opted not to follow it at all. They didn't want to give up their favorite, tasty foods, and would rather accept a dire fate than change their diet to a flavorless, restricted menu.

At the time that I enrolled in culinary school, I didn't have a full sense of how things would all come together and wasn't sure exactly why I was enrolling, but the instinctive pull to make this transition was strong. So I followed my gut and graduated from the Culinary Institute of America. The entire time I studied there, I was constantly asked why I was there at all, being a registered nurse with a Bachelor's of Science in Nursing. My parents especially, couldn't make sense of my decision to forgo completing my Master's degree. Despite all of the questions and judgment, I persisted. Plus I had a talent and a love for cooking ever since my grandmother first taught me as young girl. She had always told me that I'd find a good husband as long as I could cook. My reasons for cooking grew to be much more expansive than finding a husband, but there was still that shared bit of history and nostalgia that I harbored in my spirit and fueled my love of cooking.

Over the next decade, I used my cooking skills to help those around me, especially those who needed help with their diet. I cooked for my friends, I cooked for weddings, I hosted large gathering at my home just as an excuse to make a large meal. And I never sacrificed flavor in order to make a healthy dish. Instead I made dishes that were healthy and tasted good. I used fresh, local ingredients. I used my knowledge of food pairings to enhance and complement ingredients, and I used spices to elevate recipes to the next level.

I continued my nursing career while I cooked. In my spare time, I pursued other modalities and paths toward entrepreneurship, but nothing seemed quite right. At one point, an opportunity to become a health and wellness coach surfaced. I took to the idea right away. This was a perfect avenue for me to help people advocate for their health before they had an illness to manage. As I researched how I could make this coaching a business, I discovered the Institute of Integrative Nutrition. I joined the program right away and committed to guiding my clients on a path to a healthier, more fulfilling life. Slowly, I started to reduce my hours as a nurse in order to pursue this business more thoroughly.

My family and friends were not immediately onboard with this new direction. After all, it looked much riskier than the steady, reliable career of conventional nursing. My father had always said that a nurse could get a job anywhere and that subsequently the world would be my oyster. But for me, the pearls in that oyster were simply missing. I needed something else that nursing alone could not offer. Because of the feedback I was getting from people around me, I often doubted myself. I wondered if something was wrong with me. So many people find happiness in nursing. Perhaps I was just expecting too much?

Instead of giving in to the doubt, I decided to relocate to San Francisco. Being around all of the negative feedback wasn't helpful. I needed to focus on my mission and not be distracted by others' opinions. I remember talking with a friend who asked if I thought I was being too greedy. That question stopped me in my tracks. Was I being greedy? Was I thinking only of myself and what would make me happy? Was I making a mistake?

As I reflected on my motivations, I recalled a nurse I had worked with years earlier. One day she had suddenly left a high-paying nursing position to start a construction business. At the time, none of us understood why she would make this seemingly incongruous decision. We all judged her for the decision, myself included. But now I understood. She had a dream and a determination to do something, and she listened to it. She didn't allow the money, or the logistics or society's perception to derail her dream. She just went for it, and we criticized her for it. But a passion is a passion, and sometimes the thing we are meant to do in this world isn't rational, but that doesn't mean it should be ignored. Our gut doesn't lie – not physically and not spiritually.

In the early part of my nursing career, I worked mostly in a hospital setting. The only other place I thought a nurse could work was as a home health caregiver or in a doctor's office. I was not aware of any nurses that had their own healthcare business. As I remembered this construction-focused nurse and saw other people outside the medical field triumphantly running successful businesses, I realized my early day dreams that exposed my uneasiness were actually viable business opportunities, not just fantasies. It was all my intuition telling me that I needed to take steps toward my passion. Relaxing and listening to that voice was the scariest thing I ever did, but also the most rewarding.

I was terrified to actually take the leap and start my business. By the time I was emotionally ready, I had spent years nursing. I was burnt out physically and had gained weight. I was hardly at optimum health myself, how could I coach others? Who would listen to me? My solution was to hire different coaches for myself. Each one helped me prepare to become a business owner. It took more than a business plan; I needed to shift my thinking.

For years, I searched for the magical ingredient that I was missing in order to go into business for myself. And I finally found it. It wasn't something elusive or expensive. It wasn't something that is even rare. The magic ingredient of business ownership is hard work and dedication. I spent years waiting for a sign or a magical omen that would assure me I was on the right path or doing the right thing. But there isn't anything magical to it. It simply is recognizing what motivates and drives you, and then going all in on that thing. The success of a business is going to take blood, sweat and tears, so the thing you build better be something that you are passionate about.

There is no need to wait for perfection or the right time. It is okay to simply begin. I waited for years thinking that I wasn't quite ready. But we will never be fully ready. One of my coaches told me that I don't need to have all the answers; I just have to be two or three steps ahead of my clients. To learn this felt like such a relief. I didn't have to have it all figured out, I simply had to be motivated to learn the answers as I needed them and be prepared for just the next few steps.

Even more of my vision began to fall into place when I got the frightening call from my father that my mom couldn't move her left arm or leg. As a nurse, I knew what this sounded like and sure enough, she had had an ischemic stroke. I was grateful, it wasn't a massive stroke that would leave her unable to speak or eat, but even so, it was difficult. I stayed by her bedside for two months. It was during that time that I learned how important retirement insurance was, and how most of us are ill -prepared for any healthcare calamity, including my parents.

This was the missing piece in my entrepreneurship journey. In addition to a healthy diet and lifestyle, people needed guidance on how to be financially prepared for the health tribulations of later life. When the finances aren't there to deal with a sudden health crisis, the stress the money portion causes contributes to the problem of getting well. This was the seed of my business model. Wellness is so much bigger than just how much you exercise or what you eat. True wellness encompasses mental, spiritual and financial health. I knew this firsthand from when I was a home health nurse. So many individuals were stressed both physically and financially. At the point I was there with them in their homes, there was very little I could do. Once the bill for thousands of dollars is on the table, I can't teleport them back in time to plan for this outcome, just like once they have a terminal disease, I can't go back and advise them against past choices. By this point, it is only about the immediate ailment.

My mother's stroke was the result of high blood pressure. That's an entirely preventable and manageable disease. The issues that arose with my parent's finances were also things that could have been planned for. But there are very few resources helping us think about and plan for the future in this way. Most of walk around living in the moment and figuring we'll deal with future problems in the future. But my time as a nurse in the early days illuminated this detrimental mistake so many of us make. And for years, I knew I wanted and needed to do what I could to change this. My company, Bloom Culture Solutions does exactly this. We provide monthly training in the spirit of prevention and awareness. We help both companies and their employees by providing comprehensive benefit packages for their employees. This includes health benefits, 401Ks and health and wellness trainings. We do this all through subscription services.

What many companies don't think about is how these benefits not only help their employees but also help the company as a whole. We teach how to prioritize wellness on every level. That means less absences and less sick employees. It also means happier employees enjoying a better quality of life. And all that translates into real money for the business. Less lost income. More productive staff. Just like the body, when you care for each part individually, the whole simply works better.

There is plenty to be done on my business. I am by no means free and clear of struggle. But I finally have the confidence to move forward with confidence. I can see the bigger picture of my entire journey, and the importance of my culinary degree in partnership with my nursing background. I even see the gift in my mother's stroke. Though I would never wish that to happen, even that has contributed to my life's journey. My current entrepreneurship journey encompasses all of me, all of my passions and all of my expertise. The uneasiness that I felt as a nurse is gone because I now am having an impact on people before they are sick. I am empowering them to take their lives into their own hands, and to be ready for the unknown rather than succumbing to it.

There is power in being proactive. There is strength in taking steps toward your own wellness. I no longer feel like I'm arriving on the scene too late to help. I am inserting myself into people's lives long before they used to need me, and I finally feel like I'm doing what I was meant to do. I still am here to offer a simple and intentional touch to my clients, but now that touch is a tap on the shoulder, a gentle nudge on the back. And it's no longer one that says, "I'm here for you while you suffer;" instead it's a touch that says, "Let's do what we can now, so there's a whole lot less suffering later. I'm here to help with that."

Instead of meeting people at the hospital when their petals are wilting and they are simply trying to hold on, I now can meet them at their workplace. Here I can teach them how to bloom and to live their best life, and together we can plant the right seeds to create a better future. That is Bloom Culture. That is my purpose.

Biography

Denise Cadet is the founder and CEO of Bloom Culture, a benefit company with a membership based wellness program that works with its employees to ensure they have access to the resources they need in order to maintain financial, physical and emotional wellness. Having spent many years working bedside as a nurse in hospitals, Denise saw firsthand what the final stages of life looked like and longed to get involved with patients earlier when preventative measures could have a substantial effect on quality of life. Being born and raised in Haiti and coming to the U.S. at the age of fourteen, she was well aware of what it felt like to be unprepared and scared in an incomprehensible environment. Just like her inability to speak the language initially was a big hurdle for her, she saw that her patients' lives and prognoses were more difficult because wellness wasn't discussed and addressed earlier in life. She found satisfaction in nursing but longed to make a difference before people became sick. When Denise wants something, she persists no matter what. She went on to get her Bachelor's of Nursing at Howard University and eventually did a research study on HIV/AIDS in Swaziland that she was asked to present to the entire student body. She held the audience captive with her work despite her thick Haitian accent, a testament to her discipline and drive. Later she graduated from the Culinary Institute and completed a health coaching program. Her company is the culmination of all of her passions coming together. Today she meets her clients in the workplace instead of the hospital where she focuses on helping them achieve holistic wellness in all areas of life.

Dedication

To my Husband:

Thank you for **LOVING** me!

To my Parents:

Thank you for **INSPIRING** me!

To my Siblings:

Thank you for **ACCEPTING** me!

To my Children:

Thank you for **CHOOSING** me!

To my Friends:

Thank you for **MOTIVATING** me!

~ Katina

"Trust in the Lord with all your heart, and do not lean on your own understanding. In all your ways acknowledge him, and he will make straight your paths"

~ Proverbs 3:5–6

Dreams Realized: A Nurse's Journey to Entrepreneurship!

By Katina Dorsey, RN

There's a space between the time of our parents and that of our children where the ground seems to be less firm, the truths less true and the confidence in ourselves built on shakier ground. I grew up in a time when the belief was that if you got a good job, then you were essentially set for life. Once you were skilled in your area of expertise and got your position, you stayed there. If you worked hard, you moved up, and only if you performed poorly, or abused your role in some way, would you be terminated. It was a time when having a good job meant security.

Now, however, especially in conversations with my daughter, I can see how much times have changed. She can't even imagine being in one place forever, working for other people and doing the same thing day after day. It's an interesting contrast, but what it means is that the generation in between these two extremes - my generation - got dealt an interesting struggle. We are caught somewhere in the middle, wrestling with old beliefs and new truths in order to find a place for ourselves in this changing dynamic.

I became a nurse because I knew it to be a good, solid job that would support my family. The profession itself seemed secure. The world would never stop needing nurses. Plus, I saw firsthand how much of an impact nurses had on the lives of real people when I became pregnant at seventeen years old. My daughter was born with a serious illness and, after her birth, spent ten days in the NICU. Prior to this, I had always wanted to be a doctor, potentially a pediatrician, but after my experience in the NICU, I saw that the nurses were doing everything in the ward that I wanted to be doing. They were involved in every step of the care. I saw the doctor very rarely and just for a few minutes, but the nurses were there every step of the way, explaining their actions to me as they went along and making me feel comforted and supported as they did things to my baby that I couldn't understand.

These nurses were an inspiration to me. I knew that I needed a career that could support me, and I wanted something that wouldn't take years of schooling before I could start earning an income; I simply didn't have that kind of time anymore. There were programs in nursing that could get me into the field within a year or two. I knew that I didn't want to rely on welfare or other government assistance, and I certainly didn't want to end up in some minimum wage job. If I became a nurse, I would have job security. I would be valuable to society, I would be personally fulfilled and I would have an income that would support my family. I very much had that worker mentality. Get a good job and everything else would fall into place.

But I also grew up with an entrepreneur father. He wasn't present in my daily life, and I didn't see him often, but I did know that he was a business owner. And today, I wonder if maybe the entrepreneur spirit is something that is simply in my blood. Being an entrepreneur could have great rewards, but I grew up seeing it also as inherently dangerous. Despite their apparent freedom, entrepreneurs are on their own. There are no pensions or unions in the background to serve as failsafe's. There is only you. On the surface, it seems far less secure than having a quality job.

I also grew up in a time when entrepreneurs weren't everywhere like they are today. The Internet was coming, but most entrepreneurs were still people who needed a lot of capital to get going with a brick and mortar business. Nevertheless, the idea of this freedom appealed to me. There was something inside of me that resented always being on someone else's time and in situations that were always someone else's decision. But as much as I longed to change things, it seemed like sucking it up, and simply finding a good job, was the price to pay for the security that I needed.

And of course, life gets in the way. When my now ex-husband and I had our daughter, we were just kids. Our daughter was born while we were in high school. We both graduated that year, and by the end of the summer, we got married. We were so young that first year, and focusing on a career was not my primary focus as I simply learned how to be a parent. Just about exactly a year after getting married, my husband was incarcerated, leaving me as the sole provider. I had wavered in my schooling, but now the pressure was on. I needed to prioritize my schooling so that I could establish myself in a reliable career. I set my sights on this goal and graduated my LPN program and passed the NCLEX-PN within two years. And once I learned that my husband was going to be incarcerated long-term, I knew that I had to cut ties with him. I had to move forward and propel myself into more positive endeavors, so the relationship had to end.

After lots of hard work and sacrifice, I finally got my first job as an LPN, working for a group of family practice doctors. It wasn't the job I had dreamed of long ago when my daughter was in the NICU, but it paid the bills. Still, I wanted more. I was getting discouraged, and I knew that I needed to go back to school to become an RN in order to get more fulfilling work. I took a full-time weekend staff nurse position at a long-term care facility. This was one of the hardest jobs I ever worked, but the pay was substantial enough so that I could pay my way through an associate's degree program to become an RN. Those days were long and grueling as I balanced that full-time job with school for three years.

The thing that kept me going was reflecting on my early experience in the NICU and envisioning a life in which I, too, could have a powerful impact on my clients. I dreamed that I, too, would get to work with babies and new mothers, but it doesn't work like that in the healthcare landscape. Desire alone doesn't put you into your ideal working environment. There are all sorts of obstacles along the path - licenses to earn, classes to take, diplomas to receive. And even when you do get a job after all that, there are still lots of politics to navigate, people to know and menial tasks to complete before you are where you dreamed you'd be.

You don't get to pick and choose what department you work in. Much like other jobs, promotions and assignments have a lot to do with "who" you know. And I had entered this field not knowing a soul. I felt like I was just a pawn in someone else's game. I had no say or choice in what I was tasked to do. I was simply required to show up and get things done.

Once I did become an RN, I worked in a variety of landscapes - home health, dialysis and elsewhere - but I still wasn't satisfied. I was tired and getting burnt out. The landscape of the nursing world felt more like politics than medicine, and it was wearing on me.

By this point, I had met my current husband, and I now had two children. As I worked these various nursing jobs, I recognized that I still had the bug for entrepreneurship. A couple of opportunities presented themselves to me in which I could start businesses of my own and work from home. One of these was for a direct sales company, where I'd be educating people about sexual health. I gave it a shot for a while, but I didn't have much time to spend on the endeavor, especially when my husband went overseas to work a contract position for the military. That endeavor ended up failing. Though the opportunity might have been lucrative down the line, I also didn't have much passion for it. The thing that I had passion for was being my own boss, but it's difficult to be your own boss when you're not totally invested in the endeavor you are pursuing.

I also took another foray into self-employment when I came across an opportunity selling essential services, like satellite TV, home security and others. I earned a commission on my sales and had lots of autonomy over how I sold these things, but I had no passion at all for this type of thing and ended up stopping not long after getting started.

Suffice it to say, my failed business attempts left me feeling extremely disappointed. Those lackluster attempts propelled me right back into that worker mindset. It seemed pretty clear to me that I didn't have enough enthusiasm to make those businesses work, and had my livelihood been tied to those businesses in any way, I'd have been on pretty precarious ground. Getting a "real job" would be the safe and smart thing to do.

I eventually found a job that I loved, working as an insurance industry case manager. The job allowed me to work from home, which gave me the feeling of being on my own time, even though I was still working for someone else. However, for the first time in a long while, I felt happy. I wasn't working bedside anymore or helping people directly, but I was doing something that I was good at and qualified to do, and I felt a little of that longed-for freedom because I was working in my own space.

I got comfortable, and then I got terminated. The termination unraveled me. After losing my job, I spiraled into a deep depression and struggled with overpowering anxiety and persistent insomnia. It became difficult to do anything, but I had two kids, so I had to move forward regardless. I thought about starting my own business in response to this loss, but I was way too depressed. My previous failures had me doubting myself and only stirred up emotions of defeat and failure, which were exacerbated by the depression and anxiety I was going through. It was difficult to not be negative, but I knew that somehow I had to try to stay positive. I just felt so completely burned out. I had worked so hard to get the degrees that I had, and I continued to work hard in a job that I found meaningful, yet none of that mattered. As an employee, I was in a position where I didn't get to decide my value; someone else had that power. My superiors decided who was worth something and who wasn't, and I was subject to their whims. They could toss me aside whenever they decided it was time. That reality was frightening, and I was now living with the consequences of the trust I had handed them.

I sought out a therapist and got myself on medication, but it was a long journey out of that darkness. I worked hard to rebuild my strength and to develop a purpose of my own. I still felt that stir within me, telling me that I should be on my own, doing my own thing so this wouldn't happen to me again. But at the same time, I needed to support my family, so I did need another job. I was caught in between the longing for entrepreneurship and the need for a steady paycheck.

Eventually, I did find another job. This time, however, I didn't relax. I couldn't relax. I constantly felt at risk, like this new job could be taken from me at any time. It made me extra conscientious and cautious, but it was also uncomfortable. This was not how I wanted to live. What good was a job if I was always worried about losing it? It took about two years before I even felt comfortable enough to bring in picture frames and personal touches for my desk. It was this discomfort that revealed to me what I needed to do. I needed to build my own business on the side. I could feel comfortable in this unreliable job if I knew that I was the one deciding it was temporary. It didn't have to be temporary, because I was simply expecting the worst and for history to repeat itself. I could decide that this was merely a stepping-stone on my larger path and take some power back over my own destiny. This feeling of angst and unease didn't help me do my job; it made me nervous and on edge. I was too conciliatory and not functioning as my true self. And I wasn't alone is this feeling. This was common, especially in the healthcare industry.

That's when the seed of my business idea began to germinate. I could start a business that would promote wellness for healthcare workers. I'd focus on preventative measures so that workers didn't end up stressed out and no longer able to serve their patients. Finally, I had found a message that resonated deeply with me. That was something brand new to me - reflecting on my past business failures. Previously, I had never resonated with what I was doing. Starting a business takes large quantities of time and energy, and you simply can't invest that when you don't believe strongly in the mission. But suddenly this was no longer an issue. I had a purpose and a clear vision. I could do this, and my current job would help me get there. It didn't have to be any more than that. I could still do my best and work at this job, but my own value didn't have to be tied up in whether they kept me or not. And in fact, my goal wasn't to stay there for the long-term. This job was not where I found security. True security resided in my own abilities and skills; as long as I had those, I could be secure in this world. What a revelation.

It took a termination and long and painful dark era for me to learn how to find firm footing on this rocky terrain. I still wrestle with the mentality I grew up with, that security lies outside of myself. But then I look at my daughter and others of her generation, and I see how liberating it is to not have those old beliefs holding them back. They inherently understand that their value lies in their own abilities. They start businesses with nothing other than a smartphone. That's not to say that there is nothing to learn from the generation before me, the one that did rely on that steady job. That's where my original work ethic comes from. It's just a different world now. In this world, the only thing we can rely on is ourselves and the networks we create around ourselves. There might be many ways in which this is terrible news, that our employers don't have our backs like they once did, that it's a dog-eat-dog world and other similar sentiments. But one positive consequence that I am absolutely sure of is this: true empowerment and security lie within, and we all have the ability to cultivate and rely on this.

Connect with Katina:
Email: nursekatina2@gmail.com
Facebook: www.facebook.com/nursekatina
Instagram: www.instagram.com/nursekatina
Website: www.nursekatina.com

Biography

Katina Dorsey started her nurse consulting business when life circumstances revealed she had the unique experience and motivation to help others like her in the healthcare industry. Her mission is to promote wellness and reduce stress for anyone in the healthcare field. As a burgeoning entrepreneur, she is no stranger to hard work, and currently works for a major health insurer as a Utilization Management Nurse in addition to building her own business. Through the years, she has worked in a plethora of disciplines within the healthcare arena, including Long Term Care, Oncology, Dialysis, Home Healthcare, Disease Management and Insurance Case Management. She currently holds a Certified Case Manager designation. Katina started her career after graduating from the Licensed Practical Nurse Program at Clover Park Technical College in 1999. In 2006, she received her Associate's Degree in Nursing from Tacoma Community College. As a native of Savannah, Georgia, Katina brings the mindset of Southern hospitality into everything she does and treats every client she meets like a good friend. She currently resides in Lithonia, Georgia with her loving husband Mike, where they love hosting family dinners for their three adult children. Katina espouses the importance of work-life balance, and so when she is not hard at work, she loves to travel the world, especially via cruise ship.

Dedication

I dedicate this book to my entire family. My loving husband Lee, handsome son Luke and gorgeous daughter Emily who love, inspire me to continue to push myself and stay determined. My sisters Janet and Holly for their love and support. To my parents Herb and Pearl who have supported me and demonstrated what it means to work hard.

James 5:11 "As you know, we count as blessed those who have persevered. You have heard of Job's perseverance and have seen what the Lord finally brought about. The Lord is full of compassion mercy"

~Janel

How Student Loan Debt Lead to the Journey of Purpose and Becoming a Nurse Boss

By Dr. Janel Willingham, DNP APRN, NP-C

Introduction Hello, my name is Dr. Janel Willingham, and I am a nurse boss, author, speaker, nurse career strategist and nurse practitioner. I want to take you on a journey of how I came to be a nurse practitioner and nurse boss. What I have experienced and learned over the past 20 years in the healthcare industry has lead me to becoming a nurse boss. Nursing is what I know for sure (a nod to Oprah Winfrey, my mentor in my head). Some days, I am not sure about this nurse boss thing, but I realize that nursing school, my nursing career being an advanced practice nurse has prepared me for this role of nurse boss. I started out wanting to be a nurse since I was probably the age of five. My mother kept a book that chronicled my school years, and every year she wrote that I wanted to be a nurse. As the years passed, I continued wanting that. I think the white uniform and hat lead me, at a early age, to thinking this was someone that I wanted to become. You ask me now why I am in the nursing profession, and I will tell you it's because God called me to this career.

I like helping others in such an intimate way and genuinely like taking care of others. So, when things got hard, I would keep going because a part of me knew God wanted me to be a part of this profession. When God calls you for something, He removes or solves all your obstacles - or at least helps you through them. I accomplished this by the Grace of God, prayer, goal setting and determination. I was at a conference in the fall of 2016, and during a session, the speaker had an exercise for us to do, which was asking each other questions to precipitate growth from adversity. The question given to me was, "What is one inner quality you've discovered about yourself that helps to make difficult situations turn out?" I thought about it for a few minutes before I answered, and what I realized even more in that moment was determination was my answer. So, as you read through this book, I hope you will be encouraged to find your inner determination, pursue your goals and, if not already, become a nurse boss. When I say I have been determined to be in the nursing profession, I mean it. By any means necessary.

I have been a certified nurses assistant (CNA), licensed practical nurse (LPN), have an Associate's Degree in Nursing, a registered nurse (RN), have my Baccalaureate of Science in Nursing (BSN), a Master of Science in Nursing/Family Nurse Practitioner (MSN, FNP) and now a Doctor of Nursing Practice (DNP). The other title I hold is CEO, a.k.a. nurse boss. I am at the beginning of becoming a nurse boss, but I have already learned so much and have inspiration to help others do the same. Although my journey has been long and hard, I am thankful for the journey and proud of it! I recognize I did it in a unique way, and my nursing journey has lead me to starting my own business. I believe it makes me well rounded, a good leader and a nurse boss. I lead with caring, compassion and empathy.

I know I am looking to help others use their determination superpower to gain their professional nursing or healthcare experience and become their own nurse boss. As I realized that determination was one of the best assets I had, I decided to examine the definition and analyze what it meant to be a determined person. I want to share with you not only the definition of determination but also the characteristics I believe determined people possess. As I was writing this book, I began to try to process what behaviors I had while perusing my nursing degrees. I believe the same behaviors will guide you through the nurse boss journey. I decided there were six I could think of, and maybe I would discover more. But first read the definition of determination. Determination is defined as firmness of purpose; resoluteness; will power; strength of character; purposefulness (Merriam-Webster.com). Also, it is a quality that makes you continue trying to do or achieve something that is difficult.

Here are the top six activities I believe determined people do to become nurses.

1. When they fail at a task, they start again
2. Keep their eyes on the prize (mission)
3. Seek help (invest in self)
4. Give up wants for a season (vacations)
5. Believe in themselves even when others don't
6. Set vision goals

These activities will be the foundation of you becoming the nurse you want to be and/or becoming a nurse boss. My favorite part about the definition of determination is "firmness of purpose." When you are aware of your purpose and know that is what God called you to do, then usually a person doesn't let anything or anyone stop him/her from completion. Journey: "the act of traveling from one place to another." In nursing, it is no different. Nurses are always on a journey. Whether you are on the journey from the emergency department to neonatal intensive care unit. Sometimes we choose our journey, and sometimes others push us to our journey. I had two catalysts to my journey to nurse boss: student loans and purpose push.

STUDENT LOAN How did I get here? Well, you've heard a little bit about my journey. I went from CNA to DNP and along that journey accumulated student loans. I had to have student loans to get through college. I was an average student in high school, and there were no scholarships for average students, and my parents made too much money, so there I was no such thing as grant money for me, either. As a matter fact, I was told my first few years of college that I basically would have to have a dependent, a.k.a. a child, in order for me to qualify for a grant. So, my other option was a student loan, which at the time seemed like no big deal. I had a dream of becoming a registered nurse. So I set out to do that. This is my journey student loan, purpose and becoming a nurse boss. The student loans started my first few years at the first college, and as I continued on my journey, my student loans continued. I looked at student loans as a necessary means and realized one day I would have to pay them back, but that always seemed far away.

Fast forward approximately 20 years, and now I have student loans the starring me in the face. [a1] For the first time in a long time it really hit home that it was time to pay my loans. Now it's time to pay back my student loans but the differences now is I'm not single anymore - I'm married with children, a husband, a car, a house, credit card bills and other projects. And now I'm facing this large debt - this large burden - and it's too much to handle. Now the guilt sets in, how did I get here? Why did I get here? Why didn't I pay? And now the frustration begins as well. This is a depressing matter - I have all these obligations, and I have the dreaded student loan people sending me statements. So you open this envelope and you have the statements that say you owe $XX, XXX.00, and you have all your other bills, and you're trying to figure out how in the world are you going to pay this bill. The student loan people want $300 a month, and I'm telling them I cannot do $300 a month - I have a car payment now, that I didn't plan on having, because I was in a rollover crash, so now I have a car payment that I didn't expect. I don't know what to do. So I deal by IGNORING; a lot of us do this.

I just started to ignore the statements. I mean, I told the lady that I don't have the extra $300 a month to send them, and she said that this was about as low as they could go on the payment. I asked for a raise and was told NO. So every month the statements come, and I think I'll deal with it and I'll deal with it tomorrow. And tomorrow becomes another day. Days become months…then another month turns into a year. I realize oh well let me open up one of the statements - I haven't opened one in a while and the statement begins to say you are basically in default of your student loan in the state of Kentucky, and you have several days to get back with us regarding the matter or we will garnish your check or take away your license.

And as you know, as a nurse we work hard for a license and the last thing you want to hear is your license may be in jeopardy. So I called in panic mode, tears coming down my face, and talked with customer service. Luckily, I have not missed the deadline, and even though I was in a default, I was not at the point where they were going to garnish my check or my license and that I would be placed in a rehab, and I would pay a low monthly fee for approximately a year and then start regular payments. Thank you, God! PURPOSE The thought of becoming an entrepreneur started surfacing during my journey to complete my doctorate degree, and at the same time

I was working in a leadership and clinical role. I started pursuing my doctorate at the urging of my husband, Lee. I admit at first I thought it was a waste of time. I did not understand it and was tired of being in school. I felt like it was something I didn't need. I applied and got in. During the first few classes, I immediately realized that in this doctoral nursing program, the conservation was different and the network was different. We were discussing true change and action. I was meeting nurses in leadership roles and encouraged to increase my network at work. I was finding out that not only did I like patient care, I also liked nursing leadership. See, I believe nursing traditionally made nurses believe they could not do both. Here I was seeing patients as a nurse practitioner and sitting in meetings with hospital leadership. I realized I enjoyed this environment and this level of thinking. I wanted to be part of the solution of the problems of healthcare and the organization I worked for.

I continued working in a role of leadership and clinical practice. Time passed, and I continued to work in my dual role. Then I began to express my desire for such a role to my director. He said he would look into it. I felt since I had my DNP and had been in the role for several years, I would be great. Yes, traditionally a medical director is a role for a physician, but I was confident that they would see my value and gifts. That was a mistake (in hind-site, I should have expressed my desire to higher leadership; that is one regret). I got my DNP and received many congratulations. Things were okay for a while, then my husband had another major surgery (after his kidney cancer diagnosis), and I was presented with a contract. I was not thrilled about a contract with a non-compete clause that could limit my practice if I left the organization. I was upset and disappointed about this contract. I sought legal advice, advice from my husband, advice from friends and advice from my pastor. It felt like the walls were closing in on me. I felt like the organization that I loved working for was betraying me in several ways.

The day my husband and I met with the lawyer, the lawyer stated he was a Christian and that God told him a message to tell me. I don't remember the exact message but it basically was encouraging me to start my own business. The department continued with day-to-day activities, and then we received a new director. This was position was not posted or announced - it was most likely a consolidated effort of resources. It made the light bulb in my head shine brighter. I realized I was not going to move forward in this department or organization. This began my greater push to becoming a nurse boss.

I have not fully dove into entrepreneurship, meaning I did not quit my job - I just transferred to a more flexible position and one where I didn't share my valuable ideas. I go to work, and I work on my own business on my day off. As you read this, I want you to understand my journey to nurse boss is not fast, glamorous and currently not lucrative…but it's my journey. You will have your journey. Just a reminder that I am becoming a nurse boss or nurseprenuer. I want to encourage everyone thinking about this to go for it, and I want to help you with steps. I remember being at a conference and being told to brainstorm all your skills and talents to figure out your purpose and passions and develop programs to make money. So, this journey has not been easy, and I still owe student loan debt, but I must move forward to fulfill my purpose and pay off the student loan debt. Becoming A Nurse Boss So, you must be considering this nurseprenuer thing, since you are reading this book.

Let me give you help with a few starter points I have learned along the way. My goal in this book is to share my story about this journey and about letting others know that you're not alone with the student loan debt. I want give you a few pointers on how to begin your journey of becoming a nurse boss, whether you're doing it for student loan repayment, car payment or some other purpose. Starting off, of course you need to come up with a name, a logo and an ideal client you want to serve. I suggest that at some point in your journey you get three coaches. You will need a mindset coach, a business coach and a nursing coach. You may not be able to afford these at first, but you need to save up your money and invest in their services. This will save you a lot of time and money.

I did not know this when I started. My first conference [a2] was a mindset coach and this was very important for me - this is where I really started to lay down the possibility that I have valuable knowledge, and I did not have to give all my knowledge to healthcare organization, and then I can monetize on this knowledge.

A mindset coach is definitely a coach I believe you should have first; this helps lay down the foundation of your business and attitude towards your business. This helps you gather your thoughts, get your vision plan, find clarity and hopefully finalize on who and why you want to help your client. [a3] This forces you to do the soul-searching you desperately need. The business coach, of course, is going to help you out with the business aspect (sales, marketing) that we did not get in nursing school. Nursing school teaches us how to be nurses, not business people.

Then I find it'll be helpful to get a nurse coach; someone who is an entrepreneur and has done the work that you're trying to do. This person can help you with the business aspect but also understand you as a nursing professional. In other words, they speak your language like nobody else. So save up your money, and at the very least, throughout your journey, get these three coaches. You also need to consider going to conferences and business workshops that don't necessarily pertain to nursing. You need to network with others outside the field. When you go outside your nursing network, you'll learn many things about business relationships, sales and marketing. So, once you begin your foundation, you also need to obtain your registration within your state for business and your tax ID. It is important to obtain a bank account in your business name.

Once you have these things in place you will need to seek an accountant in the beginning ,this person will help you file for taxes at the right time, give you tax tips and keep you on track for keeping your business separate from your personal affairs.[a4] The next order of business will be to go to Godaddy.com get your domain name in your business and your personal name and "secure.com.org. "and privacy. This will insure that no one has your name as their website. Secure your social media names and began to market your product, service and your brand. I started the NP Factory to help nursing professionals and nurse practitioners with their career goals, salary negotiation, interviewing skills and social media and media training. I would get many people asking me before interview. "so now what do I say what I do during the interview?", "how much should I ask for my salary?" etc. Then I may have nurse practitioners approach me about how unhappy they are about their salary and salary negotiations.

And I realized one day, after working for several years, that being a nurse practitioner you are part of the healthcare business. No one in the nurse practitioner school tells you about the business side of being a nurse practitioner. The school's job is to teach you how not to harm anyone, how to properly diagnose and treat your clients - they do not tell you how to properly take care[a8] patients. Self-care includes knowing the salary the salary that you should negotiate for.

As nurse practitioners, we can bill in our names, and you must always keep in mind that you are of great value to the healthcare organization, whether they want to admit it or not. They make money off of you, and therefore you deserve a piece of the pie. The more we advocate for autonomy and salary, the likelihood we will have our needs met. I believe it's every nurse practitioner's job to advocate for practice autonomy and salary. You may be told "no" one day, but the next nurse practitioner may be told "yes."

Biography

Dr. Janel Willingham is a board-Certified Family Nurse Practitioner, CEO, Health and Wellness Expert, nurse coach, published author, wife and mother. She possesses a diverse medical background, and career coaching, that has been beneficial to medical practices, clients and the community. In addition, she has been a nurse for 20 years with a variety of experiences in Community Health, Prevention and Wellness, Neonatal Intensive Care, Pediatrics, urgent/acute care and Geriatrics. Janel is an extremely motivated, dedicated, empowering, caring, diligent and innovative professional. She is a proven leader in local, global and healthcare communities. She consistently demonstrates her leadership abilities serving the community daily, volunteering, participating in missions' trips, while being actively involved in professional organizations. In Addition, Dr. Janel is a sought-out nurse expert speaker on television, radio and conferences. As the CEO of The Np Factory her goal is to help nurses and nurse practitioners achieve their career goals, nursepreneurship, increase/ negotiate salary, build their brand, survive job interviews , media interview prep and self care. The Np Factory provides this by offering ,educational mastermind classes , speaking events, coaching, e books and other methods. Dr. Janel also loves to care for individuals and has recently added concierge and wellness healthcare to her brand. Dr. Willingham started out as a certified nurse's assistant in high school, moved on to obtaining her licensed practical nurse degree, associates registered nurse degree, master's degree and in 2017 obtained Doctor of Nursing Practice from Bellarmine University. She has published several E -books such as the following: The Nursing and Spa Professional Guide to Media Appearances, Make Clinical Documentation Easier to Track, and The How to Guide to Choosing A DNP/MSN Project.

Dr. Janel Motto is – "Be Determined !" Connect with

Dr. Janel www.Drjanel.com Npjwill@gmail.com

Instagram @dr.janel LinkedIN 128 Facebook: @thenpfactory @janelwillingham

Dedication

To my husband Recardo

Thank you for always being there to make sure I soar when I take flight into the unknown. You have a source of strength and a strong foundation for my soul.

You showed me what unconditional love truly means and that we are ONE. Although this story only highlights a small portion of my life I know that without you having my back none of this would be possible and it would still only be a dream.

~Oreal

To My Five Children:

RJ: Thank you being the best son and example of a big brother any parent could ask for. You ensure your siblings are taking care of no matter what it is and I thank you. You beat all the odds from the moment you took your first breathe. You showed me that at 3 pounds you were as strong as those older and bigger. You have yet to show me otherwise.

Aurianna: Mommy knows you don't like to be singled out or the center of attention, even on your birthday. However, I know I would not ever fight for some of the things I have done so hard if it had not been for you. I have watched you fight all your life to be independent and stronger than anyone could ever imagine. Whenever someone tried to count you out, you always proved them wrong. You have given me the strength to be a one women militia and I Thank you for allowing to realize I had strength I never knew existed. Mommy is amazed and in awe of the big girl you have become. Thank you for always reminding me that you are mommy's baby.

Aiden: Thank you for also being the best son and example of a brother we could ask for. You prayed for your little sisters to even be given to us by God on our way home from Disney and Universal and God answered that prayer. You took the precious gift God have us and treated it like the rarest mineral ever and I thank you for reminding me to be gentle and patient because God answers prayers.

Olivia: Thank you for being our first rainbow baby after two storms. Thank you for allowing mommy to learn to have a little baby again especially a little girl. I see the way you watch me and just remind me that it is okay to be vulnerable.

Amelia: Thank you for showing me that I am stronger than my wildest dreams. Carrying you through some of my most trying times has showed me that love truly endures all. Your delivery was the day I realized that my physical strength and determination was enough to bring a child into this world without assistance. Thank you for allowing me to see myself everyday and to have faith in his promise that trouble does not last always.

Thank you for being the most amazing, thoughtful and kind children I could ever imagine having. Thank you for trusting me to make the right decisions for you even though you don't understand why. Thank you for showing me that all of this is worth it and my prayers have been answered.

The First Step is the Hardest

By Oreal Perkins, APRN

Ever since I had children, my dream has been to be the one who puts them on and gets them off the bus every day. On the surface, this might seem like a pretty simple and manageable dre-am, but there was a time when it felt impossible. It's easy to get to a bus stop twice a day when you have nowhere else to be and when you are in close proximity to the stop...but when your job requires you to be working during both times, it seems like that dream is perpetually out of reach. After all, I couldn't just quit my job and stay home. I had to think about my family. The bus stop would cease to matter if we didn't have a roof over our heads. But still, there was this gentle tugging, constantly present in my soul, that wanted me to stop and pay attention. There was a reason this simple desire was so important to me.

As nurses, we aren't taught how to be business people. We focus on the science, the anatomy, the patient interaction and many other things, but we don't learn business. And I've gone through lots of nursing education. I have a bachelor's and master's in nursing-related fields, but never in all my schooling was I taught about how I could harness my nursing skills and apply them to a business model so that I could do what I loved on my own terms and simultaneously have time for my family. As nurses, we are taught a worker mentality that becomes ingrained in us. We are trained to work for a paycheck. Often, we are caring and help-oriented individuals, so we are easily manipulated into working harder and taking on more responsibility in the name of the patients. What we tend to lack are skills that would promote our autonomy - like knowing how to negotiate, or when to say "no."

I like to envision a true business-minded person working in the nursing industry. The minute that person is asked to see an additional patient, or to perform an extra task, I'd imagine either a flat-out refusal or an elaborate invoice addressed to the supervisor denoting a list of all the additional fees that service required. You don't see CEOs giving away things for free, or lawyers not bothering to charge for extra hours spent going through case files, but you do find nurses seeing more patients than they can realistically tend to or working extra hours in the middle of the night because people need them. The healthcare industry is set up so that nurses never consider advocating for themselves. And that's why so many of us end up burnt out, dejected and discouraged with the profession.

In the back of my mind, I'd wanted to start my own business for quite some time. I started working at a clinic in order to gain experience to go out on my own. Before long, my responsibilities had bloomed so that I was pretty much running the entire operation. Unfortunately, someone else was reaping the benefits of all of my hard work. And knowing so much about the company, I learned quite a bit about its background, and I didn't like what I saw. The company had a very negative backstory, which inspired me even more to dream about starting a company with a more positive mission and wholesome intentions.

Despite all of this, it was easy to become complacent in my role. The money I was earning was really good, and on one level, it seemed foolish to leave that security, especially when I had four children at home to think about. Luckily for me, God was fully aware of my purpose and wouldn't let me stagnate for long. I truly believe that when God wants you to move, He'll make you. And His message showed up loud and clear to me on the day a new policy was instituted. I knew - in that moment - that I had to go. I didn't have a choice. There was no time for plans or procrastination. I needed to quit then and there.

I didn't know exactly what I would do, but I knew I had to try something. Lots of patients rely on Medicare for their health expenses, and I knew that I could apply for that licensing and the credentials would be backdated to my application date. This meant I could start seeing patients immediately, even though it also meant that there'd be no money coming in right away. I also started working at two different nursing homes at night. That paid the bills and allowed me to work on opening my health care business during the day.

What I noticed right away was that everyone's first question was, "Where are you located?" I knew that answering with my home address wasn't going to work for long, and that I needed to invest in an office. Obviously, because I left my former job in such a hurry, I didn't have time to save any money or establish credit. I was able to find a place nearby that didn't do a credit check, and I jumped on it. I also got lucky again when a local doctor retired. I was able to purchase a lot of his equipment at a really good rate so that I could stock my new office with supplies. I realized that I had gotten lucky with both finding my office and acquiring supplies. These could easily have been deal breakers for my business if I had been forced to search for start-up loans or use a large portion of my savings.

Starting my business on the fly worked for me, but the endeavor was not without its hiccups. I had a huge learning curve ahead of me, and I was figuring everything out in real time. For one, Medicare payments are always behind, and before I learned to optimize my cash flow, this put me behind with my expenses. The joy of working for yourself comes from knowing that every headache that, when I resolve it, benefits my own business. I've had to teach myself how to negotiate contracts and how to manage the magnitude of paperwork that comes with running a business. None of this was easy, but it was all worth it. I learned that if you work it, it will grow.

I am grateful that I was shaken out of my complacency. God pushed me out of my stable job and into this new place that was absolutely foreign to me, but I managed to keep pushing forward and growing. My new career path afforded me the ability to do what I forever dreamed about. I now watch as my children climb aboard the big, yellow bus, and I'm there waiting for them when it pulls back up at the end of the day. What once seemed so far away and difficult to attain is now a reality.

Once you achieve the thing that you dreamt about for so long, it is amazing what other opportunities open themselves up to you. It's like putting yourself into a new place where, once you are standing there, all sorts of other paths become visible. And you can walk down any one them. Because I have the flexibility to greet the bus every day, I can now see I have other options. I can volunteer to go on school field trips. I can bring my children's lunches to the school if they leave them on the table. I can pick them up if they get sick at school. None of these things were even conceivable when I worked for someone else.

These opportunities don't only apply to the bus stop, either. Once I learned the ins and outs of setting up a business, it became easy to see how I could add on to that business or start a completely new business from scratch. Just like how getting to the bus stop seemed so distant from my position within the walls of clinic, all of my entrepreneurial dreams seemed distant as well. I had so many questions, fears and concerns. I didn't know how to take the first leap, and so all of my ideas seemed like flimsy, unrealistic dreams. They were exciting, and I was passionate about them, but I had no idea how to make them a reality. Now I have the confidence to make anything a reality if I choose.

One of my daughters struggles with severe Autism. Watching her go through her own challenges has been an inspiring and motivating force. I watched her as she transitioned to a new school. This could be challenging for any child, but because of the social impairments that come with her condition, it is even harder for her to get acquainted with an entirely new set of people and for her to feel comfortable around them.

In her own way, she struggled with complacency. It is different, of course, but routine brings her comfort. Therefore, change can be especially challenging. When she transitioned to her new school, it was difficult, but she faced it with bravery and resilience. The things that helped her fight the urge to stay or go back to old routines was making a plan. When I could prepare her ahead of time by telling her what to expect from the changes, she felt more secure. I try to bring that same bravery and resilience with me in every new business endeavor. If she can do those things, even when they are the hardest things in the world for her, I can commit to doing so as well.

For any nurse who is thinking about going out on her own, I urge you not to stay complacent. Don't wait until you are propelled out of your current situation in order to get started on your dreams. It is helpful to plan things ahead of time, while you still have an income and level of security. That is the time to start working on the details of your business, saving money and taking the proper steps. It's great to network with people who are one or two steps ahead of you in the process. That connection will give you a sense of security, because you will know what to expect. And that alone takes a big hurdle out of the picture.

That alone is a valuable lesson I learned from me daughter. We tend to define success as the ability to jump in and do something. But we do ourselves a disservice by just jumping, because often that means survival gets prioritized over doing something well. There is no shame in making a plan and thinking things through. I made mistakes that I wouldn't have made if I just started working on my business before I was pushed out. I wasn't moving, so God finally had to give me a push, but there is no reason we need to wait to be pushed. If I can inspire anyone to plan rather than jump, than my own push means even more.

The other thing that I learned is that it's very easy to start, but it is a whole lot harder to keep the business running. Statistics show that about half of new businesses fail within the first five years. Plus we will always have that worker mentality whispering to us in the back of our minds, telling us we can just go back to something easy and have that paycheck automatically deposited into our accounts each week. It might be true that nursing jobs are everywhere and that they offer stability that entrepreneurship simply doesn't. But it's a false security. There is no personal control as long as you are working for someone else. Policies can change with the snap of a finger, management can change suddenly and responsibilities can shift into something that is simply not okay with you. And usually there is nothing you can do to prevent these changes.

As long as you are working hard on your own business, you are in control of your destiny. You'll work hard to keep your doors open, to learn the skills to operate a full business and to hire the right people around you, and everything you accomplish will be yours to own. Plus new doors will open to you that you could have never imagined before.

Once I opened my clinic, I learned more than I ever thought there was to know about business. And then a new opportunity cropped up. I opened my own cosmetics line. The learning curve on this business was much smaller, because I had already put so much work into my first business. What would have seemed inconceivable to me before was now something that I had the confidence and skills to do with ease. I, of course, encountered obstacles along the way, but I had the skills to problem-solve and to move through those hurdles.

These days, I am still working on growing and expanding my businesses, but every day I get to walk to that bus with a big smile on my face. I wave as my children go off for the day, and I stand with open arms as they arrive back home. From the place where I stand at the bus stop, I see nothing but opportunity in every direction. I can work on my businesses. I can spend time with my family. I can help other women to also start businesses of their own. I can even spend time on taking care of me. But whatever I decide to do, the decision is all mine.

Oreal Perkins, FNP-C

Connect with me!
Info@orealperkins.com
Instagram: www.instagram.com/OrealPerkins
Facebook: www.facebook.com/nporeal

Biography

Oreal Perkins, is a Family Nurse Practitioner and owner of Flexhealth Convenient Care by day as she would say. She and her husband are the sole owners and the youngest in her area to open a practice as a sole provider. In addition to owner her own practice she has launched her own cosmetics line AOD Beauty and has now transitioned to developing a Health and Wellness Directory App called Providerz. She wanted to take her love for healthcare and wellness and merge the two to create a platform for people of color to have one place to find everything to keep thee well. Providerz lists healthcare professionals, products and wellness brands and services that will provide people of color the resources they need. You can download the app in the App Store by searching for Providerz and you can also get listed that way as well. In addition to the app, she uses her entrepreneurial knowledge to help other women start and scale their businesses. From startup, vendor lists to social media marketing and management she ensures that you equipped with the tools for success.

Info@orealperkins.com
Instagram: @ orealperkins
Facebook: @nporeal

Dedication

This book is dedicated to my mother, Diana Montgomery. She was my most faithful client from my grand opening until her final transition. Thank you.

With Love,

-Ray

The Nurse Boss Collective From RN to Vsteam Queen

By Raven Diana Montgomery, RN-BC

My journey has been a controversial yet fulfilling one. Innovative concepts are often controversial, and my entrepreneurship path strives to bridge two worlds that don't always complement one another. I am an amalgamation of two differing world views. I am a nurse and therefore have spent many years working in the field of Western medicine. Science makes sense to me, and I trust the knowledge I gained in my years studying to be a nurse and my practical experience working in the community. But alternative therapies, ancient healing practices and the Earth also resonate deeply with me, and I am a huge proponent for this more holistic way of looking at health. My wellness center is a place where both of these traditions reside, and I personally have seen the amazing healing that takes place when we encompass all of our knowledge and history and use it wisely, rather than banishing parts of it as illegitimate, ineffective and primitive.

Modern medicine is amazing when you look at what we are able to do, and what we have learned through years of research, but there are times when modern medicine may not be the best option. Not everything can be cured or fixed with the pop of a pill. I struggled with fibroids and PMDD (premenstrual dysphoric disorder) for years. This meant I'd have exceptionally long and painful periods, often lasting two weeks of every month, and the PMDD caused additional emotional symptoms similar to PMS on steroids. It made daily life abnormally difficult, though I learned to deal with all of this as best as I could. Once I hit the milestone of turning forty, I was no longer willing to endure these symptoms.

Eventually, however, my condition prompted me to find a natural, holistic approach to my healing that encompassed both my physical and spiritually wellbeing. That's when I came to discover, on Instagram, the healing practice of vaginal steam. Vaginal steam, or vsteam, is known in other cultures by different names, such as yonisteam, bajos, hipbath or chai-yok, and is an herbal detox that uses steam to help eliminate symptoms associated with many reproductive and gynecological problems most women face. After locating a local practitioner, I decided to schedule a session. I had an hour-long treatment with a licensed therapist. Afterwards, I experienced some mild side effects, which I later attributed to the length of the session and my hydration status, but my next cycle was an entirely different experience. I had drastically less menstrual cramps, a lighter menstrual flow and I didn't experience the strong emotional malaise I was accustomed to. I felt lighter - physically and spiritually. Connected. Grounded. Centered. Empowered. Renewed. Relaxed. And, of course, my libido increased through the roof! My sleep was noticeably improved, and I felt like I was walking on clouds for days. This was only after my first session. I was so impressed with my results that I bragged about my wonderful, almost perfect, period to one of my closest friends. As I was enthusiastically recounting my experience to her, she abruptly ended our conversation in the middle of my story. She seemed alarmingly indifferent to my newfound joy, but I later learned she was among numerous women I have since serviced who suffered silently with some degree of menstrual irregularity. She bore her shame and distress on a continual basis, and my excitement likely triggered her on an issue she wasn't yet ready to address. Of course, in true nurse fashion, I craved more information on all of it - the physical, emotional, and spiritual benefits of this practice, and how I could better serve my community by offering vsteam services.

Immediately, I started doing my research, and shortly thereafter, I enrolled in a vsteam class. The class taught me all of the mechanics of the process, but I still desired more information, especially since the idea of opening my own place of healing was percolating in the back of my mind. I had memories of my grandmother talking about similar treatments years ago, and after some research, I learned this practice could be traced all the way back to the Bible. If this was going to be something I could potentially offer at my wellness center, I wanted to know the science and history behind this ancient treatment, and I wanted to truly understand how steam and herbs interacted within the body to create these life-changing results. I was also getting even bigger ideas. I was already a religious user of essential oils in my daily life, and I wondered how their healing properties could be combined and used, in conjunction with vsteam, for therapeutic purposes. I envisioned an entire center that promoted wellness by using alternative therapies focused on addressing not only physical healing, but spiritual healing as well.

With my vision in mind, I enrolled in a second course that went more in depth about the benefits and practical applications for vsteam. Around that time, I opened my wellness center with a partner. That's when the roller coaster started. At first, it was all so exciting. We were both on board with creating a center that leveraged both our professional strengths and our knowledge of alternative therapies. And we got started planning what services we would offer, what we'd call our center, where it would be located and all of the other details. But after just a few months of working together, my partner walked away from the business, letting me know about her departure only via a Facebook message.

Disappointed about my partner's abrupt exit, I had doubts about managing the wellness center alone while juggling a full-time nursing career, marriage and raising a family of four. That, combined with my altruistic spirit, led me to share my business and knowledge with other individuals. Unfortunately, those individuals learned whatever they could from me and later left to start their own ventures. This happened so often I eventually became discouraged. All I was really doing was educating and arming my future competition. I can recall a particularly discouraging night at my wellness center and expressing my frustration to a trusted mentor, who bluntly spoke life into my situation. She confirmed my journey is MY journey. I didn't need to bring anyone else along with me. And she scolded me for sharing so much of my time, effort and information without asking for anything in return. She reminded me, as an entrepreneur, that I had bills due, just like everyone else, and it was perfectly fine to prioritize my needs; she insisted I start sending invoices for sharing my knowledge and expertise. Her words penetrated, and I knew she was right. I was worth so much more, and I needed to carry myself with this belief front and center. This was the motivation I needed to refocus. Nonetheless, my uniqueness as a healer, empath and board certified registered nurse has set me apart from others in the industry seeking to mimic my practice. My genuine love for health and wellness, and my passion to serve my community, has paved the way for me to share my God-given gifts with women on their healing journeys.

There is a special place for me in this industry, and my path is predestined. I have and will continue to educate others freely. My gifts will make room for me.

With my new perspective in mind, I continued my mission of providing holistic care to my community. Just four months into my entrepreneurial experience, I was presented with another obstacle. Surgery. Having an optimistic spirit, I figured I could manage recovery with minimal complications. Unfortunately, my surgery did not go as planned, and I experienced complications that put me out of commission for an extended period. Despite these immediate obstacles, I pressed on with faith that my circumstances would improve.

For a short period, my circumstances seemed to improve. From the time I started my wellness center and consistently through to the present, my mother was my biggest support. She came in every two weeks for her vsteam and foot detox to assist with managing some of her chronic health conditions, de-stress, and relax. She was unwavering in her support, and I always felt comforted when she walked through the door - no matter what was going on in the business. But not long after my surgery, my mother passed away unexpectedly. Losing her sent me spiraling. I fell into a depression and wasn't sure if I wanted to continue on this journey. I seriously contemplated shutting the doors of my business for good. The events of the year seemed to be telling me it was all too hard and possibly not worth it. The thing that kept me going through all this was thinking back to my mother and what she would've wanted for me. She believed in me. She was proud of my accomplishments. She used the services herself and benefited from them. Like my clients, she felt at peace the moment she stepped into my wellness center. It was her "happy place," a place of healing and restoration. She would definitely not want her death to be the reason I closed my doors. And so I stayed open to continue this journey. Keeping the doors open and moving forward - despite all the adversity - was a way in which I could pay tribute to my mother's memory. So, I pulled myself out of my depression and discouragement, and pressed onward.

As I continued on my journey, I worked nights in a psychiatric facility and days on my business. I wanted the business to succeed, but I wanted to approach it in a smart way. I still needed to support my family financially and maintain health insurance. Not to mention, I was facing another obstacle. My already fragile marriage completely disappeared with the death of my mother, and divorce was now on the table. With this in mind, I couldn't afford to make any mistakes that would force me to close my doors. I used my paychecks wisely so that I could maintain the status quo at home and still continue to develop my practice.

As I continued working in and on my business, I met so many different women who were an inspiration to keep going forward. And I can't help but see some symbolism in one of the major modalities on which I've been focusing. Vsteam is not only a healing practice, it is a transformative one, and even the steam itself is a substance that is literally in a state of transformation. Steam is quite literally the point at which water is transformed into gas. At this point in my journey, I, too, am in a state of transformation. Unlike regular growth, which comes from learning new skills, researching and adding on to oneself, transformation usually comes upon you unsolicited. My year of challenges as I've worked to open my wellness center has brought sudden and unexpected changes that have required me to transform and take big leaps of faith.

I strongly feel the challenges I've weathered have transformed me into a stronger person, a better entrepreneur and a more determined spirit. When steam is created, it literally expands, and that is what I'm doing with my career. My mission is to expand and grow with the intent to educate others in holistic care, the healing benefits of vsteam and how to safely offer the service to the community. I have successfully taught numerous like-minded women who I am confident were divinely lead to me in order to fulfill my purpose. I'm a nurse by profession and a healer at heart, and my primary intention is always to heal and do no harm.

I contemplated for months about documenting my journey in this book. I've received harsh criticism from other health care providers. The cuts ran deepest when they came from my fellow nurses who, like me, were taught cultural diversity and complimentary or alternative therapies. One of several reasons vsteam is looked at with such harsh criticism from the medical community is because there are so many people practicing it without awareness or knowledge. Many people see vsteam as a quick opportunity to capitalize on a fad, and they jump into offering the service with little knowledge about how to practice properly, its purpose and benefits and how to offer it safely. The result of this haste is the propagation of individuals offering poor information, practicing improperly and reportedly causing harm to others in the process. Additionally, people are generally skeptical of what they don't know and resistant to change, and it's easily an uphill battle I've set myself upon.

But I wholeheartedly believe in the healing properties of this modality. I've witnessed and experienced the benefits of steam when performed correctly, and I confidently understand its purpose in the larger scheme of women's health. I have treated women who seek my services as a last ditch effort to assist with conceiving or to avoid a hysterectomy already scheduled by their health care provider due to unbearable menstrual cycles. In each case, I was able to successfully assist these women in changing their scenarios (and subsequently their lives) with vsteam. Not only is vsteam known to assist in healing the physical body, it has a history of healing the spiritual body. Vsteam is known to be an effective way to assist in releasing old traumas and soul ties. Women come to me who report being raped or molested, are suffering from nightmares and severe anxiousness or who struggle with lack of motivation or pleasure in things that used to bring them joy; vsteam has assisted in releasing that trauma, hurt and pain. I believe physical illness is the manifestation of some emotional hurt or stress. In my opinion, true wellness is obtained when there is harmony among your physical, emotional and spiritual body.

My purpose as a practitioner and business owner is to bring awareness to some of the more natural healing therapies in existence. We don't have to be firmly rooted on one side or another of the Western versus Eastern mentality. We can draw upon all of our knowledge and experience. Relying on or using alternative therapies doesn't mean trusting everyone who touts a particular modality. What I promote is simply integrating all of the resources available to us and using what makes the most sense in each individual circumstance. I am interested in understanding and listening to the body and then responding with the best therapies available for that particular affliction.

In addition to offering vsteam and aromatherapy at my wellness center, I offer Reiki healing sessions. Reiki channels healing energy and complements vsteam by helping an individual release stagnant, negative energy that could potentially contribute to physical illness. Everything I do and incorporate into my business is well researched and administered with care and knowledge. And I strive not only to help others heal, but to teach other practitioners and healers how to sift through the information and tell the truth from the exaggerated claims, and how to provide therapies in safe ways.

As I continue to pursue my path toward expansion and transformation, I draw inspiration from the steam that is the essential factor in the therapies I administer. The steam is in transformation, and, during that state, is helping to heal. It is expanding and helping women let go of what no longer serves them physically and spiritually. I've shared vulnerable moments with women from different cultures, social backgrounds and ethnicities. I've shared sincere embraces and tears of joy culminating in an often unexplained transformation of the spirit. It is undoubtedly one of the most rewarding aspects of offering this service to my community. While vsteam has been trivialized, discounted and sometimes scoffed, I have witnessed this healing practice change many lives, including my own. Never did I expect the path that started from obtaining my nursing license to lead me to such a fulfilling and rewarding career. I am grateful for the doors my nursing education has opened for me and will continue to transform not only my profession and the perspective of vsteam, but also the lives of those who cross my path. My clients have christened me "The Vsteam Queen," and I humbly embrace this title alongside the title of RN. Some might say that the two contradict each other and don't make sense as a pair, but I think these two titles complement each other beautifully and represent all of me, and what I hope to bring to the world. Along my journey, I will continue to heal, expand and release what doesn't serve me so I can keep helping those who need me.

Biography

Health and well-being is a passion Raven has carried in her heart since her early years, and a motivating factor in her return to college. Raven graduated from Central Piedmont Community College in Charlotte, NC in December 2013 with an Associate Degree of Nursing.

After graduating from nursing school, Raven served the community in the mental and home health care fields. She began her career working in a psychiatric residential treatment facility with the child and adolescent population. This experience opened the door to work within the acute setting as a Psychiatric Nurse Assessor and Charge Nurse serving both the child, adolescent and adult populations. With three years of experience under her belt, Raven obtained her nursing certification from the American Nurses Credentialing Center as a Psychiatric Mental-Health Nurse.

While working to service the mental health needs of the community, Raven also serves the community as a home care nurse. Raven serves as Director for a local home care agency and utilizes her education and experience to educate her clients and staff on health and wellness within the home setting. She continues to service the community in this aspect conducting training classes and health and wellness coaching to meet the needs of her clients.

Raven is the owner of Raven Little RN PLLC and One Drop Health and Wellness Center PLLC which opened in March 2018 in her hometown of Gastonia, NC. The wellness center offers holistic products and services focused on empowering the community to take control of their health and wellness. Services include aromatherapy, vaginal steam sessions and practitioner training, Reiki energy healing, professional nurse coaching, free wellness classes, and First Aid/CPR training.

Raven's mission is to provide holistic health care, coaching and education focused on the physical, emotional, social, mental, spiritual, and environmental aspects of well-being. She is passionate about raising awareness to preventative care and the practice of alternative therapies. Raven's vision is to inspire individuals to achieve their best health possible and create healthy communities collectively.

With her mission and vision in mind, Raven published her first inspiring book entitled "Purposed to Win, A Victorious Nurse Anthology". This book shares stories of nurses and how they overcame adversity, heartache, and obstacles to triumph in their career.

Connect with Nurse Raven:

Address: 1008 Union Road Suite B
Gastonia, NC 28054
Ph. 704-671-2261 Text 704-612-0171
www.thevsteamqueen.com
Instagram & Facebook@vsteamqueencharlotte

Dedication

Mom, thank you for your love and sacrifice. You've taught me what it means to be a phenomenal woman. Chrissy, I'm so proud of the man you're becoming. Son, always remember to believe in yourself, chase your dreams, and fight every day to be the best YOU!

Living Large- A Nurses Journey Toward Resilience

By Rasheda Hatchett, MN, RN

From a young age, I walked around the world, wanting to be a nurse and not having the courage to speak my dream out loud. I never told anyone; I would quietly watch the TV show *ER* and pay really close attention to what the nurses were doing. I mastered the way they spoke and all the nursing words they used. What I didn't know was most of what they did was not real nursing at all. But it didn't matter - I was hooked. I knew to be a nurse I would have to study hard, but no one I knew had finished college, so the thought was honestly utterly terrifying. Here I was, a former special education student with little academic confidence and a dream of being a nurse with no clue where to start or any tangible frame of reference. However, I had a dream, and I was determined to make it a reality…but how? I couldn't even tell my mom I wanted to be a nurse, so how would I tell the world?

While on a job interview for a position I thought I really wanted, my truth began to burn a hole in me. I had asked some of my professional friends to help me prep with a mock interview. I was ready! I was dressed well, in a dark pants suit with sensible shoes and small silver earrings. I arrived 15 minutes early; with copies of my resume and cover letter for the panel and was ready for anything they asked. I studied the organization and prepared myself with some great questions to ask at the end of the interview to show my interest. I just knew this job was mine. As I sat there, and we went from one question to the next, I kept thinking, "Yep, nailed it!" Then they asked me, "Where do you see yourself in 5 years?" Before I knew it, that burn was a full-blown fire, and I blurted out, "I see myself being a nurse, working with underserved people." As the words began to flow out of my mouth, I tried to catch them, but it was too late - I had spoken my truth and told this panel of youth case managers that I had no plan to stay with the organization long-term, and I didn't even want to work in social services. I had blown it! One question and all my work and preparation had gone up in smoke. Though I knew I was no longer a contender for the job, I was FREE. I had, for the first time, said out loud that I wanted to be a nurse. For the first time, I set my dream free. I was twenty years old then and wouldn't actually start nursing school for 15 years.

So much happened in those 15 years that disrupted my plan to go back to school and become a nurse and I gave up on my dream at least 10 times. I began to feel unworthy and that I wasn't smart enough; I felt ashamed. You see, I was the young lady with so much potential - I was training adults on teen dating violence at 16, and considered an expert in the field by 19 - I had been featured in documentaries, commercials, been a guest on radio and when I spoke, I had this innate ability to captivate an audience. I was supposed to be successful and what I had become was a single mom living in an abusive relationship and hoping to get out alive. I couldn't see past my circumstances; I was so broken that I was an easy target to be taken advantage of and abused. How could I speak about dating violence ever again when I had become the very thing I cautioned others not be? I'm a disgrace, an imposter, a hypocrite. Then there was the guilt and shame of being an unwed mother that hung around my neck like a yolk, like Flavor Flav's famous clock, and it paralyzed me. I felt completely worthless and my dream of becoming a nurse had drifted off into the abyss. Like so many young women, I had tied my self-worth to being a single mother and my self-esteem was virtually nonexistent. Even in that dark time, it was clear to me that I had to keep fighting, I had to be resilient if I was going to get out of that relationship and save myself and my son.

It would be 3 years before I was able to completely free myself of that relationship, but one thing got me through - I had one shred of hope that I clung to for dear life: *I was good mother.* I was a born fighter and I used my love for my son and my desire to change his future as motivation to get out and stay out. However, that was the easy part - the harder thing to do was free my mind of the abuse and rid my thinking of the negativity that had been poured into me like a pitcher with no bottom. I worked on what I could with the tools I had, which weren't a lot, but my faith in God and my family got me through. I had decided to show up for myself and made a decision to live large in my own life!

I walked into my local community college with all the gusto of finally having my life back and being in control of my own destiny - or so I thought. I sat down with an advisor and began to tell her my plans for the future. I proudly told her, "I would like to sign up for the prerequisites for nursing school!" We sat and went over all of my options, and I still had one thing to figure out: childcare for my 4-year old son. She told me that in order to get childcare assistance, I had to enter a program that was 2 years or less and nursing was too long, since it required prerequisite courses before enrollment. I was crushed. I had no other options for childcare. As I sat there, deflated, I asked what my options were and she said, "The medical assisting program meets the requirement." I left, devastated, but determined to become a nurse, and nothing was going to stop me. I went home and I called a few HR departments and found that if I worked for them as a medical assistant, they would provide me with tuition assistance to become a nurse. That was it…it was the sign I needed to keep moving forward and follow my dream, even if it wasn't going to happen the way I planned.

I signed up and started 2 months later. I completed that program and had a job lined up before graduation. I began working and realized I loved the patient's, but I needed more. This was about the time my next disappointment came along to derail my plan. I found out that my chances of getting into the nursing program, while taking classes at a slow pace, were slim - the school in my area wanted to ensure that I could handle the rigors of taking multiple classes at once. I thought, "Now what am I going to do?" It felt like the opposition was literally sucking the life out of me. I just didn't have the strength to keep going. I didn't have the grit to pull myself up by the bootstraps again - I was empty. All the hope I had of changing my life and my son's life was gone; there was no point in continuing with a slim chance and I couldn't quit working to go to school full-time; I had just started!

I tried other things: a youth advocate, executive assistant, stenographer, accountant, childcare worker and wedding planner. Needless to say, none of them stuck. I kept coming back to nursing; however, I had no idea how I was going to go back to school full-time, pay my bills, and childcare expenses; or manage being a mom with a busy school schedule. What I was certain of, I had to disrupt my current life to get the life I wanted. I began to devise a plan. I would fill out the financial aid papers, look up nursing schools, course prerequisites, program length, salary and growth potential, all to be ready when the opportunity arose. However, there was still one thing that I couldn't account for: *childcare*. I still needed help paying for it and nursing was still too long of a program to get help from the state. I had no idea where my help would come from, but I knew it would. In August of 2009, my ram in the bush, my unicorn, appeared. It was the call I needed to change my life: my mom called to say, "I'm going to quit my job and start working from home." Everything inside me jumped for joy. "Yes, yes, yes!" I knew my prayers had been answered. I had the best person on the planet to be my childcare provider - my mom.

I was enrolled and was back in school the very next month. I was prepared, I didn't have to get ready, because I had stayed ready. I had no idea my mom was going to quit her job or even agree to keep my son. But I opened myself to the possibility of my dream, and I knew it would make room for me. I was certain nursing was my calling; I was born to care for others and pour life into people as they experienced their darkest times. I completed my nursing degree and graduated from one of the best nursing schools in the country. Resilience had paid off again and I was finally a registered nurse.

No matter how far I ran from my dream, it continued to chase me! I tried to fit myself into so many boxes that weren't meant for me; I tried to become things that seemed more pleasing to others; I tried to dim my light because I didn't believe I was worth my dream, but still, it chased me. Once I accepted that my gift to the world was not mine to hold and keep for a select few, but belonged to every person I touched, every nursing student I educated, every baby I sang happy birthday to, every late night lactation session, every hand I held, every mother I encouraged, every tear I wiped, every grieving loved one I held, every nurse I counseled, and every life I prayed for. That is when I was able to say, I can see my worth; I can see my value, and I can see my purpose. I saw that I meant something to the world; I had a place and it was to be the voice for the voiceless and an advocate for the discarded. I was placed here to bring hope to those that were otherwise hopeless - that was my call.

New and amazing opportunities opened to me once I realized I was enough, and I had everything I needed inside of me to be successful. My nursing career was going well, I was making a great salary, I had gotten my family out of poverty, I was able to help my mom more, and I had gotten married. I was a success by most people's standards, yet as I began to reflect on my nursing experiences, one nagging theme kept following me- though I seemed to have it all, I felt painfully alone. I was having panic attacks when going to work as I never knew when I was getting off, I was exhausted mentally and physically, I was depressed, I felt underappreciated and overworked, and I felt like I was being smothered by the very profession I had prayed for and dedicated my life to. The guilt I felt for not being satisfied was heavy, I struggled in silence and prayed for a way out, though I was certain I was called to nursing I also knew something had to change so I could begin loving life again.

The pain of losing faith in my career is what led me to my ultimate desire to embark on entrepreneurship. Leaving my 9-5 job to pursue entrepreneurship was scaring and fantastic all at the same time. I turned my nursing knowledge into a thriving private nursing and consulting business. Working as a nurse and being in control of my schedule while finally having the freedom to create the life I dreamed of and be present for my son, allowed me to show up large in my life. Through it all. there was a thread that had weaved itself through every negative experience in my life, shocking me back into action and wrapping itself around my heart after every trauma; it kept me going and forced me to get up each time life knocked me down… that thread was Resilience. I had managed to bundle every loss and turn them into lessons and bounced-back from every adverse and traumatic life experience I endured. I realized without even knowing it, I had come up with a formula to overcome. I had realized, Resilience is my Superpower!

Each of us has a set of resilience factors that help us bounce-back from adversity and move forward in life. These are the 6 steps toward Resilience that helped me live large in my lift:

1. Acknowledge your pain

   Give yourself room to acknowledge your painful experience and grieve for the changes it has caused in your life. This may involve journaling or quiet time to self-reflect.

2. Practice trauma informed self- forgiveness

   Often, we are our harshest critics and spend too much time on the negative. There is so much power in recognizing how much you've overcome and using that knowledge to freely forgive yourself.

3. Develop healthy coping skills

   Coping skills are essential to moving forward; however, they must be healthy to be beneficial. This could include physical activity, positive socializing, volunteering, and self- care practices.

4. Exercise positive self- talk

   The most important voice is your own. Positive self-talk can block out negative emotions and thoughts, freeing your mind to absorb positive affirming words. Use your voice to speak life into yourself.

5. Seek support

   On the journey of healing it's important to surround yourself with positive supportive people who have your back. This may include brunch dates with friends, or working with a coach, religious leader, or therapist.

6. Keep moving toward your dreams

    Having a dream is essential to living a full life and pursuing that dream is imperative to living large in your own life. Staying in action gives you something to look forward to daily. Having goals gives the mind an outside focus and helps to put adversity into perspective.

Biography

Author | Speaker | Resilience Coach | Entrepreneur

Rasheda is the Owner and CEO of, Panacea Nurse Delegation Services, providing education, delegation, and consultation services to adult family homes; and Rasheda Hatchett Media, LLC, a coaching and consulting firm steeped in her passion for nurse wellness.

Rasheda is dedicated to coaching nurses through overwhelm, compassion fatigue, and burnout to resilience. Helping clients bounce-back from adversity and live large. She's a member of the National Wellness Institute, Washington State Coalition against Domestic Violence, American Nursing Association, and the Nurse Entrepreneur Society.

Connect with Me:

Web: www.RashedaHatchettMedia.com

IG: www.instagram.com/rashedahatchettmedia/

LinkedIn: www.linkedin.com/in/rasheda-hatchett-mn-rnd-b50521196/

Dedication

To my family

Thank you for guidance, unconditional love, and support.

Blessings & favor to you all.

To my readers

You are worthy and you matter.

Cheers, to becoming the best version of yourself.

~Jessica

Network Like You Mean It ™

A Nurse's Journey to Entrepreneurship & Purpose

By Jessica Sinclair, BSN-RN

"The currency of real networking is not greed, but generosity." @Ferrazzi

Can I be honest with you? I truly love people. We are so magical, unique and complicated. We all have talents that can truly impact our community and legacy. I was told by a mentor to never be afraid to advocate for myself and others because at the end of the day, we are all we have. My name is Jessica Sinclair, and I am known as the Unforgettable MC, registered nurse, philanthropist, and networking queen. I cultivated a workshop called "NETWORK LIKE YOU MEAN IT" to help people learn how to maintain meaningful relationships with peers, family and community. Networking effectively continues to open doors for me. Let this chapter be a tool to motivate you to change your mind set on how to achieve greatness in your career, business and personal development.

The Start Up

My mother said I had an outgoing personality from the age of two, always waving and spontaneously saying "hello" to strangers, neighbors, friends and family. She also said that I was a firecracker and a jolly baby to be around. I was born in Brooklyn, New York, and raised in Elmont, New York. I learned the fundamentals of family and hard work from a very early age. My dad, a hardworking Jamaican native and taxi cab driver, and my mom, a courageous and fearless entrepreneur and former child day care assistant, raised my four Jamaican-born siblings and me. I am the proud aunt of four nieces and six nephews. Family is everything to us. Team Sinclair continues to help our community, family and friends. Our home was always the place where family lived until they assimilated to America. My mother's ability to take care of others back in her country never went unnoticed and her nurturing traits are definitely rooted in my personality.

I was often referred to as the "American One," which meant I was outspoken, adventurous and a risk taker. Truth be told, being the only one born in America made me feel like an outcast at times, because I could not relate to their stories and experiences in Jamaica. However, it made me extremely proud of my culture, and I wanted my parents' life to be better. That meant I had to be the best at everything I did. I did not want them to be embarrassed; after all, I was the "American One." During all my years in academia, I brought home great grades and was involved in afterschool activities to keep busy. Making my parents and siblings proud definitely motivated me to keep striving for greatness.

Real World

I would later earn a bachelor of arts in media and communication from City College of New York. My DREAM JOB was to become a powerful publicist. I worked as a publicist for about a year and a half before I realized it was not so dreamy, after all. Exhausted and drained were words that pretty much summed up my life in fashion and entertainment. I continued on because giving up is not in my DNA. I was really great at building relationships and excelled at media pitching, but I wasn't happy - RED FLAG. Then, the recession hit the industry, and I lost my job. That turned out to be a blessing in disguise.

A friend of mine who knew I wasn't happy would always say, "Jess, why are you looking for PR jobs? I think you should be an on-air talent with your personality." I wanted to, but it just wasn't the right time. Interview after interview, I went looking for public relations (PR) work. The lack of opportunities made me angry and slightly depressed. I remember praying to God, asking Him to either find me PR work ASAP or point me in another direction. I want you to know that you have no control over your life, and no matter how much you plan, the universe will have other plans.

The day my brother suggested I apply to become a medical unit clerk at a hospital, I was literally about to apply at the mall. I had so many family members in healthcare, it was the last thing on my mind. Nonetheless, I applied and ended up working as a clerk for six years. I learned medical terminology and became a unit clerk trainer. I learned leadership and delegation skills that would prove useful later in life. Doctors and nurses would complement my customer service and communications skills.

During November of my second year as a clerk, I was pulled aside by a few nurses who said that it didn't seem as if I was going back into PR, so why not apply to school to become an RN (registered nurse) and see what happens? NO, NO, NO was my response. By January (two months later!), I was taking the hardest pre-requisites of my life: anatomy, physiology and chemistry. I continued working full-time as a clerk and took weekend classes. I had no personal life for the next two years while I completed those courses. When I learned I was accepted into a nursing program, I couldn't believe it. Naturally, I read the acceptance letter over and over again.

Giving Up is Easy

Before the start of the semester each year, every student was required to pass the dosage and calculations exam for medications. It involved a lot of MATH, which was definitely not my favorite subject - at all. The exam consisted of ten questions, and to get a passing score, nine of the ten answers had to be correct; meaning, if more than one answer was incorrect, you failed. Only three attempts were given to pass this preliminary entrance exam, and if you failed three times, you'd be automatically kicked out of the program.

In my most vivid memory of this exam, I was just sitting there in math review class, sweating. I attended all of the math review classes, asked for extra math questions and even with all the prep work, I was unsuccessful in passing the exam the first time… and the second time. I only had one attempt left to pass the math exam and secure my seat in the nursing program. I had to sign a contract stating I had received academic advisement that the next math exam would be my last attempt. So much pressure was on me.

Frustration kicked in, and I swear God sent an angel to help me. He was an African American classmate who said, "You're far too intelligent to let a math exam win." I couldn't believe what I was hearing, I was so shocked and humbled. On my days off work, we practiced and worked on fifty math problems a day. I received 100% on that math exam. If it wasn't for his help, I honestly don't think I would have officially made it into the nursing program. People come into our lives for reasons unbeknownst to us. Always embrace and accept others' help, because it is so rare. Count your blessings.

Passing the NCLEX Exam

I was never a great test-taker, especially standardized testing like the National Council Licensor Exam (NCLEX). The NCLEX is a nationwide examination for the licensing of nurses in the United States and Canada. Once passed, it awards permission to practice nursing by the state. Each nursing schools' goal is to have a high pass rate, and they offer preparation classes through companies that sell study techniques. My nursing school collaborated with Kaplan. One size doesn't fit all students, so I also purchased practiced questions. I wanted to be 100% prepared to sit for this exam. I was told that the more questions you practiced, the more familiar you would become with the exam. I did questions non-stop; it became my life. In my opinion, you never feel ready to take the exam. I picked and committed to a date.

My first attempt at passing the test was unsuccessful. Rumor had it that the more questions the computer gave you, the more likely you are to pass. I answered all 265 questions of the exam. I felt defeated, but I remember telling myself, "You made it out of nursing school, you can do this."

I was still working full-time as a unit clerk, but it became clear that I needed to study more. I studied harder questions, and incorporated online videos. I asked other nurses for advice and registered again for the exam. I had to wait forty-five days to take the exam again, so I became proactive and started to look for work as a nurse. I heard back from the nurse manager on a unit of interest who said she would keep me in mind for a position. I was so nervous and eager to pass this exam.

On my second attempt, I did not spend too much time on the exam questions. I felt more confident, but I still did not pass. I told my mom that I was going to take a long break before I took it again. I threw in the towel; all my peers were posting on social media that they passed. I was happy for them, but deeply sad. I gave up and let the exam get the best of me. It wasn't in my nature to quit, but I did. I walked around, head down, for a few months.

In the months that followed, I soul searched. I talked more to God, attended church more often, broke down in tears and asked for a **BREAKTHROUGH**. I am not sure how spiritual you are, but what I know for sure that God will not give you more than you can handle. Just like it took me three attempts to pass the math entrance exam, I passed the NCLEX exam the third time around.

Nursing is Where Reality Happens

Have you ever met a person who loves to coordinate with a team, keep everyone updated on what's happening and make things fun while providing education and training? Those are some of the reasons why I became a nurse. As a nurse, it is my goal to make sure patients feel respected and accommodated. Although I loved working with people, I faced a lot of adversity being a new energetic nurse. The seasoned nurses did not work well with the younger nurses; they were set in their ways. I was lucky to have a great nursing preceptor, which made the transition from unit clerk to nurse easier.

Nurses are the glue that hold the unit together. We have to communicate, document, teach and support, which can lead to a quick burn out. I often felt like the nursing administration did not support us; it was always about the numbers. Admissions and discharges were the priority, not the nurses who provided patient care. The harsh reality of working in healthcare is working while understaffed and feeling rushed. However, regardless of the circumstances, I still made patient care and compliance my primary focus.

Since some of my beliefs weren't a priority in bedside nursing, I took the initiative to start my own business. That enabled me to make guests feel comfortable and secure and to create an enjoyable experience in an energetic atmosphere.

Facing Fear

How do you face fear? Head on, that's how! Do a dance on fear, scream at fear and shout, "I AM GOING TO CONQUER THIS." When I am filled with doubt, I mediate and fast. I let God take control over my body. I know that faith can move mountains, so I pray, "God, fix this because only You can."

I love being alone in my thoughts. When we are quiet, we allow our minds to be creative. Being around the constant noise of others can block your growth and creativity. As much as I love helping others, I had to learn to treat myself better and to listen to myself in silence. Fear is a useless emotion that will keep you from walking your divine purpose. You need a game plan to tackle fear, because it can creep it on any given day.

What does happiness look like in a fearful state? What works for me is to visualize myself unafraid; once you see it, you can achieve it. Here's an example: you are waiting in a conference room for a meeting to discuss your promotion. Visualize all the feels[a1] , take a deep breath in and it hold for three seconds before exhaling, smile (it's infectious!), cross your hands, sit tall in your seat and know you did everything in your control to reach this place. The way you see yourself, and how you think and feed your mind with positive images, is the best way for you to perform at your highest potential.

Passion and Purpose

I always knew I wanted to start my own business; it was just a matter of time. Patience and prayer were two things I needed to accomplish this. I did not want my business to be a hobby or a side hustle. It was vital to establish a business plan and take the appropriate steps to be official. I went to the county clerk office and filed the proper business paper work for Sinclair Master of Ceremonies, Incorporated. After that, I had my launch party and continued to promote, promote, promote with the help of my network.

I wanted more success, and it was difficult working a full-time nursing job and giving my business its necessary time. I left my full-time nursing job to take a few months to strategize, and it was the best thing I ever did. Only you can decide what you truly deserve and need. Never let anyone dim your light. Keep your head high and just know that, with patience and prayer, all things are possible.

I am the owner and lead host of Sinclair Master of Ceremonies, Inc. As a wedding host, I coordinate all the details of my clients' wedding receptions with style, grace and meticulous attention to detail, making unforgettable experiences. My service is different from the rest. I keep everyone updated, make all announcements and handle any concerns and issues that may arise. My clients trust me to handle everything, and it is my pleasure to serve. Due to this, I was recognized by *Wedding Wire* as a brand that demonstrated excellence in quality, service and professionalism within the wedding industry.

I also host workshops on wellness and curate health fairs as a community advocate. As a red carpet host, I generate the perfect buzz and excitement. I also engage with viewers in real-time to increase brand awareness of an event, conduct interviews and give behind-the-scenes access as a social media host. However, my brand isn't just about facilitating or hosting events. I help brands commercialize their business with my voice and give them knowledge on the power of collaboration. Building relationships by networking effectively was key to my growth as an entrepreneur.

Built on my natural abilities to put people first, I created *Network Like You Mean It* to share networking tips that helped me grow my business. *Network Like You Mean It* is an interactive workshop covering topics that sharpen and develop interpersonal soft skills, like: leadership, communication and motivation. Sessions explore the fundamentals of public speaking, preparation, collaboration and self-identity. The more knowledge participants gain around a specific skill set, the more confidence they will have when performing these skills.

My professional development sessions help them cultivate and maintain meaningful relationships with peers, family and community.

My program boosts self-esteem, volunteerism, social awareness and fortifies critical thinking. The overall goals of the workshops are to help participants sharpen the tools in their networking toolboxes, increase opportunities for internships, volunteerism, academic advancements, job placement and build confidence and credibility. My workshops also address topics such as public speaking, branding, critical thinking and stress management.

Networking Tips to Get You Started:

1. Establish Your "Why" - Knowing your "why" will help you stay focused, especially when things get difficult.

2. What You Offer - Write a list of your strengths. What do you bring to the table?

3. Do Your Homework - Research the people you want to connect with. Go deep and find out their likes and dislikes (LinkedIn, Facebook, Instagram and Twitter).

4. Set Goals - Create a vision board. What are you trying obtain? Once this is established, you will begin to create your plan.

5. Networking is Strategic - Go in knowing what you want and who you want to connect with.

6. Establish a Relationship - Networking is about building organic relationships. Think of it as dating; not every shoe fits. Be patient.

7. Stay in Touch - Follow up and be of service. Email articles, invite folks out to a mixer and ask how you can help them achieve their goals.

8. Be Confident - You are enough. Remember - you are human and not everyone wants to see you win. A NO can transform to a YES.

9. Invest in Professional and Personal Development - Learn something new each month. Knowledge is power; the more you know, the more you will grow.

10. Be Yourself - Let your personality shine. We are all unique. Don't try and be like everyone else. The right people will embrace YOU.

I hope these ten tips will help you on your networking journey. Never stop dreaming and working hard to achieve greatness. Be patient with yourself and know that you are doing your very best.

It is a true honor to create freely in this space. Thanks go to Michelle Greene Rhodes and the accomplished, professional and victorious nurses and practitioners for inclusion in this book. I hope it sheds a light on the importance of storytelling, because it can save a life. I have faith that this anthology will inspire, motivate and uplift you. No matter where you are in your journey, NEVER GIVE UP! Fight for your happily ever after. We all have trials and tribulations in life, and no one is perfect. Be gentle with yourself, and listen to your intuition. PERIOD!

It would be an honor to help you achieve networking greatness - shoot me an email at info@itsjessicasinclair.com

Biography

Born in Brooklyn and raised in Elmont, New York, Jessica is a 2007 graduate of the City University of NY (CUNY) with a concentration in communications and public relations (PR). She later transitioned from public relations to work as a medical clerk, which inspired her to become a nurse. In 2014, Jessica received an associate degree in nursing from Nassau Community College. Upon completion, Jessica was a recipient of the Nassau Community College Association Scholarship, Presidential Scholarship and Citation Award. For two years, Jessica worked as a medical surgical nurse, where she had the opportunity to innovate a patient healing initiative and complete her bachelor of science degree, cum laude, in nursing, from Farmingdale State College in 2018.

Be sure to sign up for monthly networking tips on ItsJessicaSinclair.com
Shoot me an email: Info@ItsJessicaSinclair.com
Follow me on Instagram for events and tips: @itsjessicasinclair
Collaborate with me on Linkedin: @JessicaSinclair

Dedication

This book began as a gift to me and after many years of thinking about my experience, I'm finally ready to give voice to my own narrative. Encouraged by my lovely husband, I have decided to push past my fear and reveal my greatness. These words were written for me, but I hope they inspire you.

~Casaleen

Lifting the Veil of Fear

By Casaleen Humber MS, RN, PCCN, CCM

For as long as I can remember, fear has been a consistent theme in my life. I wasn't always aware of what I was feeling, but as I've reflected about my purpose and life recently; I can see that fear was the true motivator beneath everything and was constantly present. It's almost as if I was cloaked in a veil of fear. It was a constant effort to rid myself of the fear I felt inside, but soon after it would float back onto me, bringing with it flecks of doubt and insecurity. The doubts coupled with insecurity simultaneously made me both nervous, hesitant and inspired me to develop high standards for myself. It seemed the only way to combat fear was through knowledge, observation and becoming the best person I could be. As a girl, I often felt different than my sisters and friends, because they were highly sociable and outgoing. Everyone else seemed comfortable in their respective skins and accomplished things effortlessly. I, on the other hand, always felt a crippling shyness that was so strong it prevented me from partaking in school activities, clubs and church performances. I could not explain what kept me fearful, but I knew I had to dig deeper.

My family's main resource of support was farming. We didn't have an abundance of material resources, money was ration, but they were consistently loving and supportive. My childhood overall was filled with happiness and laughter. So, there was no tangible reason for my relentless insecurity. My mother had me a few months before her eighteenth birthday. She was present but worked tirelessly to support her family and as a result I was primarily raised by my grandparents. What I observed about my mother and grandmother was enlightening. They were drastically different from me. They accomplished things with apparent ease and confidence. My mother and grandmother alike would state they were going to do something, and it would happen shortly thereafter. I was amazed by their confidence considering at the time it seemed impossible to me. I remember she once pointed to a property near a beach and said that she'd own a restaurant there one day. Not a year later, she did.

This effortless ability to do things was impressive and I knew that I possessed the ability to do the same, because I was such a natural thinker. I dreamed of traveling the world, teaching and making a difference. The actuality of making this my reality seemed like an insurmountable task which felt impossible. As a girl, I learned about the world through reading books and from the two channels on our television. Tucked away in my private corner in our modest two-bedroom house, I would hide and escape to all sorts of exotic destinations. It was not only exciting to read about places and people that were contrary to the subservient lifestyle I knew, but it was also a great way to learn about unfamiliar ideas. Reading was my gateway to competence, unveiling the unknown, but more awarely a way to combat my fear.

I always felt compelled to improve. I desperately longed to be exemplary, show my family and the world my inner truth. I needed to be that someone others could visualize as a role model. I was often told by my family that I need to be a good example for the younger generation namely my sisters. Therefore, I set high standards for myself when it came to anything that I did. Even as a child, I loved to teach and show others how to do things. Unaware of whether overthinking made me fearful or fear caused me to overthink, I became hesitant and in return feared judgement. I was always acutely aware of my shyness, longed to be bolder and self-confident. There was so much that I wanted to do, and my shyness was always holding me back from actually attempting things. Every day I would repeat affirming phrases to myself and hope that this was the day I could leave my insecure self behind.

Some of my most favorite memories as a girl were the times that I was able to get past my fear and plan things like summer school and community festivals, which I christened, "Fundays." I loved organizing bake sales where I could make and sell cakes in my community. I grew up watching my mom start and manage many businesses through the years, and I aspired to do the same. She always seemed more confident, relaxed and flexible whenever she was working on her own projects and businesses. While she taught me the basics and I knew I wanted that for myself in my future.

My grandmother essentially raised me and having spent so much time together, she became my best friend. The two of us had an especially close bond, and she was the center of my world. Just before I graduated from high school, she was diagnosed with cancer and passed away shortly thereafter. I remembered she was in high spirits when she told me the news. An inconvenient illness was not something that could shake her. She was a tough woman and seemed unshakeable. As a girl, she lost one arm to an amputation of a fracture that became gangrenous, but she pressed on, raised twelve children and did whatever else needed to be done to ensure our family was content. So, upon hearing this news, she simply took it like any other news. For weeks she used public transportation to get her daily treatments alone as she wished, because she refused the disrupt her family life. As she would often say, "No worries life must go on, I will alright."

Eventually, however, despite her positive outlook, she got a lot sicker. She was having trouble breathing and couldn't walk across the room without gasping for breath. Her breathing became so erratic that she was afraid to go to sleep and feared she'd stop breathing in the night. Her health was degrading quickly, and we eventually had to take her to the hospital. Something inside of me said that would be her last time in our home, it was a solemn and dreaded feeling. She ended up having fluid in her lungs, hence the shortness of breath. The nurses were exceptional, compassionate as they cared for her and called to daily to give us an update. My instinct had been correct, and she ended up passing early in the morning, but something about the entire experience stuck with me. I was mesmerized by how the simple care and verbal comforts of the nurses helped us during that time. They were like this angelic superhero team that was there for us during one of the darkest times we'd experienced as a family thus far.

Despite the impact that experience had on me, I wasn't thinking about actually becoming a nurse at that point. My specialty in high school was architecture and building technology. I loved to draw and worked relentlessly to become the best in my class. I was one of six females in a large group of males. The only problem standing in the way of my dream to design buildings was that professions like this just weren't seen in my community. Everyone I knew was either housewife, farmer or a local tradesman. No one in my experience became something so exotic as an architect. Without real life examples of people working in the profession, my dream seemed too far-fetched to be realistic. I searched for information and guidance to prepare myself for this sort of future, but it was so difficult to see it becoming a reality. My old fears surfaced, and I failed to see an actionable path to take me to my dream.

I moved to the States after high school, because I knew my opportunities were endless in America. When I first arrived, I didn't have a specific plan or very much money. I lived with an aunt and decided to nanny in order to save up enough funds to go to college. Initially, I wanted to go into architecture, but my research was telling me that this was a difficult path. The schools were expensive, a degree in the specialty would take years, and the jobs seemed to require connections.

My aunt originally suggested the idea of nursing to me. She knew a lot of people doing this, and she said I could be a nurse in just two years. From what she knew, the jobs were plentiful, and I could easily be making a generous living right away. As I talked to different friends, they all seemed to agree that not only would this be a good profession to pursue, but they all seemed to think that I would be great at it. Because multiple people were telling me the same thing, I started rolling the idea over in my head. I reflected back on my experience with my grandmother and remembered the impact those nurses had on all of us. Together, all of these things seemed like a sign, a spiritual push toward a certain path, and I decided to apply. It wasn't long before I fell in love with the profession.

Once I became a nurse, my life changed drastically. I started meeting so many wonderful and inspiring people. Some of them were patients, others were my superiors and colleagues. It was during my time as a nurse that my millennial tendencies started to emerge. They were qualities they I've always had, but I now saw were trademarks of a generation. I was always open and willingly love to learn about an array of topics. My interests were broad and learning a little about lot of things kept me both engaged and helped me to understand the bigger picture.

There were so many flavors of nursing that I wanted to try and then to master. I loved the fast-paced nature of the work and how things were different from day to day. I ended up working in an array of departments and capacities throughout my tenure as a nurse. I worked in the intensive care unit, burn unit, pediatrics, rehabilitation, long-term care, quality management and infection control, case management and as a nurse educator. Not to mention, I worked as a telephonic triage nurse and travel nurse; travel nursing is a millennial's dream.

To many in the nursing field, moving around that much was misunderstood. Sometimes I did wrestle with the predominant view that I should find one position and stick with it. But as the years have gone on, I've come to embrace my nature. For me, moving around to so many different departments has given me a better understanding of the whole operation. There was a time when I had no concept as to why or how using ten sheets or multiple syringes connect to the larger picture. I simply cared for the patient and didn't think about anything else. But now having worked in the departments that gave me a vantage point to understand the financial component; I have a more comprehensive understanding of how and why those things matter in the grand scheme of things. My movement has made me a better, more experienced nurse and definitely not one who is less of an expert at one thing. It has taken me awhile to come to appreciate this quality and strength in myself.

I've also seen how all this learning helps me get rid of fear. For me, the only way to eliminate fear is to learn. Fear comes from anticipating of the unknown. When we don't know what to expect, we fill that void with fear that we create. Being inquisitive has helped me to slowly remove the veil of fear that has been hovering over me my entire life. By channeling the strengths of my mother and others that I've admired through the years, I can look at new challenges without fear. I simply learn and jump in. If something doesn't work, I don't have to stay mired there. I can simply make a change and try something new. The more that I do this, the less power fear has over me. The more that I am able to do and accomplish, the more I can move toward fulfilling my purpose.

Currently, I work as a nursing professor at two different universities, and I've never felt closer to my purpose. I am often overwhelmed by how far I've come since being that young, insecure girl from the small unknown community in Jamaica. I remember when I first arrived in the States, I was too scared to walk on the streets after 7pm. Throughout the years, I've slowly taught myself how to be more confident with each affirmation that I've uttered so that now I can stand in front a room of eager nursing students and share my knowledge and expertise. I absolutely love what I am doing now, and my goal moving forward is to venture even farther onto the path of entrepreneurship.

I also took a big step shortly after Hurricane Sandy. My whole place was flooded, and I decided then and there that I needed to do something selfless and fearless. That's when I decided to volunteer in Guatemala. I went by myself to a new place where I didn't know anyone for two weeks. Taking that action, shirking away any fears and just going there was a huge step for me, and by doing it, I proved to myself that I was strong and capable.

In the coming years, I plan on working to create and develop my own workshops and programs that will serve to guide other millennial nurses on their journey toward entrepreneurship and wellness. I am passionate about teaching nurses to care for themselves while simultaneously caring for others. In addition to just teaching, I also hope to lead and inspire my students. My idea of leadership has always been that leaders show people how to do things, whereas managers just tell people to do things. I have always strived to be the former. I am not interested in ordering people around, but when I can show someone how to grow, stretch themselves and leave their comfort zone, I light up. I am excited for my entrepreneurial journey, especially having identified that fear has been the thing holding me back. Every time I have broken through and accomplished something new, it has been because I was able to overcome my fear. After lots of self-reflection, I learned that my fear can be distilled down to something more specific, the fear of judgment.

It's been an awakening to realize that the fear of judgment is something so out of my control. All of this time, I have been stressing about controlling something that was out of my hands. The solution is to simply let go of what other people think and simply live my purpose. For me, that is to teach and to lead. By setting goals, achieving them, trusting myself and believing in myself, I can actively let the veil of fear fall away. It hasn't been easy, but this journey of unveiling fear has been endlessly rewarding. The only person I can truly control is myself, and I don't ever have to allow the opinion of another to shadow the magical being that I am. I've emerged from beneath a veil of fear and discovered what's underneath. I was always afraid that what I'd find was someone insecure and shy, not quite as courageous, tenacious or bold as what I perceived everyone else to be. But I was wrong! There is only greatness beneath all that fear. I am committed to letting it shine and teaching others how to do the same.

Biography

Casaleen L. Humber MS, RN, PCCN, CCM, trail blazed through nursing with an inquisitive mind, eager to function as a well-rounded nursing professional by gaining the knowledge required to understand nursing from the bedside into entrepreneurship. to the boardroom or from the bottom to the top or vice versa. She was born and raised by her mother and grandparents on the beautiful island of Jamaica in the West Indies; the eldest of three children. She migrated to the United States to attend college and pursue her initial passion in Architecture. As a result of losing her grandmother to cancer she was deeply affected by her illness and navigation of the healthcare system. To make an impact for change through health and education she was encouraged by family and friends to embark on her nursing journey; which she traversed wholeheartedly despite a change in career pathway. She developed her passion for helping people through the exemplified activism of her mother and grandmother who taught her to consciously care and give to others in need. In every aspect of her life she wanted to teach, she taught Summer school as a teenager and consistently embodied a stark love for education.

To further challenge herself she decided to pursue a Baccalaureate in Nursing instead of an Associate degree. In 2007, she graduated with honors on the Dean's list from Borough of Manhattan Community College in New York with an Associate of Arts in liberal Arts. She was inducted into Phi Theta Kappa and the National Honor Society. Upon graduation, she attended Long Island University in Brooklyn New York and graduate.

Casaleen further obtained a Baccalaureate degree in nursing from Long Island University in Brooklyn New York and a graduate degree in Nursing Leadership from Stony Brook University also in New York. She volunteered her nursing services to the less fortunate in Sierra Leone, Africa, Guatemala and Dominican Republic. As a new nurse she started in long-term acute care then worked I every intensive care specialty. She taught nurses as an educator in multiple healthcare facilities across the country and now she is a nursing professor. She is married with two beautiful children and lives in Coral Springs Florida. Casaleen is starting her journey as nurse entrepreneur in the guide the millennial nurses on their pathway to professional and personal balance through wellness and education as a nurse coach and consultant. I am passionate about teaching nurses how to look beyond while at the bedside to grow their career or how to look back to grow their entrepreneurial ideas for longevity.

Dedication

This book is dedicated to the healthcare superheroes that often go unacknowledged.

To the CNAs, RNs, Nurse Practitioners that have a vision to work beyond the bedside.

To Vandrikha Wint, a.k.a. Vonnie. Words cannot express the deep gratitude that I owe to you for simply being there to push guide, and lead me through nursing school and beyond.

To Natasha Barthe for always seeing that entrepreneurship spirit in me, even when I was too young and immature to grasp your words of wisdom. Thanks for your continued support in all my career endeavors.

~ Flobrenne

Ordained Steps: My Journey to Nurse Entrepreneurship

By Flobrenne Joseph-Spaulding, RN

When the Lord ordains your steps, be ready to run! August 4th, 2017 I officially became a nurse entrepreneur, or *Nurseprenuer* as Michelle Greene Rhodes, coined it.

One of the biggest errors I made along my journey into launching my own business, is that after each failure, I jumped right into the next idea. I never gave myself enough time or space to figure out what was the root cause of that venture's dismay.

While I was looking for more career opportunities that will enable me to reach my goal of having businesses in the health care industry, I went on to earn my bachelor's degree in health sciences, majoring in health care administration and management. I assumed that getting a degree in healthcare management will help me achieve my goals faster. However, even then, it was not enough. Sure, they taught me through traditional lectures and practicum how to run and operate different health care facilities. But the curriculum did not include the layout on how to start a business from the ground up. Rather, it taught us how to effectively plan and execute task, assignments, create policy, and communicate with multi-disciplines as their leader, not owner. The lessons learned and knowledge gained was just a few drops in the bucket of knowledge and training that I was going to need to successfully launch my own business.

I remember entering my graduate program. I had to meet with my program advisor who was responsible for guiding me through a pre-planned pathway to graduation. During that counseling session, I was asked what my ultimate career goals were? I replied, to own and operate an ALF, Adult Day Care, Primary Care Clinic, and something with assisting elderly travel with care. My advisor chuckled, "You should select one, maybe two, businesses". I wasn't disappointed in his response, but I also was not encouraged either. I ended up completed my program as one of the top students in my cohort. After graduation, I assumed that at the graduate level, I would really find out how to start a business. So that's what I did. I enrolled in the graduate level program for health sciences, this time my track was for health care leadership. About half-way into this program, I realized that not only were my professors the same, my papers and projects mirrored that of the ones I completed in my undergraduate studies. I took it upon myself to seek advice from the admission advisors in the school of business on my campus. Again, I told them of my aspirations of entrepreneurship, and their recommendation was for me to switch to a dual MBA/MS track to accomplish those goals. But that was not what I wanted. Every day that I was in my graduate program, I felt a yearning for something else. I had this unexplainable feeling that I have reached my highest potential at this school, and that it was time for me to move toward my destiny, not towards some company's idea of what their new hire executive needs to have.

With an unsettling feeling, I decided to go to the local SBA office for help and guidance. I found out that they had an office on my university's campus, I called and had an appointment set-up within that week with a counselor. In preparation for my meeting, I gathered all the information I thought I needed to discuss the business idea I had and was ready to get started. I was sure that I'd come out of that initial meeting with the SBA counselor with a blueprint for my next business start-up. But that was sadly not the case.

The information provided was so generic that it didn't align with not only my thought process, but my business idea. And to top it off, I was given a stack of papers to take home to fill out and was told, that's what I needed to start my own business. I inquired about funding as well, because I knew how costly starting an ALF could potentially be and was again referred to fill out the packet and come back. So, for the next few months, between family life, school, and filling out this packet I started doubting myself. But I kept on pushing. I went back in for my follow-up meeting with the counselor and turned in my packet. We were in the office for about 2 hours. He went on about how he was successful at owning multiple popular food-chain franchises, and that that's the easiest business to start and get funding for. Wait!...What?...Yup, instead of helping guide me down the path for ideas that I have for myself, the counselor was trying to sell me on his idea of the best and easiest business to start. Unbelievable. I left feeling even more discouraged. I packed up my paperwork, thanked him for his time, and left the SBA office in tears.

About a year later, my best friend, Vonnie told me about a new nursing program that she was already enrolled in, that was now enrolling for their second cohort. I went to the school to obtain information about their new school of nursing and to see what the program entailed. It went from a 25 min information session, to 3 hours later, passing the entrance exam, and enrolling for the accelerated program. For the next 17 months, my only focus was nursing school. I am blessed with the overwhelming support of my close friends, my mother, my amazing children, and my wonderful husband, who all pitched in during my grueling nursing school and work schedule. In June of 2014, my best friend Vonnie, a mere 6 months after getting pinned herself, came back and pinned me.

While I successfully completed my nursing program, and graduating magna cum laude, I was unsuccessful at my first attempt in taking the state board nursing exam. Boy was that a blow to my ego. I had to learn how to depend on my family and friends for moral and emotional support. I am so used to being great at everything that I do, that's the perfectionist in me. What helped me the most, was listening to other nurses speak on their troubles and pitfalls, and how they were able to come out of it, on top.

Three years after graduation I found myself working for a great company, back in school for my bachelor's in nursing, traveling the world with my family. I was really in a great groove and was out here LIVING MY BEST LIFE! But I could not shake the feeling, every so often felt a void. Despite having everything I dreamt of, I still felt like there was more for me out there.

So, I decided to go back to nursing school. That was one of the first programs I was truly interested in, however, at that time, the nursing school schedule did not fit into my family

A few months after that meeting, a close friend of mine announced that she was pregnant with her first child.

By this time, social media had begun to take on a more prominent shape and google searches where more refined that ever. Feeling unfulfilled by my desk job, and decided to try my search

So, like many people do in this millennial era, I took to the internet. For many months, I have spent countless hours gathering data and information on how to start and run a successful business.

One of the instrumental decisions I made that has led me to build a solid nurse owned business, was hiring Michelle Greene Rhodes as my business coach. At that time, I was not looking for a business coach, I didn't even know what one was or did for that matter.

I am a woman with many dreams. I have often been told to settle on just one dream and be great at it. However, when the Lord marks your path, you must follow. He has never given me one idea. For as long as I can remember, the Lord has always blessed me with more than one way to solve an issue, or to tackle an obstacle. The key to be successful, for someone like me that have many dreams and aspirations, is to tackle one at a time, not to pick just one! It is doable.

My entire childhood I was always told that I had a bubbly personality. I was even nicknamed the "energizer bunny" in fifth grade, because once I got started, I kept going, going, and going. Fast-forward to college. It was a professor that saw so much potential in me but couldn't pass me in his course because I had, what he described as impulse control issues, I wanted to be perfect in every assignment or task that I was assigned. So, what was wrong with that? I thought that those are attributes that would want someone to have me

You see, I've always knew that I was going to be in healthcare. The oldest memory I have, I think I was about 6 years old. A neighbor, who was watching me during the day, while mutt mom worked, was watching a soap opera and one of the characters was pregnant and in labor in this episode. I remember the character screaming and breathing out loud, "Hee Hee Whooo, Hee Hee Whooo!" "She's faking it", speaking to the TV, I continued,

"She's breathing all wrong and screaming too much. She's supposed to breathe regular and just push the baby out." I remember the look on my neighbor's face, she then asked me, as she affectionately calls me, "Floflo, what do you want to be when you grow up?". I excitedly reposed, "A baby doctor. The one that help the mom have the baby in the hospital."

I knew that at that point, I had to fight hard to pursue my goals of becoming a physician and owning my own business. Along the journey through prepping for med school, I had children, moved, experienced other losses that halted my studies. However, every time tragedy struck, I was able to pick up the pieces and get back to work. I always knew that my goal was to be in healthcare, working with babies, and owning my own business.

It's no mystery why becoming a nurse is hard. It's downright difficult. However, the payoff is worth it.

It's been said many times before, that's it's through tragedy that we triumph. That what doesn't break you, makes you stronger. No true words have ever been spoken.

Biography

Flobrenne Joseph-Spaulding is a Registered Nurse, Entrepreneur, and Author of *What the __ is a Doula?*, and the new *Ordained Steps: My Journey to Nurse Entrepreneurship* a nurse collaboration book. With over 15 years of experience in the healthcare industry, Flobrenne is using her expertise to empower, educate, encourage, and inspire women to worldwide through her books and podcast.

In addition to her nursing degree, Flobrenne also holds multiple degrees and certificates including a bachelor's of science in healthcare administration and leadership, and currently pursuing her master's degree in nursing. She currently owns Elite Maternity Concierge, LLC, in SW Florida, providing exceptional private maternity, postpartum, and newborn care and services to expectant families.

A Florida native, she is the 5th child born to an immigrant single mother from the majestic island of Haiti. Flobrenne has been married for 17 years to her doting husband and together they have 3 amazing children, and currently reside in Fort Myers, FL.

For Doula Services please email elotematernityconcierge@gmail.com, or visit our website at www.elitematernityconcierge.com.

To be a guest on the Ask Flo Podcast now streaming on Anchor.fm/AskFlo, please email AskFloPodcast@Gmail.com. For all other services please email NurseFlobrenne@Gmail.com.

Acknowledgement

Always first and foremost is my Heavenly Father.

For my anchor of ancestors who allow me to get to this stage

To present people in my life who have crossed paths for a reason, season, or lifetime.

To my futures who always remind me that hope is key

Thank you for the gift of YOU.

Finally, to my fellow entrepreneurs…

Continue to Make It Happen!

PURPOSE MANIFESTO

Unleashing the Covert Entrepreneur

By Sandra D. Cleveland, PhD, MSN, RN and CEO

Last night I dreamed of freedom.

I watched myself serving others...I felt the breeze through my hair and against my skin as I wielded a hammer to help a woman create her dream home for her family through Habitat for Humanity. Scene switch: I saw myself on the beach near the shoreline learning new yoga poses and feeling the internal release that stretching and breathing provides. Scene switch: I have reestablished family and friend dinners at my house – my love of cooking and our sense of community is renewed on a monthly basis. We're talking and laughing, enjoying game nights. Scene switch: I am teaching kids, teens, and seniors to find their sense of purpose and adventure in the form of mini-entrepreneurship workshops. I see myself on the magazine covers of Black Enterprise and Essence...embracing the blessings and confidence.

My dream segues into a national book tour where I have intimate book reading and signing copies of the books I have authored. I was offering fun health and fitness events – ones that combined play with working out. I was helping others evolve and, in turn, embracing my evolution. Throughout my dream, I was smiling, at peace, and fully embracing my creativity in my own business – and the results was beyond what I allowed myself to believe.

And then I woke up {insert big SIGH}. *Craaaaappp...*

I lay (lie?) in my bed, willing my eyes to stay closed and trying frantically to go back to sleep and somehow put myself back in REM sleep so I can segue into the next segment of my dream life. And repeatedly prayed to God that somehow, someway, I'd be able to use my given abilities to help others in their quests. But the persistency of my alarm won, and I got up.

As I got to work, my prayers seemed like a one-way message to HIM. I was stuck in the minutiae of the day-to-day grind, and the dreams of last night slowly disappeared from my consciousness. I was STUCK in the fulfilling of other's dreams, steadily losing the satisfaction I normally felt in contributing. Feeling defeated, controlled, ashamed.

Bottom line? – It just HURT differently.

Memories would flood my mind of others I saw who took chances that looking from afar, took me out of my own comfort zone. You always hear about key business people and how they 'made it big' by taking a leap. But that leap feels different when you see evidence of it in people in your own world. My dad went from a career with one of the "Big 3" auto companies and decided after retiring that he wanted to become a pastor. He sacrificed, went back to school and did just that. While my mom worked, she also ventured into selling beauty products. I used to watch my brother – a guy full of charisma. Willing to take chances. Willing to fail and try again. I loved him and envied him all in the same breath. Then there was me -- I felt myself living imposter syndrome, but in a different way.

Imposter syndrome is a psychological phenomenon, defined as feeling like you're inadequate, incompetent failure, and a fraud even when there is evidence to the contrary. But instead of the standard definition listed here, I felt the same phenomenon in a different context. As I progressed in my career, I recognized that the problem was cyclical…I was brought into an organization for my gifts and talents, creating content that fulfilled the needs of the organization and meeting desired outcomes. I had the confidence in my abilities and felt incompetent and a fraud because even though I would put myself out there to take on opportunities, I was often kept to tasks that lacked opportunity to use these abilities in my current roles.

So, what was the moment that I decided to become an entrepreneur?

I won't describe it as a 'moment'…I think of it as a series of 'shredding movements'. I believe I have always had the mindset of an entrepreneur. But while there a number of movements that I might speak about, let me share a more recent one.

It was the beginning of the new academic year. I was attending the annual set of faculty meetings for "professional development" (yes, I'm putting that in quotation marks…), and the question that made me freeze in my tracks was just asked. "What are two words that you would use to describe yourself?" At other stages of my life, I would just put down a couple of words that just skimmed my thoughts – but not today. Today I was in a "enough" frame of mind. I wanted – no—needed, to allow the real Sandra to show herself. I decided to be totally honest with others, and more importantly, myself. What were the two words that I wrote to describe Sandy at this season in my life?

Frustratingly. Compliant. **Compliant:** inclined to agree with others or obey rules, especially to an excessive degree; acquiescent (Oxford dictionary, 2019). For me, this just meant a mental death trap.

Dammit…there they were…the words that swirled around in my mind and my heart.

For years, I tried to follow the rules: I was the good but fun, athletic kid who suffered with the first child syndrome – honor my mom and dad, listen to my teachers, go to church. As being one of a few minority representatives most of my life, I also carried the burden of proving that I was the best – worthy to be there. I got strong grades throughout school and frequently received awards for the effort that I gave to a cause, project, or program in which I was involved.

I continued this same philosophy during most of my career trajectory. I enjoyed learning but would take it beyond learning with the goal of making myself indispensable to the organizations that I worked. Sometimes this tactic worked, but mostly it just made me feel mentally drained.

But the rules kept changing. I kept searching for a way into what I perceived as a two-tiered club in which the bottom tier appeared inclusive, while the top tier was always elusive, just out of my reach. No matter how much I did, how hard I tried, or how docile I became so I wouldn't be perceived as the angry black woman, it was never enough.

Another incidence of this recently occurred...I went for an interview, of which I was qualified. I did the necessary prep – practiced interview questions, developed my presentation, and the like. So, when I heard the words "I'm sorry, Dr. Cleveland – we're all in shock, but you did not get the job..." (The phone call I received after going through a rigorous interviewing process), I was frustrated, but felt freedom. Freedom that I recognized that my strengths can be used outside of the expected environments. Why was that?

Because it was different this time. What was the difference? *I openly shared that I was an entrepreneur.* I no longer wanted to hide my entrepreneurial side. That's the moment I recognized my worth and purpose – and realized *I was ENOUGH*. I really started to redefine my life to reflect this. Others may have thought it was a mid-life crisis, but I prefer to think of it as my awakening through shredding. God has blessed me with a number of gifts, but I felt that the gifts were still in their boxes and wrapping paper, waiting for someone to open them up.

However, I noted my mindset adjustment wasn't complete. I noted that I was repeatedly upset and angry, focused on what I perceived had been done to me. I was trying to utilize these feelings of negativity and move towards my purpose. But what I've realized in this year of transition is that although I state I'm "moving towards" my purpose, I wasn't quite there yet. I noted that I was still having schizophrenic moments. What do I mean by that?

At the time, it was important to break through the rejections that were received and force some acceptance, if not respect. But I was like the proverbial 'round peg in a square hole'—never quite fitting in. All of us want to fit in somewhere…believe we have something that needs to be heard, have a seat waiting for us at the table with the insiders. I wanted to fit in, yet be recognized for my individuality.

What I finally started to realize in my heart was that the idea of a reason, season, or lifetime (paraphrased from Ecclesiastes 3) applied not just for the people in my life, but the purpose I'm supposed to fulfill. While that was big for me, it was really put into perspective from a meeting with a personal coach. This wonderful individual, whom I never met before, heard my story and stated, "why do you keep doing this for them? This is not your niche group!" And with that one statement, it allowed me to free myself from unconsciously seeking their permission to be me.

What have I learned from my transition to entrepreneurship?

Entrepreneurship is not a covert operation that should be put away for the convenience of others. Rather, it's an experience…an encounter that I want to fully embrace. I am proud of the unique ways I bring ideas to the table. I'm driven to fulfill my purpose and help my clients reach their purpose as an entrepreneurial servant leader.

I mention in my book, *Shred: Removing the Layers to Find YOUR True Purpose* that shredding is a vital component to appreciate, accept, articulate, and allocate your God-given gifts. There were four components in shredding that I found myself applying as I worked through this transition:

*Core – this means really listening to yourself and aligning your purpose with God, higher power, or philosophy. Strengthening the core is essential for the rest of the body to stay aligned. You have to focus on the little movements and note which ones help you stay aligned versus those that weaken the core. Likewise, for an entrepreneur, your work should be focused. It means letting go of the extraneous thoughts, words, and actions that compete with your core.

*Plateau: It's inevitable that individuals going through a shred hit a plateau. During those times, your trainer will help make adjustments to push you through the plateau...but you still have to do the work. Every entrepreneur will reach stages in their journey where you either reach level ground and just stay there or find a level of comfort at the stage. Remember there are times to lay low, but growth is part of the process as well.

*Realization and Release: those in a shred focus on listening to their bodies and minds. They realize the activities and diets that they can do, and those they need to let go of during the journey. Entrepreneurs need to do the same. We need to learn when to release those thoughts, tasks, behaviors that steer us away from our primary missions – doing the work for our "whys".

*Flexibility: muscle development is a focus during a shred – but not the only focus. We entrepreneurs need to learn to stretch without breaking, compromise without messing up our core. Flexibility has positive effects on our overall well-being by helping us use not just the big muscles we commonly engage, but those smaller muscles that help keep balance in the muscles, decrease stress, and improve mobility.

Entrepreneurs (aspiring or established) can also apply the 4 components. It is so important in your shred as an entrepreneur to identify your core, realize the items within you and your world on keeping you plateaued; how do give yourself permission to release the old and realize the new; how you gain flexibility; Release items in your life to move forward on your goals; understand that plateaus do happen. Use these as well as your past experiences and your values (your core) to help with the uncertainties in your life and conquer the deferred dreams and decisions you have or want to make. I shared the following points before – but I'm bringing them with a "twist" for those with an entrepreneurial mindset:

- Be vulnerable… you don't have to have it all together. Be willing to share your fears and feelings, and quick to acknowledge your mistakes. There is absolutely not one entrepreneur who felt confident at every stage of the journey.

- Everyone is not meant to be your audience. Your gifts are uniquely yours to give. Likewise, your gifts are uniquely geared for certain individuals to receive. When you align your core with your customers, it allows you to focus on a product or service that meets their needs.

- Once you've acknowledged your mistakes, FORGIVE YOURSELF and OTHERS. You need to create this freedom so that you can focus on the task at hand. This shredding strategy is part of realization component.

- Leverage the haters. Because you will have haters who are watching you who don't want to see you succeed. And that's okay! Rejection is part of the process. Don't believe me? Many of us have heard of the challenges that entrepreneurs such as Shonda Rhimes, Walt Disney, Oprah experienced before they found their destined purpose.

- Never stop growing – allow yourself to stretch outside of your comfort zone. For instance, you might feel really comfortable designing your products or services but try to avoid the business and marketing components that you realize also need to be addressed. Take small steps into that uncomfortable zone – find a podcast, book, course that helps you learn about the areas that make you squeamish to address. This will combat the 2nd part of the shred (plateau).

Distractions can happen, and dreams can be temporarily deferred, but work to live your purpose in whatever the situation. This applies to you too, boss. You do work to develop consistency in being a boss, but if it comes at an expense to others or you negatively, it is perfectly okay to take a few steps back and pause. I did this and am refocusing my business in a way that better aligns with my purpose.

Know that you will have struggles – but don't let the struggles be the only source feeding your desire to move in your business. Mindset really is everything. Know that you CAN do this... you don't need anyone's permission to move forward. Your vision of your journey is divinely ordered. It is unique to you – and your uniqueness is a gift. I am so excited to see what's YOUR next step, boss – and would LOVE to hear how you used the shred to move you forward. Let's talk! Reach out to me and share about your personal shred. Remember, shredding is the process to move you from the struggles to your SUCCESS. My prayer for you is that you align with your purpose in that the journey you choose to take. May your dreams of freedom come true!

Biography

Sandra Cleveland, PhD, MSN, RN, NETA-CGEI – "Dr. Sandra" as she is affectionately known, wants to transform individuals and small businesses beyond their potential and achieve desired goals. She has 18 years of teaching experience in undergraduate and graduate nursing programs. Her current responsibilities include teaching in the graduate program for the doctoral students, specifically in capstone development; online course development; curriculum development, implementation, and evaluation. Sandra has also worked as a Registered Nurse for 25+ years in various roles including staff and agency nursing, nursing administration, and as a Clinical Nurse Specialist.

Fitness is another passion – she is a nationally certified group exercise instructor. She incorporated her passions lives the principles of servant leadership as a nurse educator, nurse, her use of technology, and fitness instruction, which took her trajectory to create her business. As CEO of Tribe Consulting, LLC, she mentors health professionals through personal and professional enhancement and helps nurses help each other through the power of connection. Many nurses and nursing students share that she is an encouraging presence, creative, and note how much they have learned from her. Additionally, she offers health and wellness offerings based on the power of play, incorporating educational technology in learning, and online course creation.

She has presented on these topics at national and international conferences as well as academic publications, serves as an alumni association board member, and assists the parish nurse at her church. Her ongoing mission is to help other's reach their full purpose (Jeremiah 29:11) and feels honored and humbled to be used as a vessel for God's work. She is author of the book *Shred: Removing the layers to find your true purpose*. Dr. Sandra lives in Michigan and is a wife, mom, educator, entrepreneur, and sports and fitness buff.

Acknowledgements

First, I want to thank God for leading and guiding me throughout my entire life. I have been afforded many opportunities that I know it was no one but God that allowed me to have; thank You. I am truly grateful for the life God has given me and the ability and knowledge to become a nurse entrepreneur. I am grateful for the family He has given me.

Secondly, I want to thank the love of my life, my loving supporting husband, Terrence Sr, who gives me everything I could possibly imagine and then some. You are husband of the millennium. I could not do what I am doing without your love and support, both emotionally and financially. Thank you for being there for me and listening whenever I need an ear.

Finally, Terrence Jr. thank you for being such a wonderful son and sharing all your business knowledge with me, giving advice and making videos for me. I love you!!!

~Valerie

Unshakeable: Bitten by the Entrepreneur Bug

By Dr. Valerie E. Green

Entrepreneur Bug "The Bug" is the unrelenting, unshakeable, powerful urge to go into business for yourself.

~Dr. Valerie E. Green

I would like to say the entrepreneur bug bit me early; in reality, it should have since my father owned a mechanic shop and a trucking business, my grandmother owned a country store, my step grandfather had a garden and drove around town selling the vegetables, and my grandfather and uncles all had trucking businesses. Unfortunately, the bug shied away from me in my early years - even my son became an entrepreneur before me. I grew up in a home with a father who was an entrepreneur and a mother who was a nurse. No one would have thought that my journey would lead me to become an entrepreneur and a nurse, otherwise known as nurse entrepreneur. Because when I was a young girl, I would say, "When I grow up, I want to be a doctor and a lawyer, so if anyone sues me, I can defend myself." Entrepreneur was never in the plan nor was becoming a nurse. Upon reflection, becoming an entrepreneur probably should have been in the plan, since when I was in junior high school, I would take my lunch money, buy Big Bol candies that cost one cent each and sell them 10 for a dollar to my classmates/clients. I turned my $5 a week lunch money into a profitable business. Well, that was until my mother shut my business down.

Until recently, I did not think of self-employment as being an entrepreneur, when that is exactly what it is. I never thought of my father as an entrepreneur, I only knew he was self-employed doing two things he loved: fixing things and driving trucks. I would spend many hours under a car with my dad (probably getting oilier than he), holding the light and passing him tools like a 9/16, a socket, a monkey wrench or a Phillips head screwdriver, while he was rebuilding a motor or taking out a transmission. I also tagged along with my dad on many road trips, delivering goods in his 18-wheeler, and he would even let me drive, so naturally being a "daddy's girl" I would go into the family business, or at the very least, open a business, right? TOTALLY WRONG!!! That was not my dream. Although owning a business would come up every now and then in discussions with my husband regarding franchising a restaurant, that was his desire, not mine. I did not seriously think about entrepreneurship after my junior high enterprise went out of business, but I have discovered that it is never too late.

Although my entrepreneurship journey did not start early, it did begin by the way of becoming a military police officer and then a nurse. My parents did not push college on my brother and me even though we both furthered our education beyond high school. I did not enroll into college immediately after graduating high school because as I grew older, my sights were set on going into the military. I participated in the Junior Reserve Officer Training Corps (JROTC) from junior high school through high school. I attended JROTC summer camp in Fort Rucker, Alabama during the summers. In the 12th grade, I was the JROTC battalion commander, and I missed my senior prom to attend the JROTC competition. I was serious about going to the military. I spent my 18th birthday on the firing range, qualifying with my weapon, while others were going through the gas chamber. Although, I loved the military and it was my desire to go, when I went to basic training, I thought, *What in the world have I gotten myself into, someone telling me what to do, what I could not do, when to get up, when to eat, when to sleep and most importantly, when I could not sleep?* Of course, the military has a way to ensure you do as you are instructed to do; they hit you where it hurts, right smack dab in the pocket. Thank God, I am not one that has to learn the hard way, so I did exactly what was expected of me and with excellence, of course.

After military life, it was time to settle on a career. I started nursing school after being overseas (Operation Desert Shield/Storm), getting married and having a son. So, imagine being in nursing school with a two-year old in which family obligations came first, before any studying could be done, and being older than the majority of the students. I knew it would be difficult but doable; there were many all-nighters, but after all, my mom did it with two children and a husband. I survived nursing school, and on to my nursing career I went. I began my nursing career with my sights set on becoming an administrator. I knew I did not want to work on the floor my entire nursing career, so in my mind, I had to continue my education. I also knew I would have to work at least three times as hard as others to get where I wanted to be. I learned that early, and I suppose that is where my overachiever mentality arose. One example of this was when I applied to nursing school, I was placed on the waiting list with a 3.7 GPA. I was devastated, but I eventually got in. Another student with a GED and a lesser GPA was accepted and not placed on the wait list. I, nor she, could understand how that happened, which only confirmed my suspicious that I had to perform three or more times better. The struggle is real, for real.

Operating a business became a small whim when I began looking at the cost of assistant living, adult day care and nursing home facilities for a loved one. Others, I knew, were also having the same issues of finding affordable places for their loved ones who were experiencing dementia. I heard of individuals paying $8,000 or $10,000 a month for assistant living. I would say, "I need to open up a facility, they are making a killing from other people's adversity." I thought to myself, *I am a nurse - the residents would receive better quality care, and I could do it more economically and with a real compassion for the clients.* But where would I open the facility, and most importantly, where would I get the funds to open it? I just knew there was no way I could get the money to do that, because I thought I had to have lots of money to start a business, so I did not put much thought into it and kept moving. I know now that I had a misguided mindset.

In recent years, I witnessed people with health issues who worked for over 40 years but could not retire for financial or other reasons, then others who got tired or fed up, came into a job and turned in their paperwork to retire immediately. It appeared to be a great feeling for those who could leave anytime they were ready. Since I knew I did not want to work until I died, I started preparing for my departure and what I wanted to do in the next chapter of my life. I started thinking about how I could make sure I was not held hostage from retirement when I was ready. That's when "The Bug" bit.

Throughout my nursing career, I have been afforded exceptional opportunities and had invaluable positions that have prepared me for this path I am now on, but I have also felt looked over for positions that were given to individuals who were less qualified. As I now reflect back, those positions were not for me, I would have gotten content with where I was and would not have kept pushing forward to my goal. My goal was not to become an entrepreneur, especially at this point. But I knew I did not want to work for someone else for the rest of my life. I have said many times that I needed a job where I could come in when I was ready and leave when I was ready. I know there is no company that will allow me to do that, other than my own. Currently, I am questioning myself, why I did not start on this expedition to a business much earlier, but I realize all things have their season. So, I chalk it up to it was not my season then, but now is the time and the harvest is plentiful. Even when I think about doing something else or taking another route, or wondering if I could really do this, the Lord places me right back on the entrepreneur path.

My road to entrepreneurship has not been paved with gold but it has not been the fiery pit, either. My actual path to entrepreneurship began when I completed my doctoral degree. I was sure that once I completed my degree, I would work towards that administrative/director/CEO position and enjoy life. I thought, *I have accomplished my goal and I am done*; but it did not end at completing a doctoral degree. As life would have it, "The Bug" bit me!!!!! It was unshakeable. I could not shake it off. So, instead of working toward that administrative/director/CEO position in someone's company, it would be my own. But where do I start? How do I start? Those are great questions that deserved even greater answers. I did what anyone would do - I consulted my son and others who were already in business for themselves. By nature, nurses are very resourceful individuals, but we need help, too. During my entrepreneur journey, God has placed numerous people in my path to assist and steer me in the right direction. In these days and times, there is no need to struggle in silence; there are too many successful people who are willing to share their journey, some for free and others for a fee. In the end, it all depends on how much it is worth to you. I have heard that you have to spend money to make money, but you have to be smart about it. I have never seen the need to reinvent the wheel, just improve upon it, make it better, make it work for you. I began researching. I joined entrepreneur network groups on Facebook, not even being familiar with Facebook at the time, so again I had to consult my son regarding Facebook. I had no clue what kind of business I wanted to go into. I knew nurses could do anything, but to my amazement, I discovered that nurses were doing it all and not just sticking with the nursing or healthcare fields.

Nurses are taking the entrepreneur world by storm with their many talents, and I wanted to be a part of it. I have always thought that there were limitless opportunities for nurses, but even in that thinking, I was naïve. Nurses as entrepreneurs, this has to be the dream. I discovered that I could combine what I am passion about -

quality health care - with business. Life just does not get any better than that. That saying, **if you can believe it, you can achieve it**, is so true. Until the entrepreneur bug bit me, I felt completely satisfied in my role. I thought I would continue until God pushed me into something else, and THAT HE DID. Who would think about doing anything else when they were extremely happy with what they were doing? Why would you do anything else? There are so many people who are unsatisfied with their jobs and here I was very satisfied and still moving into entrepreneurship. Until "The Bug" bit me, I thought I would have to be dragged out the healthcare system that I work for. Now, I am ready to follow whatever journey I need to, down the entrepreneur road; I have never chosen the easy path, and I do not see myself starting now. I happen to think that is the best way to do it. I am not forced to try something else; I am doing it on my own terms and in my own time. I am doing it by choice - it is my ambition and my genuine love - not because I am tired, frustrated or burned out. So, I have to love it.

Attaining my doctoral degree was very difficult, and there was a time when I thought I would have to put completing it on hold due to a glenoid fracture. I went to the doctor because I hurt my shoulder and was in excruciating pain with just doing simple activities of daily living. I diagnosed myself with a rotator cuff tear, so when the doctor called me over to the X-Ray light, I asked, "Why are you calling me over there? That implies you see something, and you cannot see a rotator cuff tear on a X-Ray." When I heard I had a glenoid fracture, I just knew the doctor was making up body parts. If you know anything about a glenoid fracture (fracture of the socket of the shoulder joint), this type is rare and difficult to fracture. But me, the overachiever, managed to fracture mine. The surgeon told me 2 cm or less and they would not think about surgery, but mine, the overachiever, was 3 cm, of course. If I had the surgery, which would have to be done the next week because my repair window was closing, I would not be able to move my shoulder for 12 weeks, not even to finish typing my doctoral paper. In my mind, that was not an option. I had just applied for a new position, and I did not want to miss out on that opportunity. In the end, I did not have the surgery. Life is about choices, and I would not change a thing regarding my life or my choices, not even the bumps and bruises, potholes and pits, because they had an integral role in shaping me into who I am today and starting me on my journey as an entrepreneur. The military taught me discipline, loyalty, structure, determination, and, of course, being timely in completing a task, as well as how to return to my feet when I stumble or fall. Nursing taught me the importance of organization, caring, high-quality, integrity, dignity, commitment, and excellence.

Although my journey has been a blessing, I must admit it takes a lot of work, commitment and sacrifice. I still have much more work to do and I am enjoying this ride while being afraid at the same time. I heard once that if you are not scared, it's not really courage. Until now, I have never sat down and planned out where I wanted to be in a year, in 5 years or in 10 years. I am surprised that I have not planned out my goals, being a bit of an overachiever, but I have always allowed God to steer me in the path on which He wanted me to venture. That has worked for me, because I could not have planned my life or career as well as it has gone. Do not get me wrong, I am so far from being a fly-by-the-seat-of-my-pants person; I do not like knee-jerk reactions, and I would rather be proactive than reactive. I just didn't want to sell myself short. I do not expect entrepreneurship to be any easier than when I worked on my doctorate or completed nursing school; nor, any decisions be any easier than my decision not to have shoulder surgery. Whatever I face on this continued journey, I will continue to FAITH IT until I MAKE IT!!!! I must warn you, the final chapter of my journey has not been written, so stay tuned.

Biography

Dr. Valerie Green is a dedicated wife, mother and child of God. She lives by doing the right thing even when no one is looking and when she does not receive any credit. She has a passion for quality improvement to deliver exceptional care to everyone.

Dr. Green is a healthcare accreditation, compliance, and quality consultant who partners with healthcare facilities to navigate the accreditation and regulatory compliance environment. She inspires, coaches and mentors new and experience health care professionals. Dr. Green has dedicated her entire career to creating high quality, reliable systems of care and developing the next generation of nurses and health care professionals. She specializes in empowering and developing others to excel in their careers and profession.

With over 18 years of experience, Dr. Green has an extensive background in Quality Management, Performance Improvement, and Utilization Management. Dr. Green's clinical experience expands to operating room, surgery clinic, house supervisor, and acute care. Now the CEO of Green Healthcare Group, Dr. Green works with healthcare organizations to attain and maintain high-quality, safe patient care and continuous compliance by identifying opportunities for improvement, implementing effective solutions, and educating staff.

Dr. Green obtained a Bachelor of Science in Nursing and Master of Science in Nursing from the University of Mississippi Medical Center and a Doctor in Nursing Practice from Grand Canyon University. She has Six Sigma Green and Lean Six Sigma certifications.

Dedication

I dedicate this chapter to my adult children - Davina, Kenneth, and Charlene. I acknowledge the family, friends, and mentors who inspired me in any way to start this business. I have a heartfelt thank you to Linda Heitel-Dozier, my first nursing mentor, and Michelle Rhodes, through whom I wrote my first book and this one.

~Diane

A Nightingale's Journey 2 Business

By Diane Ehrig, MSN MBA RN-BC

Introduction

Allow me to introduce myself. Besides my name and the degrees, you might not have any idea that I grew up in a home with an alcoholic mother and step-dad who were physically and emotionally abusive. I ran away from home at the age of 15 and went into a foster home until I turned 18. I became pregnant at 15 and gave birth to my oldest daughter 2 weeks before my 16th birthday. My foster mom was also emotionally and sometimes physically abusive to me. One of my earthly angels at the time was my foster mom's brother, whom I call Uncle Mickey. It was though his influence that I started going to church, got baptized, and joined the choir. Another earth angel was the Dean at my high school. I could always talk to him, and it wasn't necessarily about school.

I jumped at the opportunity to travel from Sacramento (hometown) to Los Angeles on a singing engagement with a very gifted musician, singer, and songwriter. Initially, I planned on returning to Sacramento, but things didn't work out that way. I married a man I met in Los Angeles, and we had a son together. My first husband was also an alcoholic. I moved out when our son was only a few months old.

I went to school for Medical Assistant and worked in that capacity for about 5 years. At an early age, I dreamt of becoming a nurse. About a year after that first marriage ended, I met a fellow who strongly encouraged me to start my nursing training, which I did.

That fellow and I were together for about 3 years. While I was in the Nursing Program, I left that guy.

The Twenty-Year Journey

A dear friend and I were attending a church together. The pastor wanted the two of us to sing at a concert he was having in 1983. One of the band members and I started dating, and we got married two years later. I failed one of my nursing courses in 1983, but chose not to re-enroll when the time came a year later. Instead, I started working as a bookkeeper. It was something I was good at doing. I kept taking bookkeeping and accounting courses, and earned my MBA in 1997.

My second divorce happened in 1998. Although I liked accounting, I never loved it. I was financially comfortable, yet my soul was yearning for what I loved.

Two Taps on My Shoulder

One of my employers sent all the employees on the retreat in Santa Barbara for a weekend. It was at that retreat that I completed a career profile based on your personality. It simply emphasized the fact that accounting was the absolute worst career choice for me! It was because I'm such a people person, and accounting is very isolated most of the time. That was the first tap on my shoulder. Not long after that, I dropped a friend off at her house after a day of shopping. She said that she had a vision of me working as a nurse and wearing all white. By then, nurses had stopped wearing solid white uniforms years before that. It was the second tap on my shoulder. My friend's vision was a lot more poignant when, a few years later, my nursing school uniforms were solid white!

In the early summer of 2000, I bumped into a friend of my second ex-husband at church. He and I started dating. We got engaged in December, 2001. In the spring of 2002, we talked about my dream to go back into nursing and become an RN. He initially encouraged me, and I applied to a local community college. This fellow and I got married in October 2002. I rejoiced when I got the acceptance letter from nursing school in 2003. However, my third husband was adamantly against it. I was so frustrated because he originally supported me going into nursing school, which is why I applied to the school in the first place. When he expressed that he wanted me to wait another year, I had a hard time with that decision. It had already been 20 years since I interrupted my dream of becoming a nurse, and I didn't want to wait another minute! I discussed this dilemma with a friend of mine who was a good listener. She strongly encouraged me to take the leap and accept the nursing school invitation. I decided to seize the opportunity and started my nursing program in September, 2003. I wasn't able to work during my first semester, and money was going to be tight, at least so I thought. I was so relieved when my father-in-law became my financial Angel. He significantly contributed on a monthly basis for six months, which supported my continuing the nursing program. Ironically, my husband was actually angry that his dad was financially supporting me.

Early 2005-Graduation

By early 2005, my husband and I were arguing nearly constantly. My grades started slipping, and I refused to let anything stop me from achieving my goal of becoming a nurse. I decided to leave him and move out. I was blessed with another earth angel, one of my classmates, who rented out one of her bedrooms to me. I'm so grateful that I was able to graduate on time in June 2005. I passed the RN licensure exam in September, 2005.

My First Job as an RN

I started working at Cedars Sinai Hospital in Los Angeles. I was working nights. I noticed that the classes we were required to attend were only scheduled during the daytime. It was a huge disruption to what was a normal sleeping pattern for me and my night shift coworkers. We experienced fatigue, grogginess, and other physical symptoms. My question was: why weren't any required classes scheduled at night when night shift nurses were normally awake?

A Peer Review Commentary

I started taking an online Bachelor of Science, Nursing program in 2006. My Cultural Nursing class required a term paper. I asked my former nurse manager to review it for me. When she completed her review, she commented that I should get that paper published! I was strongly encouraged to do so. That research paper was about some of the physical and emotional difficulties that night shift nurses faced as a result of attending required courses in the daytime.

The "All About Caring" Workshop

During this workshop, I completed an assignment that was pivotal. It was to write about something you were super passionate about, and imagine that you got to experience it. I wrote about implementing some education for the nurses that was scheduled on night shift, and the impact that it had on the nurses. I imagined that I got a letter from the president of Cedars-Sinai acknowledging me for a significant contribution to the nurses. While I was reading it to the other attendees at the class, I was literally in tears. Wow!!!

A Nightingale's Journey 2 Business

I discovered that almost all facility required nursing education was scheduled in the daytime. I started researching how many other facilities and nurses were experiencing the same thing. I became a Basic Life Support instructor, and began marketing myself to hold these classes at night. My first attempt was in late 2010. I had little to no support; I had no mentor; I hadn't developed any of my own courses yet, and I didn't know how to market my services. I was so discouraged about that, because I was getting so many positive comments from the night shift nurses themselves. However, it was the nursing leadership at those facilities who delayed or simply didn't respond to my communications to them.

Keep Swimming!

This business venture was going to be a massive undertaking. However, I knew that nurses who worked night shift needed and wanted classes scheduled at night! There were few and far between times where a night shift nurse could attend a class during the hours they were normally awake. While working on my Master's degree, I knew I wanted to expand on the research I had done during my Bachelor's program. I was inspired by my mentor's comment to get that research paper published. I had a lot of personal experience, as well as that of my peers which encouraged me to keep going. As part of my Master's Capstone thesis, I wanted to offer required classes at night and see how doing that impacted job satisfaction. When my night shift coworkers heard that I would be offering two classes at night, they jumped at the chance to become my participants! Although I didn't get paid for doing that, I learned some valuable lessons during that process. This work did get published on www.AllNurses.com. It's called "Night Shift Nursing Education and Effects on Job Satisfaction", published in December, 2013.

Speaking About Speaking

In early 2019, I completed a workshop for nurse authors offered by Michelle Greene Rhodes. I am excited to say that I wrote my first book while I was working with her. The book (chapter) you're reading now is my second book! Michelle is all aboutmentoring nursing entrepreneurship, becoming an author, and public speaking at workshops, conferences, and seminars. I am grateful to say that I have my first nursing education contracts where the training is all conducted at night. I also completed the Speaker Academy offered by Michelle Greene Rhodes.

It's important to remember that you're never alone. I know now that going it alone is why wasn't successful the first time around. It's important to have a plan, it's important to have a coach or mentor, and it's also important to have accountability to your plan. For me, it is also vital that I acknowledge my Lord and Savior Jesus Christ for His influence in my life. Throughout my life, He has sent me numerous Angels in human form to tap me on the shoulder, kick me in the butt (metaphorically), and pray for me. Michelle Greene Rhodes and her nurse entrepreneur tribe have done all of the above!

Many of the nurses with whom I have spoken over the years have mentioned that they have an idea of how to do things better at their jobs. Some have invented products or come up with processes that save time and lead to improved patient outcomes. Others have written books, like the one you're reading, talking about how they got started in business. I highly recommend hiring a business coach to support you with identifying what you want to do, who you want to serve, who will pay for it, and how much you might get paid.

You have a book in you! Write the book! Write your vision! Invest in a coach like Michelle who will guide you to achieving your business development dreams. I am so grateful to be part of this 30-author collaboration project. Life is NOW! I'm so grateful that I connected with her, and that I invested in myself to get the coaching which resulted in my previous book and this book. Working with Michelle, I also got very clear on my target market, and who would pay for those nighttime nursing education courses. I was blessed to also get access to the other authors who contributed to this book, and other amazing nurse entrepreneurs. These amazing nurses are all now part of my tribe. We encourage each other, hold each other accountable, refer business to each other, and give one another feedback.

My first book is called A Nightingale's Journey, and is available on Amazon and Kindle. My website is www.NightNurse.Academy. Write the book, start the business, make an impact!

Biography

Diane Ehrig is an RN who has been licensed since 2005. She obtained a Master of Science, Nursing Education, and an MBA. Diane has three adult children and lives in the greater Los Angeles area.

She is a speaker, singer, and a published poet.

She is the CEO of Nightnurse Academy.

Connect with her at www.Nightnurse.Academy

Dedication

Dedicated to all the amazing people who positively impacted my life prayed and empowered me for greater. Keep inspiring and standing in the gap for others to live in their truth and purpose.

There is no ME without WE!

To my amazing children, Erica, Terrian, and Cornelius, I'm deeply grateful for your love and patient as we GROW and GLOW together!

To my Momma, Janice, thank you for your unwavering support and prayers. You are my wind!

To my sisters Andrea and Felicia, who is no longer with me, contributed so much to my success. Thank you!

~Kecia

Tending to the Spark: The Power of Dreaming Big

By Kecia Hayslett, RN

I never felt like I had permission to truly dream big. In my experience, big dreams were reserved for other people - people with more luxuries and less responsibilities. For me in my life, it seemed impractical to spend time fantasizing about an elaborate future when what I needed to worry about were the more tangible and pressing issues right in front of me. I needed to keep things modest, worry about doing my job well and maintaining it so that I could provide for my family. Anything beyond working, taking care of my patients and supporting my family were not important enough to spend my already limited time on.

Nevertheless, I always had an entrepreneurial spark buried somewhere inside of me. This spark turned to a burning flame after an enlightening interaction I had with a patient of mine. She was in her late thirties or early forties when I met her, and had just had a baby less than a year earlier. I was assigned as her nurse for the day on the afternoon that she was being diagnosed with cancer. She was sobbing when I saw her for the first time and could hardly catch her breath. The only intelligible words that she could manage in between her sobs was, "what about my daughter," which she repeated over and over.

I sat down beside her and in a calm but sturdy voice said, "Can I ask you a question?" She nodded. I looked at her and said, "The decision we make today will say a lot about how you live your life going forward so my question is this: What do you want to see happen?" To this day, I am not sure what compelled me to ask this as there was a part of me that felt it was too much, too big of a question to ask, but I asked it anyway. I wanted her answer because I felt like whatever she said would help me and the entire team provide her with better care.

The silence that followed seemed to last forever; it ballooned outward into the room and it seemed like everyone and everything in the space was holding its breath. Finally she answered. She said, "I just want to be with my baby." She had just gotten a divorce letter in the mail and in it were threats that her daughter would be taken away from her. Hearing about her prognosis on top of this already detrimental news was too much for her to handle, and it didn't seem to her that being sick would make her case of being with her daughter any stronger.

I took this all in and said, "Okay, I can't make any promises. I don't have a magic ball, and nothing will happen by tomorrow, but if you work with us, we'll work with you. We'll try to work toward a future that includes you and your daughter."

That was the beginning of five cycles of chemotherapy for her. The cancer was a powerful one, and she was physically weak. By the fifth cycle, she was extremely sick. I arrived at work one day and was walking down the hallway where her room was when something told me to turn around and go back the other way. I didn't question the voice and simply turned around. I found her lying in bed. She couldn't talk, and was just staring into space in distress. I looked at her and held her gaze. I decided to simply stay with her in that moment. Suddenly, she started to code. I was still looking at her and as the staff rushed into the room, I said, "You shall live and not die." Shortly after I uttered those words to her, the staff whisked her away.

Later that week, she was readmitted to the floor, and I went to her room to check on her. She was still weak and sick, but looked much better than when I had last seen her. She pulled me aside and said as if it was the most urgent thing, "You have no idea, but you saved my life. I couldn't speak, but I could hear. When you said that I'd live, I knew I could hang on."

Her words blew me away. I couldn't believe that something so simple as saying a few words could mean the difference between life and death. I felt so empowered and full of service, and that's when I knew that I wanted do more like this, but I wanted to do it for myself as part of my own business. What was only a small urge before now became a full-blown burning desire within me. I now understood the power of dreaming big. I had always equated big dreams with self-gratification. It had almost seemed selfish to want and work toward big things for myself. But this experience showed me that dreaming big wasn't about just me. When you give yourself permission to dream big, you allow your influence to grow in the world, you elevate your purpose to a place where it begins to affect others for the better, and you make a difference for many people. When I step into my true purpose, I can live a life in which others benefit too because we don't live in a vacuum. It is only when I am living my best, true life that I can be of most service to others. When we don't dream and instead resign ourselves to living lives based on obligation and duty, we are depriving the world and everyone in it of our true gifts and talents. I had never before seen my dreams in this light before, and I was finally ready to take action.

I didn't know business at all, but I knew that I could help others. That's where I began. My first real business was a Home Care Agency that I started while still maintaining my job at the VA hospital. Because I was so excited to get started so that I could have this affect on other people, I didn't do much planning. I truly found myself standing at a cliff, and I jumped without even looking at what I was jumping into.

I don't regret taking the leap, but I've learned a lot during the process. For those of you, like me, who find yourselves in jobs that pay the bills and are hesitant to dream big, I would recommend that you keep those dreams alive and well. Keep your day job for the moment and really plan your approach to entrepreneurship. The job that you are currently working has value, and part of that value is fueling your entrepreneurial endeavor. Be grateful to it for what it is. There is no need to distort its important in your life. Usually, we see our jobs in one of two ways. Either it is the bane of our existence, and we are resentful, either consciously or unconsciously, that we are obligated to go there every day sacrificing our happiness; or we are so grateful for the job that we give it more importance than it deserves. We decide that we owe everything to the job and work tirelessly to do well and move up. When we become too reliant on the job, we can be blindsided when changes happen. In these instances a layoff or a role change can sabotage our entire self worth.

The healthy mentality is to understand that a job is ephemeral. It can be taken from us at any moment and is out of our control, but we don't have to be in that position forever. During the times when we are working, and the money and the hours are good or even average, we have something providing us with money and experience, that can help us make that leap into entrepreneurship. We've got respect for the job, but we're not reliant on it. We know that true job security comes from inside and what we can do. And we can make the most of it offers us when it gives us something. And then when we are good and ready, we can step away on our own terms.

The journey of transition is another thing I learned. It is vital to define, in no uncertain terms, what the destination looks like. Vague ideas about owning your own business won't cut it. Write down what you want your business to look like. Will you have employees? Is there a certain income that you need in order feel secure? Is there another threshold that would mean you are where you want to be? As best as you can, envision what your life will actually look like when you are at your at your destination. You can have a few different tiers. There will be a certain point in your business when you know you can quit your day job and be okay. There will be another if you want to grow your business to a particular size. The most important thing though is to establish some landmarks for yourself so you know when you get to your destination.

It's not unlike setting a destination in your GPS. The only way to know when you get to your destination is to type a location in and start driving. If you start driving without doing this, you won't have any idea when to park the car.

Once you're on your path, it's important to stay productive. The easiest part of entrepreneurship is starting a business. The hard part is actually keeping it running. Things come up, and life happens while you're building a business. Problems don't just wait for you to be ready to solve them; they show unexpectedly all the time. This happened to me for sure. After all, I was still a single mom as I was building my business, and life was relentless. There was always something new to deal with.

I hadn't planned a thing, so I was constantly dealing with things like navigating insurance, paying rent, and acquiring supplies. There was a point when it felt like serving the clients was getting lost amidst everything else that was going on around me and required my attention. There was always something that needed to be done, and it's important to prioritize and get all of these things done. Ignoring issues or concerns doesn't make them disappear. They'll resurface eventually, and most likely as much bigger problems. It's helpful to figure out an organizational system that works for you, and then stick to it. Neglecting things for too long will only cause problems.

It's also important to find a mentor in your field that is at least a few steps ahead of you on the path to entrepreneurship. There are constant challenges surfacing every day, and when you are building something of your own, it can be very lonely. Now you're finally your own boss, but that means you are the only making the decisions, bearing the consequences of those decisions and celebrating the victories. Having a mentor means having someone to share the solitary trials and tribulations with. It means getting feedback and advice. And it means averting problems that they've already experienced and solved. Having a mentor is invaluable to anyone attempting to start a business.

After hearing all of this, it might sound like entrepreneurship is more trouble than its worth…and it is…if you choose something that is not meaningful for you. Whatever avenue you pursue on your entrepreneurial journey, it must be something you are passionate about. You are going to invest a lot of blood, sweat and tears into whatever you do, so the trick is to find something that truly lights you up. I knew that I wanted to recreate that powerful patient interaction all those years ago, so I knew the work I was putting into my business was going to be worth it. But if I didn't have that drive, it would be no different than working a regular job for someone else.

There will be days when you are working a day job and then will have to put hours into your own business. Other responsibilities will tug at you. And tough decisions abound. It might mean saying, "no" to hanging out with your friends at the wine bar after work or staying up extra late so that you can see your child's baseball game and work on your business. None of this is easy to do. What's easy is to brush off your dream and say you'll worry about it tomorrow. But tomorrows add up fast. The only way to ensure a better tomorrow for yourself is to put in the work in the present. The only way to maintain your effort and level of sacrifice is to truly love what you're working at.

Entrepreneurship is not for everyone, but if you have something calling you or if there is a dream that you've been dreaming and have been scared to go after it, follow it. Only you know what you were brought to this Earth to do, and it would be tragic if you pushed that away because somewhere along the way you learned that dreaming big was a dangerous game, something not meant for you, and best left to other people.

If you have a dream, do whatever you need to do to work toward fulfilling that dream. There is no dream that is too big. And dreams don't just serve the person dreaming them. Big dreams make the world a better place for all of us. That's we gain the power to really help others and touch lives in ways that matter. The worst thing that can happen when you dream big is that you fail; but every failure gets you closer to success. And if you can do something once, you can do it again.

I once helped a woman with just my words, and in return she helped me to go after my dream. Because of her, I will get to help others like her in my own business. Because of her, I jumped at the chance to find joy and improve my life, but that is not the end of the road. When I am living my true purpose and when my joy is overflowing, it is landing on everyone around me. When one person dreams big, everyone benefits. Dream big, make plans and be who you are meant to be. It's worth it.

Let's connect on www.nurseentrepreneurmastery.com Facebook group. It's a lively and inspiring community for nurses and about nurses.

Biography

Kecia Hayslett is Chief Manager and Master Coach of Soulful Nurse consulting. Here she coaches High Achieving Nurses on how to package their knowledge and experience so that they can make a quantum leap toward their passion.

She has built her brand on the foundation of uncovering one's true purpose. She uses her platform to educate and empower individuals who wish to start their own businesses. She is also a provocative thought leader and personal growth teacher who prides herself on empowering women with an entrepreneurial spirit and a desire to do more with their lives.

Kecia is no stranger to adversity. She picked herself up after having been divorced and homeless with three children in her early twenties. Through her faith in Jesus Christ and her own perseverance, she graduated high school, earned her LPN certification and studied nursing at The College of St. Catherine University where she graduated with an RN degree in 2004. She worked part-time as an LPN for a home health care business and full-time as an RN for the VA Hospital prior to opening her first business, Arms of Compassion Home Health Care in 2014.

She spends her free time volunteering around the world where she helps with medical missions in developing countries. She is also a noted international speaker, author, Certified Health Career Coordinator and Nurse Aide School Coach. Audiences respond to her engaging speaking style, as she is known for delivering compelling messages with compassion, humor and truth. Everything she does, she does from a space of authenticity and love, and she is relentless about sharing this authentic love and support with as many people as she can.

Dedication

"It takes courage to live your dreams." @RN2CEO

I am so grateful and thankful that I have the opportunity to share my story with other amazing nurses. I hope that you the reader will be inspired and encouraged to do the same.

Regards,

Sharon

At the Right Time

By Sharon Addison, RN

We sometimes have that one moment in time when we make a decision to move ahead or stay in the same places and spaces. It's that moment when you know that if you don't make a decision now, you will have missed the opportunity to reach your goals. It's not that you won't ever achieve your goals, it's just that the timing is off. Life goes on. New challenges arise and you continue to make your mark during the seasons of your life. Some people get an opportunity for second chances, while others may allow fear to drain them of their creativity and deflate their courage. Some will use their children or circumstances to not pursue their dreams or even invest their time in learning something new. I am mindful of those who may need someone to stand in the gap and hold the space for them. Some may just be at a place where all they are able to do is listen to an audio, read a book or sit in a seminar. We all had to start some place. It takes courage to follow your dreams and be willing to say you're taking the entrepreneurial leap AT THE RIGHT TIME.

Think of a moment that you took that leap into entrepreneurship. Can you remember the moment of uncertainty mixed with excitement, trepidation and "WHAT THE HECK am I going to do when it comes to paying the bills" kind of emotions? Some will tell you they jumped into entrepreneur after getting fired from a job that no longer liked them and they no longer liked. Many entrepreneurs will take the leap, while others will make a plan; some will continue to wait until everything is lined up in their favor.

Unfortunately, the latter seems to be the least realistic. The question I am asked the most is when did I know that it was the right time to say bon voyage and sail off into the sunset from my job? As for me, it has been a process of signs, nudges and support from like-minded progressive individuals who believe in the possibility to live a life that serves them and the world. We also have those who inspire us to be our greater selves. It may be a parent, a teacher or mentor. Start to pay attention to comments and conversations. Words spoken can shape the reality of your future. Evaluate your conversations and be intentional about how and who you share your dreams with. Be willing to do the work surrounding your success in life and business.

While reading these words, know that I hold the space for your dreams and the lives you will touch with your genius, while making this world a much better place. In the meantime, hold the vision of the legacy you will want to create as you continue to thrive in the endless possibilities of being a successful entrepreneur. If you have not yet experienced your pivotal moment, know that it's right around the corner. It's the moment that will test your tenacity to either go forward or stand still.

My pivotal moment came from a family member who knew it was time my siblings and I took the entrepreneurial leap. She held the space for me to be able to wrap my head around the possibility of living the life I deserve. She also nudged me out of my comfort zone towards the journey of discovering a higher version of myself.

It all started when I received an invitation to go to Jamaica for a few days and hang out with my mom, who was visiting relatives and who had promised me that she would have lunch with me at the hotel of my choice. So, I decided to spend a few days with her and see my aunt and other relatives.

I got on a plane heading to Jamaica on a Tuesday to return back on a Friday. I didn't feel this task needed more time. I just knew it was going to be super special, and indeed it was. The memory of spending an afternoon on the hotel balcony, overlooking the Caribbean Sea, having lunch with my mom and aunt, will forever be etched in my memory. It was a beautiful, clear day and the ocean was calm. The waves gently rushed to the shore and the sounds became the backdrop to the words my aunt shared with me.

We had one of the most heartfelt conversations that would change the trajectory of my life and how I showed up in how I serve others. "It's time your brothers and sisters and you have your own businesses. You are all talented enough to even go into businesses together. Your sister, niece, cousin and you are all nurses. You all have enough education, knowledge and experience to start your very own business. It's time. You've all served others well, but I know it's time to build a legacy. If anyone can do it, I know that you can."

Well, this conversation had me putting my hot spicy jerk chicken back on my plate. This was no normal conversation. This was someone who, when she speaks, always speaks into the lives of my siblings and me. I like to say that she dreamt our future. It took me back to the time when I worked for a few major airlines. She somehow understood that I loved to talk and would go the extra mile to make people feel comfortable. Aunty was clear that I loved traveling, seeing the world and having new experiences.

Up to this point, I had been on a quest to find my purpose. I invested in self-development courses, walked on hot coals and even travelled as far as Soweto, South Africa to serve others. Being in Johannesburg and Cape Town South Africa was life changing. It was an amazing experience that got me connected with the motherland. I've had reservations of owning a brick and mortar. I always knew that no four walls could contain me. I wanted to be the philanthropist and health care advocate that could make a difference in this world. I shared my desires and concerns with my aunt, and she understood. Aunty told me that it takes money to be able to have more impact and still have my flexibility. "You always loved to be up and down flying - but first, make sure you have something solid. You will even be in a better position to help others. So, baby Shar Shar (that was her nickname for me), when you go back to the United States, get in motion because it's time."

I spent the next few days being still. Early morning swims, walks on the beach and embracing the idea that I was called to do more. I started to step into the dream that my aunt so eloquently painted with her words. I started to see myself as she saw me. Open enough to accept the challenge and bold enough to fulfill the dream. Living life with no regrets. Allowing what is and anticipate with grace what is to come.

My personal philosophy, first, is that I believe it is possible. Second, I see the vision - along with the support - needed to experience it all. I then step into the dream and live it before it even exists. To me, the second time around is the even sweeter. This is what keeps me grounded when it comes to setting goals and maintaining the momentum. I, too, knew that it was time to re-evaluate how I showed up as a parent and re-evaluate some relationships. This would take a whole mindset shift, and I knew that the time was now.

My time in Jamaica had me reflecting on my showing up for our daughters. The job of their dad and I was to make sure that they became productive citizens and decent human beings. Yes, we made sure they were given the opportunity to be their best. I look back with gratitude, grateful for the seasons, and shed a few tears because it was time to allow them to fly. I am glad they were my why and not my why I can't.

I look back at that time in Jamaica with so much love and extreme gratitude and the realization that it was a changing of the guards. It was time my siblings and I leave the nest and step into the world of being entrepreneurs. Each person's journey is unique and will take different routes, but we will all end up at a place called destiny.

After returning to the states, I hired myself a business coach and decided to allow myself to be supported to be that change agent. I no longer worried about holding on to a position that I had obviously outgrown. Even my co-workers were very much aware of this. We'd had a few conversations about the fact that I was a part-time employee with a long-term entrepreneurial mindset. One such conversation with a particular nurse still rings true to date. She said I should go and write my books, speak, preach, travel and be in the places and spaces where my gifting could and would touch lives in different parts of the world. I took her advice and have not looked back since.

A downsizing of my department gave me the option to walk away with no regrets. There was no desire to stay or be transferred elsewhere. This to me was an easy way out of having to quit. I know I may not be the first to have had this particular dilemma. We sometimes stay in spaces and places that stifle our creativity and drain our courage. We sometimes come up with excuses that, because of our children and other obligations, we can't do it. How about having them be the reason why you do it and how to make it all work.

For those of you reading this, I am honored to hold the space for your dreams and the life you deserve. There are many who came before us and blazed trails that opened up a path for us to make our mark. We stand on the shoulders of those who came before us. They actually dreamt our lives for us. They thought and spoke into the future. Circumstances may have been different for them, but this time around, the ball is in our court. This story is as much about you as it is about me. Our dreams and desires are no different. We all want good health, love, peace, joy and prosperity in our lives. We want to treat our neighbors as we want to be treated - with love, respect and yes, the human touch in all we do. If you agree with me, then we understand each other.

I know for sure that I am standing on the shoulders of those who came before me. My destiny is intertwined with the dreams and desires of those who stood on this planet before me. From the bedside to the boardroom, to classrooms and stages, we carry the essence and fingerprint on our legacy of our dream keepers. It is up to us to allow ourselves to be supported and carry the torch. We also must allow ourselves to identify the individuals who can help make the dream a reality. We must also keep in mind that the dreams and desires we have require we share our gifts without reservations or fear of losing it all. After all, there is more to gain, expanding the legacy of the dream keepers who came before us.

In conclusion, I took the next six months to complete a prestigious leadership program, made peace with the decisions of my daughters (regarding their career choices) and strengthened my relationships with family and loved ones. Eighteen months to the exact date, I launched my HealthCare and Wellness Boutique style agency. I also expanded my coaching business and embarked on My Ultimate TRIP to Success US Tour™. I wrote down my vision and posted it in plain sight so that each morning, when I looked at It, I ran the play through my mind, reinforcing that it's our duty to respectfully embrace what is and forever shall be. I now teach my clients to do the same.

Being an entrepreneur takes guts, and it's exciting with many twists and turns. I've found that you will flourish more in a sandbox with other entrepreneurs who are ready to play full out. Making a decision to want more will make room for abundance to flow in all areas of your life. When you invest your time, energy and resources to something meaningful, you will eventually show up as a better version of yourself. Know that you are worthy of your dreams and the lives you will touch along the way.

Make bold decisions and align your success with other successful people. Have an accountability partner and a few coaches to support your dreams. Be willing to surround yourself with people who are in a space to create and add value to those who support your products and services. Always put people first and remember to celebrate your wins. Sometimes it may take a little longer to get to your original target, but be willing to re-evaluate, change course if you must but never give up. Entrepreneurship takes discipline, team building and being clear on your personal vision and mission. Leadership skills are essential in leading a successful business. Be willing to know as much of your business as possible and be willing to scale at the right time.

No one can say for sure when the right time will be. Get ready to gain clarity around your plan. Be willing to re-evaluate and listen to good sound advice. Develop the discipline that it will need to take you closer to your ultimate goal. Let your why be your driving force. Let the work that you do have meaning and purpose. What you desire must have an impact to make this world a much better place. You will find that doing business will become more manageable when you set strong personal and professional goals. Continue to review the plan for your business, and be willing to invest in the resources that will support your growth.

One of my life lessons learned was not celebrating out loud the accomplishments of the company that was birthed out of my aunt holding the space for me. I've learned to truly celebrate wins no matter how small or great they may be. My aunt Eunice single handedly held the space for her daughter, her two granddaughters, my siblings and other relatives. I encourage you to show up more boldly. Know that you are supported and that there are so many who really want to see you win.

Biography

Sharon Addison, RN, also known as @RN2CEO is the founder of the Caribbean & Global Women of Power Summit, an annual live event that empowers and unite women across the world. She is also the founder of **Your Awesome Power Within** ® Academy which offers personal and professional development programs and resources.

Known as "Your Awesome Power Within coach, she works with a select group of faith based professional women who are business owners and have a heart for humanitarian and philanthropic work. Her mission is to inspire professional women to lead extraordinary, rewarding and fulfilling lives. She does this through her speaking, coaching, workshops and empowerment retreats.

Addison is a best-selling author and the host of the award winning SpotlightOnGospel.org radio show and visionary of the virtual Spotlight on Prayer ministry. An avid traveler, she has travelled as far as South Africa, Central America and the Caribbean on good will and medical missions.

She resides in New Jersey with her family and is the current

Executive Administrator of their boutique style health care and wellness company

IG: @RN2CEO
FB @ RN2CEO
Twitter: @RN2CEO
LinkedIn @AddisonMedia
WEB: AddisonMediaGroup.com

Dedication

This book is Dedicated to My Mother, Thelma Rogers.

All My life I remember you putting me in Environments and Auxiliaries That Enhanced my Life and for that I am Eternally Grateful.

I exist because of YOU!

Thank you for your Tireless Sacrifice to Your Children!

"Ain't No Momma Like The One I Got"

Making A Definite Difference

By LaTonya Mims, CRNA

Ever wonder how you get to where you are and what milestones lead to who you have become? What pinnacle events happened in life to make you think and behave as you do? As an adult, I have this overwhelming desire or call to help others in a special way. No matter how I try to suppress it, it remains there, so I decided to trace some of my steps to find out when this began.

Since Elementary school I have been an academic scholar; however, I had this one big issue…I talked a lot. And guess what, it was frowned upon in class by my teachers. I always seemed to want to "help/boss" my classmates. My teacher's favorite report to my mother was "she is so smart but talks too much." So of course I received many "timeout" moments for these infractions. Little did I know that my mouth would be used to engage and ignite women throughout my life's journey. This is one of the reasons I encourage parents to explore and cultivate their child gifts and talents because some negatives can be molded into positives over time. Today I'm very grateful for the opportunity to be able to use my voice to make a definite difference.

In high school I continued to excel. I received significant Honors, Accolades, and Awards such a Louisiana Girl State, Caddo Parish Student of the Year, scholarships totaling over $300,000 including West Point Academy, Valedictorian, and so much more. While theses honors were great, it was around those years I decided I wanted to live a life that counts in a memorable way. I wanted my Thumbprint to be recognized in a magnificent way. Above everything, I wanted my Life to Matter Significantly, so I began connecting with people I thought were exemplary. One of my earliest mentors invited me to Keynote speaker at her Women Empowerment event. She constantly told me "You are In Training for Reigning" and I just trusted her tutelage. It was in preparation for this event I coined the phrase "It's Time to Make a Definite Difference" which was over 25 years ago as I write this. After that, those words seem to stick with me and it became my mantra. I can hear the words ringing in my ears and realized these very words would govern how I lived aspects of my life. Before long I was being called "A Definite Difference Maker" by family, friends, and coworkers. I went on to name my scholarship "The Making A Definite Difference Scholarship Award".

As a young PICU nurse, I was always optimistic, caring, and open to new adventure. I enjoyed the challenges of my job as I volunteered to float to other units in the hospital. There was one particular assignment that would change my life in a remarkable way forever. On December 23rd, 1998 I was the admitting nurse for three years old boy who was basically agitate, inconsolable, and febrile. He was admitted to the PICU for IV sedation and monitoring which couldn't be done safely on the pediatric floor. I was his admitting nurse right before my &PM shift change would occur. Little did I know, I would report to my 7AM shift the next morning and his skin had begun to totally sluff off his body and he was paralyzed and intubated in less than 12 hours. It was something about that little boy that captured my heart. Not only was I his nurses every day I worked, but me and my family and church family began to visit him regularly. He was so sick that his mother asked me to be his guardian mother because she couldn't be there. Of course, I eagerly accepted and began loving on him even the more. I can't tell you how many times the Chaplain came to pray with us because "he might not make it through the night". He had the most outstanding pediatric intensive on this side of heaven and the entire PICU team was Relentless in his care. We continued to release our faith and believe God for Miraculous healing daily for his life. ShaRon stayed with us from December 1998 to August 1999. The entirety of events could not be told in this chapter, but Trust me when I tell you God is a Miracle Worker. My amazing mother became ShaRon primary caretaker in the hospital so I could continue to work and support our family. The expected outcomes projected by some doctors were dismal at best such as he would be slightly mentally retarded after suffering a stroke and seizure. He might not walk properly and needed to be enrolled in a "special" school. ShaRon was discharged from the hospital with his mother and I visited him daily. After about 2 weeks, his mother made the tough decision to give me guardianship him. Fast forward 21 years, Sharon played little league baseball although he is legally blind, he graduated from private Christian high school, has attained an Associate's Degree in General Studies, an Associate's Degree in Health and Human Services, and currently pursuing his Bachelor's degree in Social Work. I am so grateful for the opportunity to encounter and help navigate this young man's journey.

I'm grateful to say that I have committed to a life dedicated to serving and making an impact in lives of those I encounter. I started this work of ministry, mission, and serving at such a young age.... way before there was a Facebook, Twitter, LinkedIn, Snapchat, or Instagram. I remember being a volunteer in high school to help disabled and autistic kids in my school. Looking back even further, when I was in elementary and Junior High School, my mother would take me to North Louisiana Rehab with BellSouth Volunteers Pioneers of America once a month to serve by feeding and play therapy for the resident in the facility. I know those early years of selfless service helped me to into the woman I have become. I'm especially grateful to God for the ability to come into relation, Serve, and Connect with thousands of nurses and other healthcare professionals through social media.

Inquisitive as I was growing up in nursing, one day I received a patient from the OR but I was captivated by one particular person and how she commanded the room. She was giving report and obviously in charge of the patient transfer from the OR to PICU. I overheard her say "I'm Denise the Nurse Anesthetist". I had never met a Nurse Anesthetist but read about the profession my senior year in nursing school. I went over and introduced myself to her. She obliged me by answering all my pressing or uncertain questions. She told me the admission process at her school, Texas Wesleyan, and gave me the office number and secretary name to contact. I was so overwhelmed in that moment but I went over to the computer to look at the school website. Then I immediately called the school to request a paper application because this was before the days of online applications. I did exactly what she advised for my application process. I believe in not reinventing the wheel if someone is successful in what you desire to accomplish. She was the definite difference maker I needed at that time in my career. I applied to her school, interviewed there, and received my acceptance letter 9 days later in February 2000. I was flabbergasted because I was told "no one gets in anesthesia school" on the first attempt and in that moment my son was back in the PICU and now I have a new hurdle to cross. And to my amazement, he was discharged home and ready to start kindergarten in Fort Worth as I started my first semester in nurse anesthesia school that August. So now, I tell everyone who asks "is CRNA School hard?"... My response is always, "If one person has accomplished it, that proves it can be done and is possible for you!" If you think you can, you can! If you think you can't the opposite is also true.

Now I passionately serve in many arenas in the field of nurse anesthesia to help groom other students and nurses who are interested in the field of anesthesia. I allow nurses to shadow me at my job to see what I really do. This allows them to ask questions, explore possibilities, and make an intelligent informed decision based on relative insights and information. One powerful motto I truly believe is Exposure Expands Expectations Everytime. I've have guided several nursing students and nurses on their nurse anesthesia journey and help them get great jobs. I must say it is Extremely Rewarding.

I strive to live a life of relationships that cultivates Growth, Service, Great Experiences, and Contribution. I want to look back on my life and celebrate the Impact I have made in the lives of others. Selfishness is an enemy to any Definite Difference Maker end game. I look for ways to be Resourceful and provide Assistance to others. I've always been fueled to do and have more. I believe the more you know, the more people you can help. I wanted All My

Friends to Win! As a nursing student, I insisted my brother's then ex-girlfriend not quit college and come to Grambling State University with me and start over. She did just that and became Miss Grambling 2000 and graduated from college and is an Entrepreneur. I remember at 23 rallying two of my closest friends to go back to graduate school with me because we could set trends for those coming behind us. Now two of us are Certified Registered Nurse Anesthetists (CRNA) and one A Pediatric Nurse Practitioner and we are now pushing our children in the same manner.

As an S.I.S.T.E.R.S. International Inc. Board member for the past 19 years, I've been blessed with the opportunity to empower, inform, and bring wholeness to girls and women. Serving this organization faithfully has allowed me to support women coping with Emotional, Physical, and Spiritual challenges. Through S.I.S.T.E.R.S. International Inc. I was afforded the opportunity to serve and minister to People in South Africa in a powerful way.

For the last two years, I also am actively involved in Restoration Crisis Center Therapeutic Home which provide safe place for young ladies to refocus, regroup, and recharged so they can be restored. I absolutely love being a role model of what is possible for young ladies. I've always understood the need to mentor, tutor, and coach others as a way to 'bridge the gap" to what is possible in life. I believe every one of us have a Gift that is on the Inside of us that World Need.

Through the power of visualization, I would see myself make Huge Impacts on People.

Characteristics of a Definite Difference Maker

1. Servant Heart
2. Love and Compassionate
3. Contagious Passion and Energy
4. Empathize with Others
5. Purposeful Intent
6. Believe in Power of Change
7. Want to make Impactful Contribution
8. Optimistic for A Better Future
9. Legacy Oriented
10. Vision Driven

How to Begin Making A Definite Difference Maker

1. Live a life focused on People not Money
2. Live a life Worthy of Duplicating
3. Live While You're Living
4. Tap into Purpose outside your Job
5. Start with One
6. Don't delay another Minute

Living a Life of Significance is the greatest call I believe One can Achieve. Making a Definite Difference Make Energizes My Heart and Soul. The positive affects made on one person allows them to impact the life of another which creates a Legacy of Positive Change which can't be underscored. When this happens, long after I am gone, the Footprints I made in the Sands will continue to make its Mark. It's Time for You to Make a Definite Difference!

Biography

As an International Speaker, LaTonya has touched the lives of many through service, inspiration, engagement, and empowerment.

LaTonya is a native of Louisiana, but her professional career sends her on many travel assignments. As a Certified Registered Nurse Anesthetist for 16 years, she is afforded the opportunity to connect with her patients in a unique way. LaTonya has created a lifestyle brand as a Queen Influencer, who understands that her purpose is to intentionally make a difference in the lives of others. She is energized to serve and volunteer her time and talent to help others reach their maximum success potential in life. She is affectionately known as the "Queens Queen" by friends and colleagues. LaTonya uses her influence as a Confidence Curator, an Advanced Practice Nurse Consultant, a Health and Wellness Enthusiast, an International Speaker and as an Author, to Ignite a Fire in their lives of others!

LaTonya serves in many teaching and training roles within ministry to Mankind. She is also a Board Member of SISTERS International, Inc., where she has served for over 19 years with compassion for women and children from all walks of life, who are in crisis situations. She desires to ignite the God given potentials inside them through mentorship.

LaTonya graduated from Grambling State University in 1995 with her Bachelor of Science in Nursing. She received a Master's in Nurse Anesthesia from Texas Wesleyan University School of Anesthesia in 2003. Currently, she is a Certified Registered Nurse Anesthetist who works independently in Texas and Louisiana. Her drive and determination keeps her striving to reach the next level in her professional career path as she pursue her Doctorate in Nursing Practice. She has served on the National Board of Professional Nursing Organization.

LaTonya is the mother of one son and 9 Amazing Guardian Children.

A passion of LaTonya's is helping children grow into their full potential Scanned with CamScanner academically, which she takes very seriously. Her strong belief and love in their continued educational experience prompted her to start the Making A Definite Difference Scholarship, that awards deserving high school students who excel academically, to pursue their life and career goals.

You can stay connected with LaTonya on multiple social media platforms:

Facebook: @LaTonya Mims CRNA
Facebook: @Queens Empowerment Academy

Instagram: @fitgasgirl
Instagram: @thequeensempowerment

Twitter: @latonyamims

SnapChat: @fitgasgirl

Dedication

I thank God for another opportunity to share my personal and professional journey in hopes to encourage and inspire woman across the globe. To my parents and siblings who continuously encourage and pray for my success as I lay my flowers on my journey of entrepreneurship. To my immediate family the true unsung heroes who allow me to share my time, space and expertise with others. You all are truly the real MVPs. Thank you for allowing me to be a legacy with you all. Always remember, now thanks be unto God, which always causeth us to triumph in Christ, and maketh manifest the savour of his knowledge by us in every place Cor. 2:14.

Love your Daughter, Wife, and Mom

~ Vikki

A Journey on an Untrodden Path - A Nurse's Story

By Victoria Y. Buggs MPH, RN

Hey everyone, I am here with exciting news to share about my journey as a Nursepreneur. Since my last book *The Good, the Bad, the Victory: Threefold Reflections*, where I wrote about some phases in my personal life and business career that made me dig deep within myself to remain resilient and relevant, I have secured a spot in the marketplace and entrepreneurship. My journey has not been all peaches and cream; however, I would not change it for all the tea in China. One thing that I've learned is never to lose sight of your goals, dreams, and aspirations. Networking and collaborating with other entrepreneurs has been a huge factor in my recent success, and I can't wait to dive in to share some valuable nuggets with you. My prayer for everyone seeking to become an entrepreneur is that this book would be inspiring and uplifting to you. I believe that my business is a ministry that touches the hearts of people, changing their lives for the better. While reading this book, I hope that you would pick up the flowers that I have laid on my path and encase them in the most solid vase within your hearts and mind. Please use these nuggets as you venture on your journey to entrepreneurship.

A Sheep in Wolves Clothing

Back in 2016, I met a woman at a home investment seminar, and we kicked off pretty good. She informed me that she was very vast at entrepreneurship and small businesses, and she had a wealth of knowledge on proposals and contracts with the local and state government. We discussed how we could connect and how to get my business off the ground and running. Together, we drafted a business development plan for which I paid, and a signed a contract of services. She seemed very helpful and very intense and never showed that she had any ill intentions. Then, she offered me a position or, rather, a seat at the table – it was a significant contract with the government. Yet again, having little knowledge in the contract field, I asked her for her help, and she provided me with information. We involved several people as we worked on the contract and finally submitted a contract proposal. Right after this, I received an invoice for $3200 for services that I never requested or had rendered. Neither did I sign a contract for services.

On the journey of entrepreneurship, you would quickly find out who is for you and who is against you and who has an agenda for you and your business. I learned that this lady had no real intentions of good for me or my business and that when she saw that I had a couple of business certifications, she took advantage of me. I allowed it, I opened the door and let her in so she could take advantage of everything that I possessed, and she charged me for it. During your entrepreneurship journey, know those who labor among you and know who is in your circle. Do background checks on the individuals that you solicit support from, check their testimonies and check their referrals. I didn't have any information on this lady; all I knew was that she knew people and she introduced me to people, but she was a scam. Because of that situation, I began to be very watchful of who I trusted with my business, I began to treat my business as my baby. I have three children, and I would protect them with my whole heart and being - with my business, I do the same. Should anyone make a comment about my business or if anybody appears to try to jeopardize the operation or add themselves to the business without good intentions, I become very offensive and guarded. I become very protective.

Several people would offer their services to you with bad intentions, like wolves in sheep's clothing - like that lady who never showed me that she was only out for the money, and I never saw the sirens of her agenda or her intentions. This is not limited to family and friends.

Rules to follow:

1. Know who labors among you. Ask the questions - what is your experience? How long have you been in business? Seek expert testimonies, results of research, and reviews. Take your time to make a decision.

2. Many local resources are available to assist you in developing business plans and contract proposals. There are free business centers and women business centers across your local area, do your research, and know who to contact.

3. Never grow desperate. Anytime you meet a new person, go in knowing that you are informed of what you would like to do and what you would like to accomplish. Let the person know

what you expect of them and what they should expect of you. And with cost, always put everything in writing; get a business lawyer, and have them review all of your documents.

This experience was an eye-opener for me. Beware of wolves in sheep's clothing. My experience was that once I told people about my business, business idea, goals, and vision, I began to attract more friends and people who seemed to have my best interest at heart. I quickly learned that the world of entrepreneurship and small businesses could be a dog-eat-dog world – you would have those who would pray with you and those who would prey on you.

Adapt and Overcome

According to Webster's dictionary, 'adapt' is the root word for 'adaptation.' To adapt means to fit in or make suitable for a purpose, while to overcome is to conquer a difficult situation or task. I am an overcomer! Repeat after me, "I am an overcomer." Listen, I am going to say this one time and one time only. You and only you are responsible for your success. Becoming an entrepreneur is not an easy task, and you must put in the work to see the results you dream of. As a Nursepreneur, it took me a long time to find how and where I could and would fit my CPR business in a saturated industry. Nobody is responsible for making your brand or niche perfect but you. It's your vision, your dream, and your baby, so get to work.

In a previous book, I mentioned that when I first received my nursing degree, I moonlighted at Womack Army Medical Center and Bon Secours Hospital. I was super excited about learning and operating in the full capacity of a licensed nurse. While working at both locations, I quickly found out that it was up to me to ensure that I chart properly and to know where all the equipment was located, the medication room, etc. At both locations, I worked on the telemetry floor, which was pretty fast paced, depending on what type of patients were there. As a newbie, it felt as though nobody had time to answer any questions or help me out because everyone was busy handling their patient load. I am pretty sure some of you have felt the same way throughout your nursing career. After a month of working at Womack Medical Hospital, I learned that I needed to work a little harder by spending some extra time on the floor to get acclimated to my environment. Many can identify with me that nursing school didn't teach us everything we needed to know, and sometimes on-the-job training is required to get a better understanding of processes and procedures. I am using this analogy because it's the same way in business. There's only so much you can learn through reading and the help of others. Entrepreneurship is a hands-on task. It takes the application to be successful. I believe if you can answer these questions, you are on your way to operating a successful business:

1. What is the purpose of my business?

2. How hard am I willing to work for my business?

3. Am I applying the knowledge I received from reading to my business practices?

4. Am I being honest with myself about dedicating the time I need to operate a successful business?

5. Have I aligned myself to fit in a space that seems to be difficult?

Embrace the Challenge(s)

While walking on this rugged road of entrepreneurship, I've faced many challenges. One specifically was asking for help. I had many things in my head, and there just wasn't enough room to hold the ideas, visions, and dreams. I actually could see how I wanted to operate my business but did not know how to get it out of my head and put it on paper. I began to ask people for their opinions and recommendations about my business - people that had no clue about how to operate or manage one. I attended numerous training and programs and began to get frustrated, feeling that I should have had a grasp on the business concept already. We've all been here, correct? During this time in my business career, I decided I needed to make a change. The Department of Veteran Affairs (VA) offers many programs for disabled veterans. As a disabled veteran, I was most interested in the Vocational Rehabilitation Self-Employment track. I worked with a counselor to clearly define my business goals. We discussed what I wanted to do with my business and came up with a plan of action to make it happen. The counselor informed me of a program called Center for Business Acceleration. I enrolled in the program and dedicated 19 hours a week to be successful. In the meantime, I also searched for a business coach. Luckily, I crossed paths with Michelle Rhodes. In conjunction with the two forces - the Center for Business Acceleration and Michelle Rhodes - I was able to complete a full business plan detailing how I would strategically proceed in being relevant in my business and generating revenue that resulted in me having five figures a month; also, I received a grant. Challenges build character, so embrace them. Here are a few nuggets for you to remember:

1. Relevancy is vital; keep learning.
2. Tell everyone about your business. Networking is key in entrepreneurship.
3. Behind every closed door is a new opportunity. Go get it.
4. You have to put in the time and work to see quality results.
5. Recognize that there would always be challenges. Learn how to embrace them. We all go through growing pains. Seek help from those who can help you.

The Marathon Continues

The journey of entrepreneurship can be long, unpredictable, daunting, and rewarding. Often, I find myself reflecting on why I'm here and how I arrived in such a magical place. I remember the day I was accepted into Howard University's Nursing Program; I was so proud to be granted the permission to learn and earn a degree from such a prestigious university. Through all the sweat, tears, and long nights, I was going to graduate with a nursing degree. While I was faced with adversity in my military career and nursing school, I am constantly reminded that it will be the same as an entrepreneur. Just like I overcame those obstacles, I will overcome the valleys in entrepreneurship. Ten years later, and I feel the same way from nursing student to nursepreneur! See, operating a business is no joke, and neither is running a marathon. I've learned that you must have a marathon mindset to reach your full potential as a business owner. You must fully assess and understand your daily operations, to include strengths and weaknesses (personal and professional), in order to be successful. This may take time. However, having a positive and can-do attitude can go a long way. Find out where you're truly lacking, humble yourself and ask for help. Marathons are held on roads. Depending on the location, you may encounter a hilly or flat land. Depending on how you've trained, you must decide on whether or not to take the hill with all speed ahead or cruise as you make a decent downhill. Regardless of how you proceed, know that you will need both strategies to finish the race successfully, so pace yourself. I know that I'm an over-thinker and my thoughts can linger on for hours or even days. I have self-doubt about whether I've made the right decision or if my flyer is conveying my message to my intended audience. Time is more money, so being productive versus unproductive beats any indecisive day. In the military, we use to do after-action reviews (AAR). AARs were conducted to reflect on what happened, what was supposed to happen, what went right, what went wrong, and how we can improve. Like marathon runners and entrepreneurs alike, conducting performance base analysis is essential for growth and development. As you push and not lose sight of your why, you must remember that your faith, commitment, dedication, and perseverance will be your strength when facing the unknown. Many successful entrepreneurs can tell you that they've been where we are running to get to and they didn't get there overnight. Just like myself and other entrepreneurs, we can't be successful on our own. You truly don't have to succeed solo. Remember, you are never alone.

My Why

I have a family I owe everything to. Many don't understand that God has charged me with many things on this earth, and one of those charges is to live with purpose. I didn't have the ideal childhood and my parents didn't feed me with a silver spoon; everything that I have and will ever have is because I earned it. Each day that I rise, I thank God for another chance to be a hope and example to someone who doesn't believe they can accomplish their dreams. Most importantly, my faith has allowed me to press on even when I thought I couldn't; thanks be to God who causes me to triumph. The journey of life is so unpredictable as we lay our own flowers on our God-given paths leaving a legacy for our families. My family has allowed me to follow my dreams as they are my best supporters and cheerleaders. My husband and parents, especially, consistently encourage me to live my best life while denouncing fear and doubts. The legacy that I am praying to leave behind is one that knows how to generate wealth, to be a giver, an encourager, and last, a risk-taker. Following your dreams comes with a price, however, living a life of freedom, peace and prosperity is priceless. I continue to break barriers and live a life that reflects the image of Christ because it is not by my own power that he has graced me with this life. I take nothing for granted and every day, I remain thankful for his mercy.

Dedication

This book is dedicated to my loving

Mother, Mary Alice Davis, CNA

We made it……

This is my Year to Grow: Journeys and Strategies for Nurse Entrepreneurs

By Michelle Greene Rhodes, MHS, RN

Just thinking back to three years ago, 2016, I would not have thought that I would have come this far. Absolutely not one of us have a crystal ball and cancel foresee the future, so we never quite know how a new venture will roll out. Yes we can plan, we can create outlines, we can set dates and goals and gather facts and figures. But the reality of it is that we often have no clue about what is around the corner. Just like as when we take a plane or ride a boat, we just never

know how the trip is going to be. So, I am happy to be able to continue this entrepreneurial journey and walk alongside some powerful nurses that I've met along the way. Over the course of three years I have now helped numerous nurses start businesses, Be it public speakers, or become authors. But I have to a secret to tell you. I lost myself in the process along the way. So welcome to the point in my journey where I expose the growing pains. The purpose of my chapter is to just inspire you to greatness, encourage you to keep on keeping on and yes to make your dream life your reality!

But do we understand the intricate balance that is required to keep all of these energies in sync? I learned the hard way and continue to learn this about myself, in spite of the task at hand. I have genuinely fallen in love with my schedule, I enjoy blocking off time for myself now, and my relationship with my family is better daily.

Communication is the Key

This entrepreneurship journey has made me better, as I no longer hold my feelings inside. It is taught me how to yes work hard towards my goals and help others, yet easily say no. It is taught me how to speak up for myself in a better way, while learning how to speak clearly. It has taught me that my time is not my own What has the journey taught you? *Let's briefly discuss communication, growth, and time.*

Communicate and speak your mind, point blank. It's so easy to hold back, to hold grudges or to simply stay where we are. When it comes to business, this is something that we cannot afford to let happen, as we know there is no growth there. We must keep communication clear especially during the growth process, especially if we're going to have teams carrying out work for us. Take the time to study communication and I would ask that you do a personal development assessment to really learn yourself as to how you handle situations, how you communicate things, and how you resolve conflict. Make communication acorn measure of your business.

Growth

When it comes to growth – its an important thing because you and only you in your heart if your business is growing or floundering. But how do you know? What measures do you watch and when do you know to accelerate or pivot? Knowing your organizations KPI's (key performance improvement) numbers have helped me get on track, cut the fluff and step up to the plate. I knew I had to dig deeper into my products/services in order to keep and attract ideal clients.

What number do you need to pinpoint down in order to know that we have successfully met a goal?

How do you know how much time is to be allotted in the strategy in order to make things happen? What performance indicators show that you are on the right track and we have the data to prove it? Will we check on our progress once a month, once a quarter or once a year?

There are various ways that we can do these things, of course ultimately this can only reflected in your business plan based and upon your business strategy. Be sure to take the time to reevaluate your progress, check your profitability and see if you are hitting milestones along the way towards your set measure of success.

Time is the great equalizer

Business owners often say I would rather lose money than time, as I can always make more money. I am here to encourage you to be mindful of the second, hours, years that you might think that you have left. Let's not be arrogant and assuming that we have time, as it is promised to no one. My job is to push you, pull you, stretch you to your highest and greatest self. So, what can you do to redeem the time? Or make the most of the time that lies ahead? For me being pushed to be more mindful of my schedule and plot out everything on a calendar, has really helped me. This business is just way too busy to fly by the seat of my pants, so I had to sit down and find tools and software that would help me maximize my day. I encourage you to do the same, and do not be lazy about it. You'll find that you'll actually make more money in your business if you're able to prioritize, streamline, and optimize. I would be curious to see what your business look like a year from now once you implement these changes. Please let me know.

In summary I wanted to share tips this book that would help you along your journey, yes we have all learned how to start the business in my first book, "RNterprise" but now I felt it was time to stretch out, and I have deeper to share with you some key lessons that I have learned along this journey. It is help me towards my destination, but I can tell you that I have not fully arrived yet.

Oh, a couple more thoughts about growing pains:

First things first

Know who you are selling to. Once you know your niche and target market-you know how to speak to them and talk their language. In 2018 I was trying to coach everybody that would listen, and I had a shift within my mind that it narrowed this thing down, and work with people who are truly serious about launching their business and growing the business. So, I had to put a cap on 10 per group and work with them all year long as opposed to just six weeks here or 30 days they are. They are now in the midst of working more efficiently and I see better outcomes as a result of this streamlining process that helps my clients get better outcomes.

Stay tuned for the Nurse Entrepreneurs Society!

Secondly

Set your money goals and work backwards. I think sometimes new entrepreneurs make it so hard on themselves by focusing on making one and then moving "on to the next". Never truly building relationships with others, or truly building a customer experience. I have witness business owners who miss out on customer service opportunities to win a lifelong customer, who might continue to buy from you for a lifetime. But if we have not dug our heels into our programs and services, looking at things from a customer point of view, and discovering where could we improve – we miss the mark. Our improved outcomes, which will in turn -make you more money along the way- is the goal of the goals. I'm excited to share that once I found my magic number that it seemed to help everything fall into place for me. I pray over my business daily and by setting my intention on meeting a certain number, it feels as though God is divinely making that happen. Speak life and know your numbers!

The buck stops here

Lastly, I would say relationship building has done more for my business than anything else. But uniquely and intentionally aligning myself with certain organizations online and off-line, money has floated to my business effortlessly this way. Be sure you have gotten your branding tight, you know yourself, and what you bring to the table. When you do meet someone who knows more than you, if they see the potential in you, most times will try to help you rise to the next level. It is only because I have presented myself with my groundwork complete, when they are ready to have me join their team, it is very easy to do because they know my work. So have your work and be ready to move when the opportunity presents itself. Winning goes to the prepared!

This is your year! Now the fun really begins…….

Biography

Michelle Greene Rhodes, MHS, RN, CCM, CMCN
Michelle Rhodes Media LLC
Healthcare Coaching and Consulting

Inspired by her passion for mentoring and coaching, she assists nurses startup and grow as entrepreneurs. As a Consultant, Michelle and her team assists

Organizations with Corporate Wellness initiatives, Schools of Nursing with elective curriculum development for "Nurses and Business" and hospitals incorporate Intrapreneurship into their Nursing culture.

She has gone to enjoy a 20+ year career in Nursing, Authored six (6) books, and now speaks on various Health care topics that affect her community.

A former Population Health Manager with a Managed Care Organization, Michelle is described as extremely detailed, organized and creative this Nurse has become the "go-to" source when it is time to construct a health-related programs and approaches that will solve problems. She is a passionate and highly engaged workshop leader. Coach Michelle is a Wellcoaches trained Coach and VA Certified Mentor, and Certified Managed Care Nurse.

Her Nurse Consulting firm displays passion for entrepreneurship and intrapreneurship facilitation within Healthcare.

Some of the highlights of her career have been:

* Assisting hundreds of professionals to meet their goals

* Leading workshops Nationally and Internationally

* Serving on NonProfit Boards and Local Community Service Organizations as Chair and Co-Chair of Health

* Leading Strategic Planning Sessions for the upcoming year

* Served as a ANCC Pathways Reviewer, selecting level of criteria met for determinants of a "Healthy Workplace"

* Certified Mentor by the Veterans Health Administration

* Certificate in Health Promotion and Workplace Safety by University of Southern Indiana

* WellCoaches Motivational Interviewer and Health Coach

* Graduate of Veterans Florida - "Veterans Entrepreneurship Program"

* Certified CoStarters(TM) Facilitator- Startup Workshops

Her speaking topics include:

"The difference between entrepreneurship and intrapreneurship in Healthcare"

"Health Challenges for the Black Female"

"Dare to chase your dreams"

"Personal Branding for Nurses"

"Curriculum building for Nurse Entrepreneurship"

If you are looking for an experienced healthcare professional, who is passionate about these topics then book this speaker is for your organization.

Please connect with Michelle at:

www.MichelleRhodesMedia.com

Resource List

By Marylyn R. Harris, RN, MSN, MBA

Marylyn R. Harris is a Healthcare Cybersecurity Consultant, former U.S. Army Nurse and Social Entrepreneur. In 2010, Harris (and her children, Jamaar and Amaara), founded the first Women Veterans Business Center, a non-profit organization headquartered in Houston (TX). The Center's mission is, "to educate and empower Women Veterans (and Military Families), to start and grow professional careers and 'wealth-generating' Veteran-Owned Businesses." The Center has outreached to over 25,000 Stakeholders to date and assisted hundreds of Veteran owned businesses to launch and scale.

Harris began her nursing career in 1980's as a nursing assistant, Army Medic and Licensed Vocational Nurse (LVN). She earned a bachelor's degree (BSN) in Nursing from Prairie View A & M University, a master's degree (MSN) in Psychiatric Nursing from UT*Health* School of Nursing (Houston) and a master's degree in Business Administration (MBA) from the University of St. Thomas (Houston). Harris' reach spans across five continents, (N. America, S. America, Asia, Africa and the Caribbean), where she has helped thousands of patients to heal. Harris' rich Nursing experiences include, Medical-Surgical, Oncology, Neurology, Psychiatric, Prison, Missionary Service and Nursing Education. Harris is a highly sought after Adjunct Faculty Member, Executive in Residence and Invited Speaker at several Schools of Nursing and Schools of Business.

Harris currently holds membership in numerous civic, military, professional and community organizations. Harris serves as a National Appointee on the VA Research Advisory Committee (RAC) for Gulf War Veteran's Illnesses. In 2019, Harris received several noteworthy awards and scholarships to include, Prairie View A & M University *Alumni Award*, Four Chaplains Memorial Foundation *Bronze Medallion*, Zeta Phi Beta *Woman of Excellence Award*, Congressional Black Caucus Veterans BrainTrust Award, *BlackHat USA Scholar, Grace Hopper Scholar, ISC2 Scholar and ICMCP Scholar*. Harris was named a *"Diversity in Business Champion"* by the Houston Business Journal (2017), a "Houston Hero" by the Houston Chronicle (2015) and the 2013 "Veteran Business Champion of the Year" by the U.S. Small Business Administration (SBA) Region VI. Harris is the Author of two books, (2010) '25 Free Resources Every Texas Veteran Needs to Know' and (2011) '25 Free Resources Every Texas Woman Veteran Needs to Know." In 2013, Harris was honored as a ***"White House Champion of Change"* by President Barack Obama**.

Marylyn R. Harris

Resources for Women in Business

1. Women Veterans Business Center
   "2020 Women Veterans TECH Careers and TECH Business Initiative"

2. U.S. Small Business Administration (SBA)
   Women Owned Small Business/Economically Disadvantaged Small Business Programs

3. Women's Business Centers (SBA)
   https://www.sba.gov/business-guide/grow-your-business/women-owned-businesses#section-header-0

4. America's Small Business Development Centers (SBDC) Network
   https://americassbdc.org/
   *Veteran Business Outreach Centers (VBOCs)/Service Core of Retired Executives (SCORE)

5. The Women's Business Enterprise National Council (WBENC)
   https://www.wbenc.org/

6. Women's Business Council
   https://www.nwbc.gov/

7. 'U. S. Chamber of Commerce II Women's Chamber of Commerce

8. U.S. Department of Labor (DOL) – Women's Bureau

9. Business and Professional Women's Foundation

10. Institute for Veterans and Military Families (IVMF at Syracuse University)
    Entrepreneurship Bootcamp for Veterans (EBV) with Disabilities/ EBV for Families

www.ingramcontent.com/pod-product-compliance
Lightning Source LLC
Chambersburg PA
CBHW032058090426
42743CB00007B/165